Edith Wharton's Social Register

Also by Claire Preston

SIR THOMAS BROWNE: Selected Writings (*editor*)

EDITH WHARTON: *The Glimpses of the Moon* (*editor*)

Edith Wharton's Social Register

Claire Preston
Sidney Sussex College
Cambridge

First published in Great Britain 2000 by
MACMILLAN PRESS LTD
Houndmills, Basingstoke, Hampshire RG21 6XS and London
Companies and representatives throughout the world

A catalogue record for this book is available from the British Library.

ISBN 0–333–74622–8

First published in the United States of America 2000 by
ST. MARTIN'S PRESS, INC.,
Scholarly and Reference Division,
175 Fifth Avenue, New York, N.Y. 10010

ISBN 0–312–22557–1

Library of Congress Cataloging-in-Publication Data
Preston, Claire.
Edith Wharton's social register / Claire Preston.
p.   cm.
Includes bibliographical references (p.   ) and index.
ISBN 0–312–22557–1 (cloth)
1. Wharton, Edith, 1862–1937—Political and social views.
2. Literature and anthropology—New York (State)—New York–
–History—20th century.   3. Literature and society—New York
(State)—New York—History—20th century.   4. Darwin, Charles,
1809–1882—Influence.   5. James, Henry, 1843–1916—Influence.
6. Social Darwinism in literature.   7. Social values in literature.
8. New York (N.Y.)—In literature.   I. Title.
PS3545.H16Z77   1999
813'.52—dc21   99–16599
                                                              CIP

This book is printed on paper suitable for recycling and made from fully managed and sustained
forest sources.

10   9   8   7   6   5   4   3   2   1
09   08   07   06   05   04   03   02   01   00

Printed and bound in Great Britain by
Antony Rowe Ltd, Chippenham, Wiltshire

For my parents
R.S.P.   A.C.P.

Contents

List of Abbreviations

Lewis R.W.B. Lewis, *Edith Wharton: a Biography* (New York: Harper and Row, 1975)

Letters R.W.B. and Nancy Lewis, eds, *The Letters of Edith Wharton* (New York: Simon and Schuster, 1988)

Benstock Shari Benstock, *No Gifts From Chance: a Biography of Edith Wharton* (New York: Charles Scribner's Sons, 1994)

Yale The Edith Wharton archive in the Yale Collection of American Literature, Beinecke Rare Book and Manuscript Library, Yale University (YCAL MSS42)

Page-references to Wharton's published and major unpublished works are given in the text using the following abbreviations, which refer to the given editions.

AI *The Age of Innocence* (1920) (New York: Collier Books, 1992)

B *The Buccaneers* (1938) (London: Everyman, 1993)

BG *A Backward Glance* (New York: Appleton-Century, 1934)

C *The Children* (1928) (London: Virago Press, 1985)

CC *The Custom of the Country* (1913) (Harmondsworth: Penguin Books, 1987)

CSS *The Collected Short Stories of Edith Wharton*, 2 vols (New York: Charles Scribner's Sons, 1968)

DH *The Decoration of Houses* (1897) (with Ogden Codman) (New York: W.W. Norton, 1997)

EF *Ethan Frome* (1911) (Oxford: Oxford University Press, 1982)

FD *False Dawn* (1924) (New York: Appleton and Co., 1924)

FF *Fighting France: from Dunkerque to Belfort* (1915) (New York: Charles Scribner's Sons, 1915)

FG *A Further Glance* (Beinecke Library, Yale Collection of American Literature, unpublished MS)

FL *Fast and Loose* [1877] (Charlottesville: University of Virginia Press, 1993)

FT *The Fruit of the Tree* (1907) (London: Virago Press, 1984)

FW *French Ways and their Meaning* (1919) (New York: Appleton and Co., 1919)

GM *The Glimpses of the Moon* (1922) (New York: Appleton and Co., 1922)

HM	*The House of Mirth* (1905) (New York: Charles Scribner's Sons, 1905)
HRB	*Hudson River Bracketted* (1929) (London: Virago Press, 1986)
IB	*Italian Backgrounds* (1905) (New York: Charles Scribner's Sons, 1905)
LI	*Life and I* [n.d.] (Beinecke Library, Yale Collection of American Literature (unpublished MS)
M	*The Marne* (1918) (New York: Charles Scribner's Sons, 1918)
MF	*A Motor-Flight Through France* (1908) (DeKalb, Illinois: Northern Illinois University Press, 1991)
MR	*The Mother's Recompense* (1925) (New York: Appleton and Co., 1925)
MT	*Madame de Treymes* (1907) (New York: Charles Scribner's Sons, 1907)
NYD	*New Year's Day* (1924) (New York: Appleton and Co., 1924)
OM	*The Old Maid* (1924) (New York: Appleton and Co., 1924)
R	*The Reef* (1912) (New York: Appleton and Co., 1912)
S	*Summer* (1917) (Oxford: Oxford University Press, 1982)
SF	*A Son at the Front* (1923) (New York: Charles Scribner's Sons, 1923)
Sp	*The Spark* (1924) (New York: Appleton and Co., 1924)
TS	*Twilight Sleep* (1927) (New York: Appleton and Co., 1927)
WF	*The Writing of Fiction* (1925) (New York: Charles Scribner's Sons, 1925)

List of Plates

Preface and Acknowledgements

'By and bye I shall be a classic,' says a Mrs S. in a notebook sketch; '– brr, how cold that sounds! –...and one is sold in sets and put on the list of the hundred best books. – I foresee the day when I shall be as lonely as an Etruscan museum.'[1] This remark, eventually given to the famous novelist Mrs Dale in Edith Wharton's short story 'Copy' (1901), is a prescient indicator of what Wharton would come to colonise as her special fictional territory as she wrote herself into a version of Mrs Dale. The chill of the relict – for her stories are populated with the remaindered remnants of once-powerful civilisations, families, and sensibilities – is her ambient atmosphere; the preserved specimen apparently her preferred subject. To Judge Robert Grant (fellow novelist, and author of one of her favourite books, *Unleavened Bread* (1900)) she explained herself as a 'great...believer in the objective attitude', and praised his own fictional practice in terms which mirror her own modernism: 'consistent abstinence from comment, explanation and partisanship...confidence in the reader's ability to draw his own conclusions'.[2]

In 1900 Wharton had published some short fiction, but not a novel; her own handling of 'the objective attitude' was still largely before her. The aim of this book is to examine the sources and consequences of that attitude. What some of her critics identified as *froideur*, or as an empirical remoteness from her subjects, obscures the modernist basis on which Wharton constructed fictions. As she complained on more than one occasion, 'American and English reviewers of fiction are so disinclined to recognize that novels may be written from a dozen different standpoints, and that the "heart-interest" need not always predominate.'[3] And 'heart-interest', indeed, was never the source of her art: in spite of her sex, and her preference for women's stories and protagonists, Wharton's work is difficult to place within the conventions of '*women's*' writing; she is influenced instead by social fictions and by non-fictional work in biology and evolution, anthropology and sociology. She is compelled by her subjects as she would be by an article on amphioxus or by an Etruscan potsherd: the declined civilisation of Old New York summons from her an antiquarian rather than an emotional interest, friendly but detached; the withering of Lily Bart takes place in what feels like a social laboratory in which Lily's mutant experience is measured against the control-group of ruthless Trenors and Dorsets; her portrayal of what she

xii

calls buccaneers registers her astonishment at and admiration for their exotic adaptive behaviours, her description attaining the clarity of a scientific report about an uncatalogued species; in her expatriate novels, Wharton uses her abiding sense of alienation to promote ideas of limits, boundaries, and pales among the European tribes, and incidents of transgression and invasion which disrupt those frontiers, disruptions centred obliquely on the aftermath of the Great War.

Scholars and champions of the emergent turn-of-the-century American realism have tended to dismiss Edith Wharton's fiction as outside their domain, housed as it is in mandarin style and dealing, almost exclusively, with social élites rather than with the experimental linguistic surfaces and fashionable working-class *données* of early and high Modernism. But Wharton is indubitably within the early Modernist tradition: and the purpose of this book is to situate her style and themes in the context of prevailing new intellectual fashions which included sociological and anthropological writing, and developing work from the slightly earlier scientific revolution of the mid-nineteenth century.

Bearing in mind some of the principal ideas of these disciplines, the book is organised into four distinct essays whose themes are inter-related: Chapter 1, 'Tribes', establishes the idea of boundary in the form of Whartonian socio-genetic and onomastic relations among families and individuals; these in turn constitute some of the essentially 'tribal' ideas which are extended by Wharton to the spatial and the aesthetic in the form of architecture and interiors, neighbourhood, and geography; and of taste, profession, language, and behaviour. Wharton develops a carefully structured binary cosmos of apparently simple but actually elusive and complex oppositions such as 'within/without', 'done/not done', and 'accepted/ outcast' which function in her work almost as natural laws, and which are the governing forces behind her social tragedies. Through her experience of America, as described in her autobiographical and critical writings, I suggest ways in which her observations also proposed to her many associated themes: the idea of tribe allows her to frame principles of outcasting, expatriatism, and transgression to which the subsequent essays of the book are devoted.

Chapter 2, 'Outcasts', considers Wharton's use of Darwinian metaphors of survival and adaptation, and connects these with the already established spatial arrangements which are so prominent a feature of her work. Lily Bart is a central figure of non-adaptive specialisation; the consequences of her insufficiency are figured in anthropological ideas of marginalisation, liminality, and placelessness. Lily's outcasting is, in a sense, impersonal, merely biologically necessary rather than governed by volition or intention; the tragic agent of *The House of Mirth* is thus less human than environmental. In contrast, other marginal characters successfully abide in their liminality by situating themselves near the centre of the tribe in roles required by its social eco-system.

Chapter 3, 'Buccaneers', invokes the work of Thorstein Veblen to analyse Wharton's most vigorous and shocking character, Undine Spragg. Transgressive and grasping, Undine represents the buccaneer invader whose function is partly to expose the flimsiness and vulnerability of tribal boundaries. If Lily Bart and other outcasts are incapable of resisting the centrifugal tendencies of tribal membership and are inexorably marginalised, the buccaneer character desolates tribal boundaries in ignorance and will. The essay relates Undine and *The Custom of the Country* with the flourishing genre of money-novels and the terrifying blankness of money-figures, but also connects that blankness with the images of whiteness, vacancy, and transparency which settle on tribal women. The vacancy of a May Welland compared to that of an Undine Spragg is an analogy of the dessication by money of the old, fragile tribal limits and decencies, limits which in the Modernist world of the first 25 years of the century are practically impossible to maintain.

Chapter 4, 'Expatriates', considers two themes: displacement in Wharton's fiction is generally the afterlife of the buccaneer, and in American expatriatism she continues and enlarges on the behavioural horror of the buccaneer, unmoored by this phase even from the rigour of money-making. But buccaneer expatriatism is even more powerful a symbol of the depredations of the Great War. Wharton's own experience of the war in France defined and refined her sense of place and belonging, and this was accomplished partly through her observation of American expatriates during the crisis, and her remoter sense of home-grown American attitudes and behaviour after the war was over. Her relation to America is at once more complex *and* more simplified as a consequence of her expatriate status and her devotion to a country not her own. Her disdain, more profound in this phase than in any other, is an index of the delicacy she perceived in the relation between native and visitor, insider and outcast, sympathiser and plunderer.

In the writing of this book I have been greatly indebted to the Beinecke Library of Yale University for granting me, in the form of the Donald Gallup Fellowship, the opportunity to use the library's extensive Wharton papers, and especially to Patricia Willis (Keeper of American

Manuscripts) and to Steve Jones of the Beinecke staff; to Jonathan Edwards College of Yale University, and most particularly to Barbara Goddard; to David McKitterick, Wren Librarian of Trinity College, Cambridge, for allowing me to consult the Gaillard Lapsley papers; and to the Cambridge University Library. I taxed the resources of the Hawthorne–Longfellow Library of Bowdoin College more than was right for a part-time user, and I am eager to register my thanks to its good-humoured staff. Part of Chapter 3 originally appeared in different form as 'Ladies Prefer Blondes: Edith Wharton, Theodore Dreiser, and the Money-Novel' in *Soft Canons: American Women Writers and the Masculine Tradition(s)* Ed. Karen Kilcup (Ames: University of Iowa Press, 1999). I have been allowed to present various papers on Wharton to the British Association of American Studies conference of 1995, to the 1996 'Reading the Nineteenth-Century Domestic Space' Conference at King Alfred's College, Winchester, and to the Edith Wharton Society Conference of 1997 in Lenox, Mass., as well as to the Cambridge University American Literature seminar; Charmian Hearne and Julian Honer at Macmillan have been helpful and kindly editors; Colin Fairweather scrupulously proof-read and indexed. Sylvia Adamson, Adrian Poole, the late Jeremy Maule, and Patricia Zampini gave literary help and advice; Bob Boutilier, Victor Buchli, and Elizabeth Flowerday and Michéle Thomas answered questions about zoology, anthropology, and dressing cases (respectively); Angela Preston investigated photographic permissions and Richard Preston checked references; Kevin Jackson, the late Tony Tanner, and Anne Barton read and commented helpfully on substantial parts of the manuscript. The Master and Fellows of Sidney Sussex College, Cambridge, granted me invaluable sabbatical leave which allowed me to complete the book. Kevin Jackson gave patient and positively alcine encouragement, in this as in all things. Finally, in the dedication I record the life-long debt which it is an honour to owe.

1
Tribes

She used to say that she was embogged in New York society up to her neck; fortunately her head was free.

Robert Norton [1]

The force of negation

'"For pity's sake, don't destroy my last illusions"' (*AI*272)

In an early draft of her autobiography, provisionally entitled *Life and I*, Edith Wharton recalls her discovery that babies come from people and not from flowers. Excited and perplexed, she attempted to communicate this great news to her mother. She was informed by the formidable Mrs Jones that such subjects are 'not nice' for little girls. 'I was left', writes Wharton, 'with a penetrating sense of "not-niceness"' (*LI*34). In the published form of this work, *A Backward Glance*, she describes other such interdictions: her playmates were selected by her mother for their 'niceness'; moreover, her extraordinary habit of 'making-up' (composing stories aloud but – eccentrically – alone) was performed at the expense of these nice friends, whose company became supererogatory, making such fictional activities, in consequence, 'not-nice' (*BG*35). From an early age, it seems, Wharton was aware of a contention between the impulses of her imaginative gifts and the dictates of her tribe.

'Not-niceness' is an odd litotes which seems to summarise an essential linguistic and behavioural demarcation in Wharton's fiction. It represents an impoverishment of vocabulary, in which the opposite of a thing is formulated merely as its own cancellation. It is the evasion of particularity (what is 'niceness', *exactly*, and how far would one have to go not to be nice?). Non-logical and 'indeterminately evaluative',[2] it represents the

1

linguistic atrophy of her fictional tribe, the locution of a group which succeeds in making 'other standards non-existent by ignoring them . . . a force of negation which eliminated everything beyond their own range of perception' (*HM* 76). Not-niceness is certainly something real and dreadful, but it remains mysterious and unformulated: only those who are indisputably 'nice' can recognise it and define it, putting the not-nice at an inherent tautological disadvantage. Niceness is like a very expensive diamond – something you can't have if you need to ask the price. The semantic opposite of 'x', expressed as the category 'not-x', is a descriptive evasion which relieves the mind of imaginative, verbal, or social exercise. This evasion is a kind of restrictive antithesis which in semantic terms leads nowhere.[3] In *A Backward Glance*, she described her Episcopalian background as *not* 'fissiparous' (*BG*10), a term from T.H. Huxley's biological writings by which she refers to the endogamous kinship alliances within her caste; the 'not-x' phrase itself corresponds to biologically tautologous, genetically enclosed, self-replicating matrimonial practice.

Of the secretary of the National Institute of Arts and Letters, which invited her to become a member in 1917, Wharton begged to be known as 'Mrs Wharton' rather than 'Mrs Edith Wharton', the latter, to her ear, 'associat[ing] me with vendors of patent medicines and other categories of females with whom I have no affiliation'.[4] When replying to fan-letters addressed to her as 'Mrs Edith Wharton', she usually made a point of prefacing her thanks with the elaborately polite *assumption* that she was indeed the intended recipient, as if there might be some other, vulgar, novelist known by that title, a title, moreover, suggesting divorce. Not only was she *the* Mrs Wharton, hardly requiring the specificity of a first name, but she was also thus cloaked in the impenetrable correctness of her matrimonial title and position. She could be addressed as 'Mrs Wharton' (or as 'Mrs Edward Wharton'), but never as 'Mrs Edith Wharton'.[5] The difference between the two forms of address is a nuance in the language of 'not-x', one in which – whatever her ironies about it – she was fluent.

In a letter to the dramatiser of *The Age of Innocence*, Wharton complained of a younger generation unattuned to 'the allusive, elliptical & metaphorical.'[6] The figure of 'not-x' is the allusive in its most inscrutable form, yet it is the very index of the kind of expressive hurdle her own writing had to clear to achieve its richness and precision. Wharton's attitude towards 'not-x' is therefore deeply ambivalent. It can stand for several things: it is a form of exclusion, of shibboleth; it is a kind of intellectual canalisation; and it is a richly inflected and now quite dead ancient language. Her attitude towards 'not-x' (that is, her elliptical fluency in it and her irony about it) are both in play in her tribal writings.

A well-known painting by Eastman Johnson reifies the linguistic convention of 'not-x'. 'Not at Home' (c. 1870s) shows an interior, the view extending from within a dim inner vestibule and staircase towards a daylit, outer reception room beyond. [Plate 1] On the shadowy foregrounded staircase near the focus of vision a young woman, head down, scuttles up to the next floor. With its allusions to Dutch genre painting, this scene is compelling and occult, especially with its hieroglyphic title, a reference to a convention hardly comprehensible in an age of nuclear families and servant-less dwellings. With the tradition of paying calls still well-established, and the appropriate days and hours rigidly defined in Wharton's young womanhood, one could either be 'at home' to receive visitors, or 'not at home' – unavailable to all callers or to certain unwelcome ones. The phrase 'not at home' can be literal or conventional – the latter in the case of Johnson's young woman. She is hurrying away from the public room into which, we must suppose, some caller is being shown by a servant. There is a good deal of tension here: 'Slatternly parlour-maids', says Wharton, '. . . said "I'll go and see" to visitors calling at an hour when all right-minded persons are conventionally if not actually out' (*HM* 47), ruining the illusion of absence by literalising the snub. The ritualised gestures of card-leaving which accompany call-paying seem especially recondite. Calls (actual visits) and the leaving of cards (tokens standing for visits and sociable intention) had an exact economy, which insisted on a call for a call, a card for a card. Dropping off a card without actually calling was one way of letting a superior new contact decide whether or not to respond, thus ceremonially acknowledging the obeisance due from a socially inferior woman to a superior one. A superior woman, on the other hand, might initiate social contact with an inferior one by honouring her with a card or a call, which it was then the recipient's happy duty to acknowledge with a card or a call in return. The absence of a response was a meaningful vacancy, a way of declining further acquaintance. An initial call (a bolder gambit than card-leaving if originating with the obeisant woman) invited a return call, which like a card could be neglected by the recipient. The protocol, in other words, leaves decision in the hands of the visited rather than the visitor. The hierarchical significance of calls is at the heart of the *impasse* between Mrs William K. Vanderbilt and Mrs William Astor: the latter, as queen of the Four Hundred, had refused to know Mrs Vanderbilt or any of her tribe; but when the celebrated Vanderbilt ball of 1883 was announced and the Astors were not asked because they had not been introduced to the hosts, New York waited breathlessly until Mrs Astor decided to leave her card at Mrs Vanderbilt's very shortly before the event. Invitations were duly issued; Old New York had ceremonially prostrated itself before the New Money.[7] Even calling hours obeyed an understood pattern of difference. Ceremonial calls (paid to offer thanks for entertainment or gifts) were expected between about three and four in the afternoon; semi-ceremonial calls (as perhaps are May and Newland's visits to various family members on the occasion of their engagement in *The Age of Innocence*) between four and five; intimate visits from close friends occurred between five and six.[8] Lily Bart in *The House of Mirth*, for example, waits expectantly for Lawrence Selden to appear at her aunt's house late in the afternoon, and when instead Simon Rosedale turns up with an unwelcome proposal of marriage, she remonstrates with herself for having neglected to inform the servants that she is not at home except to Selden; but they are both to blame: Rosedale is not an intimate, and violates the rules by calling at a time inappropriate to his connexion with Lily. She cannot flee Rosedale, and he is not alive to her *froideur*, or, apparently, to the conventions of calls. The young woman in the Johnson picture may be escaping the consequences of some such lapse. The furtive quality of being officially unavailable is discomfiting and peculiar for all concerned, a quality aided in the painting by the crepuscular lighting of the main subject. As an oblique depiction of this strange convention, the picture is itself a hieroglyph, a visual token of the abbreviated expressions of 'not-x', a scene which requires decoding. 'Not at home' must have been a locution well known to the young Edith Jones: a prominent card displaying the phrase can be seen standing on the hall table in a photograph of the interior of her parents' Newport house. [Plate 2]

   In Wharton's own generation matrons partly solved the embarrassing delicacy of conventional unavailability by devising the curious ritual of regularly leaving their cards without lingering to see whether they would be entertained by a potentially 'at home' hostess, the cards serving to notify their recipients that they were to consider themselves as having been called upon. Some old-fashioned women were apparently astonished and outraged that such visitors 'did not ask' whether they were in or not (*BG*83). This kind of behavioural vacancy or absence – in which the conventional token becomes ascendant over the action it was originally meant to express – characterises Wharton's own fictional approach: so much is left to surmise, to be worked out by triangulation. We must ply our way, for instance, through such crucial obliquities as the true nature of Olenska's marriage and flight (elopement, or escape with the secretary?), the tangled matrilineal loyalties which complicate Old New York's attitude to and treatment of her;[9] the delicate evasion of sexual consummation in *The Reef*; the insolubility of Lily Bart's death (accident or suicide?); the shrouded fact of Arthur Wyant's attempted murder of Dexter Manford in *Twilight Sleep*; the shady details of Elmer Moffatt's financial career in *The Custom of the Country*; Lilla Gates's past ('Lilla behaved really badly' (*MR*60) is all we are told) in *The Mother's Recompense*; Hayley Delane's unacknowledged friendship with Walt Whitman in *The Spark*; even the slight initial mystery of Lizzie Hazeldean's infidelity to an apparently adored husband. And even when events are made clear to us from the outset, many of her stories rest upon the unsayability of certain crucial facts: the motherhood of Charlotte Lovell and the unrequited love between Clement Spender and Delia Ralston are virtually inadmissible, even by the two women who share a household and raise the child together in *The Old Maid*; Kate Clephane's long-cold affair with Chris Fenno cannot be confessed to anyone, even at the price of lifelong torment in *The Mother's Recompense*; the origin of Ethan Frome's terrible lameness is a kind of rural mystery which the unnamed narrator, a visiting outsider, ferrets out of laconic, phlegmatic villagers.

This procedure by indirection or negative definition produces a binary system in which the individual in society is categorised as either 'in' or 'not in', just as things and their opposites are often presented by a simple cancelling device – 'done' or 'not-done', 'nice' or 'not-nice', in the terms of Wharton's mother; 'at home' or 'not at home' to social callers. One way of establishing tribal enclosure entails definition of boundaries, pales, and margins (spatial and linguistic); to step beyond the boundary is to leave the defining conditions of tribal membership, to become marginalised or obliterated, to become not-nice; it is to become, in essence, unknown, invisible, non-existent; 'not-x' is merely nothing at all. This is the 'force of negation', the quality and condition of 'not-x' which Wharton *depicts* almost as tangibly as Eastman Johnson does; it is often actualised in her stories, where the unsuccessful or the unusual are literally cancelled by being sent out of the enclosure, or else forced to inhabit conventional personae devised by the tribe to contain their difference. Ellen Olenska, Kate Clephane, Lily Bart, Annabel St George, Lewis Raycie, and Martin Boyne are all ceremonially (and in Lily's case, literally) unpersoned, cancelled by the tribe 'without effusion of blood' (*AI*335). But Charlotte Lovell, Lawrence Selden, Hayley Delane, Fanny de Malrive, Sophy Viner, Charity Royall, and Gerty Farish remain within the margins under the (often false) titles of old maid, literary eccentric, bluff sportsman, sacrificing mother, adventuress, legitimated orphan, poor cousin. Although these margins and boundaries are initially abstract, such attitudes and ideas are ultimately substantiated, realised, visually imagined. When Lily Bart and Lizzie Hazeldean become not-nice, their closest friends and relatives ruthlessly cut them. Lizzie's cousin-in-law deliberately approaches her at a party in order to give her the cold shoulder in public, an insult so visible, so strategically obvious as to be nearly unbelievable. Falsely rumoured to have become 'compromised', Lily suddenly becomes a non-person, someone her friends 'do not know'. Her cards are not acknowledged; neither is her physical presence in New York in the same restaurants, on Fifth Avenue. The only people who continue to have intercourse with Lily are themselves social marginals, unworried by loss of caste or attainder by association – Lawrence Selden, the man who has the air of looking on from outside the gilded cage; Sim Rosedale and the Sam Gormers, social climbers; Carrie Fisher, the energetic double divorcée and social fixer; Gerty Farish, the impecunious relation of fashionable New York; and Nettie Struther, the redeemed 'fallen woman' whose baby gives Lily such comfort.

Wharton's inherited tribal lexis should not have encouraged her to imagine her way into not-niceness, since it is the language devised by those who wish to avoid the unpleasant at any cost; it is perhaps indicative of her personal tribal deracination (expatriate, divorced, childless, at odds with or out of sympathy with most of her family, her closest ally among them the divorced wife of her elder brother) that her imagination would not be content with an unexamined, untested binary simplicity; instead, she developed it as a mode of characterisation where distaste and sarcasm are converted into a profound and horrifying absence or blankness. Her best novels and stories are mostly about what it means to be 'not-x', so much so that the magazines in which some of them were first to appear considered them at times 'too strong' for their readership.[10]

The tribe of Old New York is governed by a precise sense of niceness and not-niceness in its social decorum, a binary stringency which determines (in another typical expression) what is 'done' and 'not done'. In the opening scene of *The Age of Innocence*, we are introduced to this dialectical code through a range of details, all proposed as unyielding, unexplained, communally and tacitly subscribed to as if they were natural laws. The setting (the old Academy of Music) is understood to be the 'correct' place to hear opera, partly because it has excellent acoustics, but mainly because it is too small to admit 'new people'.[11] Gounod's *Faust* is favoured by Old New York as one of 'their' operas, and they hear it nearly every season, just as they go to Newport every summer; certain scenes are always listened to (the Daisy Song, for instance), others never; and only Adelina Patti, they think, should sing Marguerite (it is Nilsson on stage, however). There are more general rules: one should never enter a box during an aria; one should never arrive early at the opera; and one should go only on the 'right' night (Monday or Friday). Indeed, 'what was or was not "the thing" played a part as important in Newland Archer's New York as the inscrutable totem terrors that had ruled the destinies of his forefathers thousands of years ago' (*A14*). Here is that binary locution – 'done/ not-done' – virtually at the opening of the novel, a locution which leaves us, as outsiders, to do all the work of sorting out the nice from the not-nice.

It is in this scene that we and Newland are introduced to May Welland and Ellen Olenska, the binary pairing of women who will command his life. Monopolising his attention is May, his fiancée, 'a young girl in white' whose ecstatic reaction to the love-scene on stage between Faust and Marguerite, whose bearing, dress, blush, and bouquet are all exactly 'the thing' expected of a newly engaged young woman (even if *Faust* is '"one of the most unclean of the whole unclean batch" of operas'[12]). The Daisy Song invariably commands the attention of the New York audience; being performed as Newland complacently observes his future wife, it consists in this scene of its striking phrase '*m'ama . . . non m'ama*', uttered by Marguerite as she plucks the petals from the flower. The dilemma which will consume Newland in the course of the novel is whether, indeed, he loves May or not, and 'He loves me . . . he loves me not' reiterates the 'x/ not-x' equation of which May, the characteristic, typical Old New York specimen, is so exactly and primly the emblem; it could be May plaintively destroying the flower as she wonders about Newland's constancy (although, as a 'not-nice' thought, his constancy is never publicly questioned). When the phrase is next heard, eighteen months later in the story, Newland has long since been infatuated with Madame Olenska, and he will stare at her empty seat at the Opera House as he listens again to the aria. The analogy seems suddenly to have shifted or deformed itself: the structure of Marguerite's Italian phrase echoes that of 'x/not-x'; and by this time we are acutely aware that in such an equation May is 'nice' and Ellen is not, a binary opposition already clear in Olenska's outlandish clothes in the first scene.

From the outset we are compelled to wonder what analogy between the Marguerite–Faust and the May–Newland courtships is being proposed. The Daisy Song is subtly refracted through the story as the *leitmotif* of Whartonian obliquity: does the recurring *Faust* theme suggest a Mephistophilean Olenska who has practised upon Newland, tempted him to sell his soul and lose the world for her (as Old New York thinks)?[13] The real Mephistophiles is the cunning and manipulative May, who compels him to sell his soul to Society, for respectability; in a Marlovian *Faustus*,

May would be the ephemeral Helen of Troy who turns out to be a phantom. The *Faust* story is also characteristic of Newland's self-dramatising sensibility. He sees himself, first and last, toiling in the meshes of an unmeant destiny in which his one chance of escape and redemption is renounced; and it through Newland's eyes that we see and hear *Faust*.

In other ways the binary simplicity of 'x/not-x', so confidently reported on the surface of this scene, is undercut by sudden distortions deeper down. The stage and the audience seem partly to mirror each other in the Marguerite–May simile.[14] Marguerite's name is also that of the flowers she holds; and daisies, in the period's language of flowers, always symbolise beauty and innocence – appropriate enough for Marguerite and May; but May carries lily of the valley, a phyllanthographically unstable blossom: 'return of happiness' in one reading,[15] but 'the heart withering in secret' in another, more sinister one.[16] May, ensconced in the centre of Old New York's most characteristic scene and meanings, is fraught with ambiguities, doubts, shadows in which the accidents of wealth – flowers, opera-plots, leisure itself – become unreadable hieroglyphics, portents, agents of tragedy.

Next to May in the first scene, and exciting much comment from the Club box where Newland stands, is her first cousin, unnamed and indeed unnoticed by the narrative for some time after the vision of May. She is merely 'a slim young woman' with an unusually theatrical gown and head-dress of whose eccentricity she seems unaware, and it is not until after a digression on Lawrence Lefferts's authority on 'form' and Sillerton Jackson's on 'family' – not, in fact, until the next chapter – that she is named as 'poor Ellen Olenska', a woman in flight from her husband (a *foreign* husband), whose reputation for being 'not-nice' was established long ago, when she made her debut at eighteen in a black dress. We quickly learn that her tastes in art, literature, and clothes are advanced, that her sense of what is 'done' and 'not-done', 'nice' and 'not-nice' is shockingly deficient, regrettable, and ultimately intolerable to Old New York. In the course of the novel we will be asked to mark May as the symbol of all that is nice, predictable, and done; and Ellen as the opposite of these, a distinction clear enough, in the terms of x and not-x, to Old New York; the actual distinction, however, is not so manifest.

The deaf and dumb asylum

> '"You never did ask each other anything, did you? And you never told each other anything."' (*AI* 356)

The New York of *The Age of Innocence*, Wharton observes, exists 'in a . . . hieroglyphic world, where the real thing was never said or done or even thought, but only represented by a set of arbitrary signs' (*AI*44). The severe caesura of 'not-x' is actually one of its most voluble locutions. So ingrained are tribal nuances that its members communicate more commonly by glances, silences, tacit assumptions, and an 'elaborate dissimulation' (*AI*339) which Newland feels as 'a deathly sense of the superiority of implication and analogy over direct action, and of silence over rash words' (*AI*335). These 'faint implications and pale delicacies' (*AI*16) obviate language itself, so that the code can be reduced by May on one occasion to a significant but speechless glance conveying a long, complex paragraph of subtle but specific semantic content (*AI*267).[17] So oppressive is this habit of implication that essential things can never be said outright: Newland is repeatedly taxed with his own inarticulacy, unable to express his feelings to Olenska, incapable of countering Sillerton Jackson's mistaken allusion to an affair between Olenska and Beaufort, unable to correct his family's belief in a liaison between himself and Olenska. Delia Ralston in *The Old Maid* cannot hear of her cousin's illegitimate pregnancy 'without a shudder of repugnance . . . such things . . . should not have been spoken in her bedroom, so near the spotless nursery across the passage' (*OM*33); such revelations seem to put 'into crude words all the trembling silences of her own heart' (*OM*43).

It is not merely that language has been rarefied to an obliquity useful because efficient; it is that a huge category of expressive utterance (the 'unpleasant') has been deemed unhearable. This is the world whose Episcopal Church has amended 'the coarser allusions in the Marriage Service' (*OM*5), whose congregation has adopted a compromising attitude which makes their city 'safe friendly hypocritical New York' (*OM*41), where the 'genteel monotony of . . . the surface was never stirred by the dumb dramas now and then enacted underground. Sensitive souls . . . were like muted key-boards, on which Fate played without a sound' (*OM*4). Ellipsis, 'not-x', is silence, muteness, dumbness, suffocation. Charlotte Lovell is unusual in insisting: 'Let us call things by their names' (*OM*111).

Julius Beaufort's own history, to take a case in point, though apparently well known to the women of the tribe, must by common agreement be kept shrouded in mystery, or at least unarticulated; his past is yet another instance of the Whartonian narrative caesura, whose silence we are left to supply with detail and meaning. His wife, the former Regina Dallas – one of the tribe – has to exercise great tribal delicacy to avoid looking like one of her husband's kept women; '"it takes all Regina's distinction not to look like . . . like . . ."' (*AI*258) is a remark quickly dropped and left unfinished since it cannot be completed without the introduction of a 'not-nice' thought; it is nonetheless perfectly understood by its auditors. The last scene in the novel has Newland in late middle age regretting 'the stifled memories of an inarticulate lifetime' (*AI*357), a cumulative store of such repressions which is the key to the tragedy of the novel.

In her essay 'Visibility in Fiction' Wharton argued for a specificity of characterisation which defends individuality 'against the overwhelming encroachment of events'.[18] Dickens, Thackeray, and Trollope are among the novelists she considers to have evolved characters whose verisimilitude or *vrai semblable* lets them stand out in their uniqueness against the monotony of type. Among the specificities she approves are names, idiomatic peculiarities, and gestures such as Julius Beaufort's, whose shocking visibility enjoins a rigid verbal ellipsis in his prim observers. By this standard the Old New York character is incapable of maintaining its visibility for long, since everything – dress, opinion, speech-patterns, manners, habits, noses, even names – are entirely generic. Henry and Louisa van der Luyden are examples of 'invisibility': so profoundly and respectably of their type, class, and tribe are they that they have virtually disappeared into a ghostly existence in their mausoleum-like house. The world they inhabit has been thinned and rarefied into 'super-terrestrial twilight'; they bear the most typical of Old New York names; even their complexions are almost transparent, perspicuous; they are not individuals but totems. Going to call on them for social guidance is like consulting a source as impersonal and as mystical as the Delphic oracle.[19]

Visibility and transparency are figured in tribal nomenclature, and the simplest way, in Wharton's novels, to distinguish the tribe from the outsiders is by its onomastic categories. Compare the outlandish, unique, highly 'visible' (even Dickensian) 'Undine Spragg' or 'Elmer Moffatt', 'Sim Rosedale', 'Eldorada Tooker', 'Coral Hicks', 'Agathon Carver', 'Alvah Loft', 'Gladys Toy', and 'Indiana Frusk', with 'Ralph Marvell', 'Lawrence Selden', 'Newland Archer', 'Charlotte Lovell', 'Sillerton Jackson', and 'Reginald Chivers'. Outsider names are odd or funny, often because they possess semantic qualities as common nouns; they are as bizarre and as noticeable as the often-remarked American habit of spitting in public, and they have no genealogical relation to their bearers – they sound like fanciful inventions which observe no tradition.[20] The reverse, however, is true of Wharton's gentry. As in Balzac, Trollope, Thackeray, Conrad, and even Joyce, her conventional family names recur in various novels, reinforcing the sense of tribal enclosure and genetic inevitability. Indeed, these onomastic choices obey the high-caste habit, still extant in America, of using surnames as male first names: hence Newland, Thorley, Sillerton, Dallas, Van der Luyden, Lovell, Manson, and Lefferts all appear as first *and* as last names in Wharton's novels. There can be comedy in this, as when Mrs Lefferts Rushworth and Mr Lawrence Lefferts turn up on the same dinner list; or when Fanny, the child of the disgraced Beaufort and his mistress, Fanny Ring (rather than of his wife, Regina Dallas) reappears as the daughter-in-law of Newland Archer, married to Newland's eldest son, Dallas (an example of genetic *ex*ogamy being delicately manifested in the onomastics of social *en*dogamy); or when the founder of the Ralston family, John Frederick, daringly christens his first-born son Frederick John. But there are significant tragedies encoded in them, too. Clementina Lovell Ralston, the illegitimate child of Charlotte Lovell, has her parental history embedded in her name – her father was Clement Spender; her adoptive mother, the woman who thinks of Tina as the child she might have had with Clement, is Delia Ralston. This mystery, however, is never unlocked by genealogically adept Old New York, though it is plain enough to the acute observer. Newland Archer, christened with his mother's maiden name, encounters his wife's grandmother, Mrs Manson Mingott, who advertises in her married patronymic an alliance in her dead husband's family which gave him a last name as a given name (perhaps *his* mother's), Mrs Mingott ('plain Catherine Spicer of Staten Island') claiming his family rather than her own less moneyed and less respectable antecedants. The Countess Olenska tells Newland Archer of her childhood infatuation with his cousin, a Vandie Newland (by the logic of Whartonian onomastics, this must be *Van der Luyden* Newland).

Leffertses, Spicers, Jacksons, Mingotts, Newlands, Chiverses, Mansons, Ralstons, Dagonets, Halseys, Vandergraves, Lannings, and the near-divine van der Luydens, not to mention Rushworths, Dallases, Thorleys, Merrys, and Archers: these 20 or so names are welded into a coherent though complex nomenclature across several novels (*The Custom of the Country*, *The Age of Innocence*, *The Old Maid*, *New Year's Day*, and *The Mother's Recompense*), in which the males bear them either as first or last names like badges or secret handshakes which allow them to move within the tribe and to enjoy its privileges. They denote important alliances through kinship and marriage; they are inscrutable to all but the initiated, who decode them as they would read 'an ancient geographer's map of the Hyperborean regions' (as Wharton puts it in *The Reef*), where only a few features stand out in the blankness, such as 'the Everards of Albany' (*R* 136).

Wharton's mother was famous for having helpfully replied, when asked which Mrs Jones she was, 'I am *the* Mrs Jones'.[21] That her mother should have considered herself the natural and obvious bearer of that imperious definite article only confirms the forbidding rigidity of the code: in her reply we may read the observation: 'if you must ask which Mrs Jones I am, you can't possibly be someone I *know'*. Mrs William Astor and her niece, Mrs William Waldorf Astor, were celebrated for a preposterous nomenclatural war in the late 1880s to decide who would be *the* Mrs Astor. Each instructed her friends to address their summer correspondence with her to 'Mrs Astor, Newport'; the confusion was majestic.[22] Alice Gwynne Vanderbilt (wife of Cornelius II) was ridiculed by Wharton for insisting, like Wharton's mother, on being *the* Mrs Vanderbilt (Wharton alluded to her assumption of aristocratic airs by referring to her as 'Alice Mrs Vanderbilt'[23]); Wharton's own insistence on 'Mrs Wharton' probably owes something to the need of those *grande dames* to establish some uniqueness in the clutter of individuals all using the same names.

Old New York maintains its tribal boundaries in part through linguistic obliquity. Newland's son admires his father's generation 'for knowing more about each other's private thoughts than we ever have time to find out about our own' (*AI*357), and this almost telepathic – or at least instinctive – capacity is reinforced by tribal nomenclature. That obliquity, or telepathy, also promotes a kind of invisibility which is mortal to the sort of characters likely to hold our attention as fictional protagonists. Ellen Olenska and Charlotte Lovell *must* erode or disappear lest their visibility threaten the quotidian niceness of the tribe. Wharton's notion of visibility helps identify the problem of Olenska herself: she is entirely, radiantly 'visible', from the way she does her hair to her unusual European clothes and Frenchified English to her taste in interior decoration and her reading and social habits. The vinelike curl lying on her cheek, the 'perverse' dress, sheathlike and fur-trimmed, which makes her look like a Carolus Duran subject – she is full of these 'delicious details that made her herself and no other' (*AI*309). Olenska comprehends the dangerous visibility of the non-conformist; but she also evinces a gestural language of restraint, denial, and sacrifice which is the opposite of the complacence, the careful hiding away of the 'unpleasantness' which she represents to Old New York. At a performance of Dion Boucicault's *The Shaugraun*, Newland savours, as always, a particular scene:

> The actress, who was standing near the mantelpiece and looking down into the fire, wore a grey cashmere dress without fashionable loopings or trimmings, moulded to her tall figure and flowing in long lines about her feet. Around her neck was a narrow black velvet ribbon with the ends flowing down her back. When her wooer turned from

her she rested her arms against the mantel-shelf and bowed her face in her hands. On the threshold he paused to look at her; then he stole back, lifted one of the ends of velvet ribbon, kissed it, and left the room without her hearing him or changing her attitude. And on this silent parting the curtain fell. It was always for the sake of that particular scene that Newland Archer went to see 'The Shaugraun'. (*AI*113).[24] [Plate 3]

This scene, so intensely and concretely imagined, depicts remoteness and distance. Its effect depends on our visualisation of her dress, her posture, and the description of her ribbon. Its highly arresting gestures are emblematic of tribal New York: nothing is said; everything seems to be experienced at a remove; the image of Molyneaux kissing the unaware Claire ffoliot's ribbon sums up the distancing, the muted reactions and tastes of Newland's world. Kissing the dress, not the woman, is pure 'not-x', the action – like that of a card for paid call – metonymising some more direct and forthright gesture. 'In its reticence, its dumb sorrow, it moved him more than the most famous histrionic outpourings' (*AI*114). The scene on this occasion especially – but mysteriously – reminds him of his leavetaking from Olenska after his first visit to her house; many scenes later, he will commit an analogous gesture of passion, frustration, distance, when he kisses her shoe a few moments before receiving the news of his now-inexorable wedding date with May.

The kissing of a ribbon can stand for the stifled ethos of Newland's own background, but (and this is why it reminds Newland of his visit to her) even more powerfully it acknowledges the bravery of Olenska, who also sends her lover away, choosing to limit her own desires in the interest of a higher and more abstract good – the ease and happiness of Newland and May, and the New York she misreads as generous and friendly. Olenska is a heroic figure: she represents an anti-tribal visibility, and yet it is hers to teach its most representative member a pragmatic lesson couched in the tribe's own virtues of silence, absence, and restraint.

And Newland is very much in need of instruction. On a walk in Fifth Avenue he sees the highly illuminated Julius Beaufort from a distance,

on his doorstep, darkly projected against a blaze of light, descended into his private brougham, and rolled away to a mysterious and probably unmentionable destination. It was not an Opera night, and no one was giving a party, so that Beaufort's outing was undoubtedly of a clandestine nature. (*AI*100)

Here is that oppressive linguistic obliquity pitted against outrageous visibility: Newland is struck not so much by Beaufort himself as by his *destination*, which cannot be named. This destination is in fact, as we already guess, the house of Fanny Ring, 'our one...professional' as someone describes her in *New Year's Day* (*NYD*136), an expensive paramour who drives her loud canary-yellow brougham in the upright precincts of fashionable New York, whose presence is elaborately alluded to by outraged ladies of that group. Even Archer's acknowledgement of her existence is signalled by an evasive mental picture:

> Archer connected [Beaufort's destination] in his mind with a little house beyond Lexington Avenue in which beribboned window curtains and flower-boxes had recently appeared, and before whose newly painted door the canary-coloured brougham of Miss Fanny Ring was frequently seen to wait. (*AI*100)

He cannot, even to himself, allow this house to be described straightforwardly as 'Fanny Ring's house', despite the raucous evidence of yellow, of ribbons, of theatrical lighting; instead it is, in his thoughts, the house where her carriage is often seen, her carriage and her dwelling (like Claire ffolliot's kissed ribbon in *The Shaugraun*) essential, load-bearing metonyms. It is the sort of house to which the sort of man Beaufort is would go to visit the sort of woman Fanny Ring is known to be. The priggishness of the New York code is nowhere more expressively signalled than in these private, timorous musings of Newland Archer. The vaunted crystallinity of New York air ('anything less... seemed stifling' (*AI*94)) feels more like fog, an opaque mist of things that cannot be admitted, an obfuscation more suffocating than the grimiest urban smog. Significantly, Beaufort seems to escape the charge of impropriety through a gymnastical mental exercise which separates act from agent. All the guilt is associated with his destination and its appurtenances, rather than with the man himself. Fanny Ring is ostentatiously and elaborately cut by Old New York, a New York perfectly willing to countenance Julius Beaufort himself. Wharton's sense of this prim evasion and blatant hypocrisy was almost certainly learned from her mother; she recalls in *A Further Glance* the demi-mondaine of her childhood who had such a yellow equipage, 'whose identity was never to be discussed' (*FG*6–7).

The etiolation and repression of New York language is brutally foregrounded by both Ellen Olenska and Lizzie Hazeldean. When Newland proposes that they run away together, Olenska asks,

"Is it your idea, then, that I should live with you as your mistress –
since I can't be your wife?" ...The crudeness of the question startled
him: the word was one that women of his class fought shy of. ... He
noticed that Madame Olenska pronounced it as if it had a recognised
place in her vocabulary ... (*AI* 289–90).

Even at this climactic moment we find Newland referring his experience to the mores of his background, where women 'of his class' don't
use terms like 'mistress'. 'Mistress', like so many other desperately
important ideas, is an unsaid word. Lizzie Hazeldean, never an insider,
bluntly tells Henry Prest that she was never more than his mistress,
his prostitute. '"Mistress! Prostitute!"' exclaims Prest. 'Such words
were banned' (*NYD* 144). In *The Mother's Recompense* Enid Drover querulously objects to the word 'female' as used by Dr Johnson. 'Is that
word being used again? I never thought it very nice to apply to
women, did you?' (*MR* 97). Mrs Drover dislikes the not-niceness of
'female'; but Newland's mother's generation reserve even the word
'woman' for the fallen, the outsider, the reprehensible (*AI* 84). The
understood 'nice' word is, of course, 'lady'; mere 'women' do not exist
in polite society.

This stultifying, horribly polite world and its tribal pressure is the
story's tragic agent. Newland's sense of his own oppression, of being
muffled or gagged, is evoked by constant reference to enforced dumbness, to attenuated patterns of expression which are occasionally burst
by impulsive gestures such as the kissing of a ribbon, or a shoe, or
the uttering of the word 'mistress'. New York 'hates scenes', insists on
the performance of important actions ceremonially or ritually (in other
words, metaphorically and non-linguistically), from the formulaic 'Grace
Church wedding' to the conventional period and costume of mourning, to the ostracisation of offending members. Everything is performed
to secure the conviction that 'nobody knew anything, or had ever imagined anything' (*AI* 335). Shoes and ribbons and other accidents of personality and purpose become the only expressions of the unspoken, the
unspeakable.

The images of suppression are especially urgent in *The Old Maid*,
the novella which could stand as companion-piece, or coda, to *The Age
of Innocence*. Delia Ralston gave up her passionate attachment to the
'not-nice' world some ten years before the novel opens, and the story is
thus entirely set in that emotional aftermath which in *The Age of Innocence* is only its *envoi*. The consequences of Delia's renunciation – of an

impecunious American artist based in Rome in favour of a completely conventional marriage into one of Old New York's 'safest' families – become fully clear when Delia helps to rear the so-called foundling child who is in fact the illegitimate daughter of her cousin Charlotte and Clem Spender, the same artist Delia forsook. This child comes to represent for Delia the life she might have led, 'her forfeited reality' (*OM* 130). Like Newland Archer, Delia is aware of 'the trembling silence of her . . . heart' which her cousin Charlotte keeps 'putting into crude words' (*OM* 43), of 'the dumb depths of [her] own past', which consist of 'feelings she had never uttered, ideas she hardly avowed to herself' (*OM* 102). The fact of Charlotte's momentary union with Clem Spender and its secret consequence is 'as close to the surface as a corpse too hastily buried' (*OM* 117), one of the 'dark destinies coiled under the safe surface of life' (*OM* 120), one of 'the blind forces of life groping and crying underfoot' (*OM* 129). Charlotte herself, whose suppression is not, like Delia's, of self-knowledge, but of impropriety, is pictured as a stopped-up volcano, with molten lava struggling to break through a granitic surface, and 'no issue for the fires within' (*OM* 118).

The depiction of 'genteel monotony . . . stirred by dumb dramas now and then enacted underground' (*OM* 4) insists, troublingly, on a not-nice world lurking underfoot, not beyond but *below* the 'nicest girls' in the 'nicest sets', a sinister underworld that is either like a fiery hell, or a shadowy deep inhabited by 'things' imagined as monster-like, titanic, threatening, dark, resistless, which exist in coils or in corpses. One of these shadowy monster of 'not-x' is sex, of course, and the power it exerts to overthrow caution and decorum in young ladies. Charlotte obeyed its power and is – though in secret – a fallen woman, the conundrum of an 'old maid' with carnal and maternal experience. Another monster is the green-eyed kind: Delia rejected Spender and opted instead for the propriety of a safe and dull marriage rather than a passionate and precarious one, and an unspoken premiss of the story is Delia's sexual jealousy of Charlotte, who took for herself what Delia was afraid to have. Each pays the price of her choice with a torment: Charlotte's, the agony of unacknowledged motherhood; Delia's, the disturbing sense of being a stranger to her own life, a third person in her daily experience, constantly ambushed by the clandestine world of feelings which she can hardly articulate even to herself. The corroding silence they maintain between themselves relegates that jealousy to a place out of conversational bounds, and erects for each of them a high wall of circumlocution which is imprisoning.

Boundaries and bounders

'What is life, indeed, without curtains?'[25]

In *A Further Glance* Wharton discusses at length the decorating taste of her mother's generation, a set of details which amounts to symptoms of attitude, a concrete evocation of ritual behaviour. In the brownstone houses of lower Manhattan:

> the tall narrow windows were hung with three layers of curtains (*rideaux de vitrage* through which no eye from the street could possibly penetrate, & over these, lace or embroidered tulle curtains richly beruffled, & draped back under the velvet or damask curtains which were drawn in the evenings). This window garniture always seemed to me to correspond, symbolically, with the superposed layers of undergarments worn by the ladies of the period. . . . They were, in fact, almost purely a symbol, for in many windows even the inner 'sash-curtains' were looped back with wide satin ribbons, in order to allow the secluded dwellers within a narrow glimpse of the street; but no self-respecting mistress of a brown-stone house could dispense with this symbolic window-lingerie. . . . (*FG*9)

In other words, the complicated triple-tiered window-treatment is less a practical than a social requisite: it defines the hierarchy of seclusion, the brownstone-dweller able to see out, but the street forbidden to gaze in. The world without is framed, upholstered, domesticated by frills and velvet, dressed up with the primness of an Old New York maiden in her heavy veils and petticoats. The actual, like the rhetorical, window-dressings of Old New York are fascinating: elaborate, immovably fixed in gilt cornices and looped back almost like stage-curtains, curtains convey to the outside world only the merest glimpses (and these tightly manipulated and controlled) of the inner world of the tribe. They also provide a heavily edited, strongly mediated 'view' of the outside world. The window itself is a powerful image for Wharton: she invokes it constantly to propose a narrowing of experience and perspective. She likens Old New Yorkers to the shopkeepers and petty merchants from whom they originate, putting 'in their windows the wares there was most demand for, keeping their private opinions for the back shop', where they invariably fade and decay (*OM*7). In 'Mrs Manstey's View' and in *The House of Mirth* Mrs Manstey and Mrs Penniston are fenestrated by necessity and habit. Ann Eliza's world in 'Bunner Sisters' seems defined by the paltry articles in her little shop window, and the great moments of her life consist of looking at things in other windows, including the clock she buys from the man who will ruin her sister and herself; old Mrs Clephane in *The Mother's Recompense* reminds her daughter-in-law of 'the Dutch ancestresses to whom the doings of the street were reported by a little mirror' (*MR*44). Delia Ralston in *The Old Maid* casts a puzzled glance at an outer world which blurs into vistas of 'the undifferentiated and the uninvited' (*OM*132). The pathos of the uninvited or the ostracised gazing out at the crepuscular ritual of lighting up the New York streets is embodied in Mrs Spragg and Kate Clephane, who reverse the wistful image of the face looking in from outside by being isolated from the world's goings-on in their splendid, damaging luxury. As Wharton says in *New Year's Day*, looking out of the window is 'a Dutch habit still extensively practised in the best New York circles' (*NYD*8).

Other features of interior decoration collude in fictional meaning, and Wharton deploys them with the remoteness of an anthropological investigator. Her mother, like all the correct ladies of Old New York, maintained a vast collection of bric-a-brac in showy vitrines in the drawing room:

> Our mothers . . . really knew about two works of art – old lace, & old painted fans. In both cases the eighteenth century tradition was still unbroken, & in nearly every family there were yards and yards of precious old lace, & fans, of ivory, chicken-skin or pale tortoise-shell exquisitely decorated. But as to any other *bibelots* a universal ignorance prevailed. . . .' (*FG*9–11).

'What would the New Yorker of the present day say to those interiors, & the lives lived in them?' Wharton asks (*FG*8). Almost unintelligible, they are like recovered fragments of early human society, most bearing the label 'use unknown'. Old New York, as Wharton remembered it, had made a cult of its own past, so that the carefully tended domestic collections of its women become for her an emblem of what Anna Leath in *The Reef* thinks of as her husband's carefully classified museum of existence, memory, and manners (*R*93). No wonder Mrs Penniston in *The House of Mirth* regards breaches of etiquette and decorum in terms of housekeeping: not-nice behaviour is like 'the smell of cooking in the drawing-room' (*HM*204), or like leaving the carpets down all summer (*HM*199). Curtains and vitrine-collections, like housekeeping rituals, are fetishised symbols of tribe, but amount, after all, only to frail barricades against whatever lies beyond their 'impenetrable domesticity' (*HM*58).

Like the limited vocabulary of niceness and not-niceness, the behaviour of its linguistic adepts is formalised in precise spatial and social
terms. The marvellously wrought opening scene at the opera in *The Age
of Innocence* introduces some of these key patterns of behaviour and
belief.[26] The opera is a showcase of social specimens: the men go there to
gaze at the women; the women to look at the clothes and jewels; the
immensely rich Mrs Julius Beaufort uses the opera once a year on the
night of her ball, going there to demonstrate the brilliance and efficient
reliability of her domestic appointments in the hours before her sumptuous entertainment is to begin;[27] non-tribal New York, ignominiously
seated in the stalls, goes to marvel at the great and the good ranged in
god-like splendour in the boxes. Newland goes there to observe and to
show off his intended bride.

We are shown the interior of the opera house from Newland's point of
view, from the various boxes he visits as he makes his way, leisurely, to
the box where May Welland is sitting with her mother and Ellen Olenska.
The amphitheatrical horseshoe of its architecture promotes intersecting
gazes across the space above the stalls, and we are treated to a veritable
opera of glances, as Newland looks at May, May gazes at Newland or blushes
into her bouquet, the salacious Larry Lefferts comments like a chorus on
the women, especially Olenska, and Newland watches Lefferts looking at
her. Everything about this scene is filtered through a kind of narratorial
double lens, as remote and clinical as the metonymic gesture of grand
ladies peering through their jewelled lorgnettes: people in this scene seem
to frame and assess each other, and their objects of contemplation are
reduced to types or representations, mannequins displaying family jewels,
family alliances, and thus family honour. The opera, one of Old New York's
essential rites, is where ceremonial containment of individuality within
such categories can be most effectively accomplished. Newland, for
example, comes to the opera to assess the effect of his beautiful fiancée
in her setting, among her family and friends, as an 'engaged' woman, a
view of her he has not had before. Newland, like his friends in the club
box, is a connoisseur of May rather than a lover; he is most pleased with
her the less he knows her; he can best appreciate her from a distance.
Newland will marry May only to find out that there is nothing there,
that there *is* no muted keyboard, no dumb drama waiting to be called
out of the depths of May's soul; this is because he has fallen in love with
an image, an idea of May, rather than with her reality, abetted by his
sense of form rather than by any powerful inclination. The view of May
at the opera – remote, radiant, pure – is the one he selects, with a Pygmalion-like intention of moulding her, forming her tastes, guiding her

experience, revealing the world to her untutored eyes. But May is no Galatea: what she is at the moment of their marriage is what she will always be; she is the price Newland pays for anticipating pleasure as 'a subtler satisfaction than its realisation' (*AI*4). This sense of filtration, of remote observation, of deferred or oblique experience, is a frequent effect in the novel. Filtration stills and deadens event and detail, packages reality safely at one remove, a technical replication of the bleached and dim emotions and enthusiasms of Archer's society. The impulse which prompts Newland to hang back in the box to observe the observers is the same which dictates that Mrs Manson Mingott's relations will claim 'other engagements' on the evening of her party for Ellen Olenska, which invokes the phrase 'not at home' not literally but conventionally. Again and again Wharton notes that the tribe requires mystification, only asks not to hear anything unpleasant. When the taboo against unpleasantness is flouted, boundaries are broken, and the violation sends the valetudinarian Mr Welland to his bed with a fever and gives Mrs Manson Mingott a mild stroke which at first renders her speechless. The raw facts of unconventionality and visibility literally debilitate Old New York and force it to withdraw behind the defences of the sickroom.

Essayists had been writing almost anthropologically about America since the initiation of the Republic. Alexis de Tocqueville noted the difficulty of erecting social boundaries in a democracy, the presence of which can only be detected by close observation and analysis;[28] the title of Frances Trollope's *The Domestic Manners of the Americans* (1832) suggests a disinterested but needful investigation of a foreign tribe; it casts a cold eye on everyday matters such as the arrangement of interior space and urban landscapes.[29] Even Thoreau's journeys to and records of Cape Cod, the Maine woods, and the local rivers of eastern Massachusetts bear the hallmark of this tradition of American social anatomy.[30] In Wharton's own day, her friend Paul Bourget was producing the anatomical essays on American life which would eventually be gathered as the book *Outre-Mer* (1895);[31] and, most significantly, Thorstein Veblen's *The Theory of the Leisure Class* (1899) established the science of sociology by treating sardonically of the American rich in the methodology and terminology of a field-study of neolithic bushmen or south-sea islanders. All these writers, implicitly or explicitly, acknowledge the existence and power of tribal grouping, custom, and taboo.

Edith Wharton's fictional and autobiographical tribal writings are nearly always couched in an extensive anthropological vocabulary and set of images. Her ear detects, for example, the flat vocal quality of New Yorkers of Dutch descent in comparison with those of English derivation (*BG*52–3). Newland Archer, in the clutches of his in-laws, compares himself to a wild animal being ceremonially displayed by its trappers; and he senses their disapproval of his association with Ellen 'by some deep tribal instinct' of allegiance and enmity. When the families of May, Newland, and Ellen realise the peril to the newly-weds, they join forces to eject the offending member (Ellen) from their midst in a 'tribal rally around a kinswoman about to be eliminated from the tribe', a ceremonial rite of rejection (*AI*334). In their penultimate meeting, Ellen and Newland rendezvous in a gallery of the art museum (chosen because nobody ever goes there), a room filled with Trojan antiquities, 'small, broken objects, hardly recognizable domestic utensils, ornaments and personal trifles made of clay, glass, of discoloured bronze and other time-blurred substances' (*AI*309). The gallery holds the remains, the incidental detritus, of some long-declined tribe, its cases a physical emblem of the anthropologist's and the archaeologist's impartial investigations suspiciously similar to the random assemblages of bric-a-brac in the maternal vitrines of brownstone New York, whose poor fragments likewise suggest the ruin of Newland's life, the paltry satisfactions and broken dreams which will constitute his future in New York, the ultimate futility of New York's traditions and beliefs. The shards and pieces of the Cesnola Antiquities are foreshadowings of the 'mere grey speck of a man', the relic he finds himself to be in his late middle age at the end of the book, 'compared with the ruthless, magnificent fellow he had dreamed of being' (*AI*354).

We know that Wharton read Herbert Spencer, Edward Westermarck, and Paul Topinard, all early anthropologists and sociologists.[32] And although there is no direct evidence that she read Veblen,[33] in *Twilight Sleep* the new money of the protagonist derives from auto-manufacture in a place called Exploit, an important Veblenian term. In *The Custom of the Country* she has Ralph Marvell referring to Old New York as 'the reservation' and visiting ethnological exhibits at the museums; Newland Archer has read books on Primitive Man. Her own *French Ways and Their Meaning* (1919) is effectively a sociological tract for US soldiers stationed in France. Wharton's delineation of the American *haute bourgeoisie* familiarly uses sociological and ethnological jargon and concepts.

Veblen refers late-Victorian American manners and behavioural decorum to the vestigial presence of tribal status-hierarchies, 'symbolical and conventionalised survivals representing former acts of dominance...

a symbolic pantomime of mastery on the one hand and subservience on the other ... '.[34] Elaborated symbolic behaviours, such as call-paying, card-leaving, and introductions, which constitute the very currency of extended social transaction, are, in other words, remote and distanced from their original meanings, as stylised and coded as the glance through the lorgnette or the kissing of the ribbon.

Veblen goes on to observe that manners acquire, with higher civilisation, a sacramental or ceremonial character, the breach of which requires exorcism, such as the one which separates Newland and Ellen forever.

Tribal membership is usually posited by Wharton as gestural (as in elaborate window-dressings), behavioural (as in calling at the correct hour), and sometimes even genetic (there is the Hazeldean heart; the Sillerton gout; the Wesson liver, infirmities as honourable as the Hapsburg lip which distinguish the clans in *New Year's Day*). The bounds of tribal identity are imagined as high walls which closely guard a citadel; but these walls are more insubstantial than curtains, and the citadel, thoroughly examined, turns out to be the repository merely of pathetic snobberies, gossip and hypocrisy which leavens the undeniable 'good in the old ways' (*AI*347). Wharton's regular allusions to the severe observations of social science (and, as I will propose in Chapter 2, to evolutionary theory), remind us that it will not do to be sentimental about any particular set of tribal rules, as Newland is at the end of *The Age of Innocence*: after all, 'there was always a traitor in the citadel; and after he ... had surrendered the keys, what was the use of pretending that it was impregnable?' (*AI*259–60). Tribal regulations are invisible until they are tested, violated, and finally overridden; only embattled are they perceptible; only when questioned or under threat can they be examined and discussed. A phrase of Erving Goffman's is useful here: such violations are a form of 'remedial exchange' in which the damage is recompensed in the clarification and verification of social patterns and hierarchies.[35]

Biographical writing about Wharton of the last 30 years can leave us in no doubt of her troubling yet liberating sense of deracination. Inculcated with the ineradicable sensibility of tribe – in its codes, its pales, its linguistic nuances – she wrote her way to social and financial freedom only to spend much of her subsequent literary career recreating its higher arcana, extracting from its recollected stultifications a coherent design, a received social order against which individual desire and the assertion of self could be picked out in bold colours, in which that same desire might also be sublimated. What the social, tribal design provided was a framework in which to explore the idea of disorder, a concept to which she cannot help awarding equivocal merit. The votaress of well-run households, precise domestic arrangements and engineering, good manners, and meticulous prose admires and regrets the vanished civilisation of her childhood, its carefully tended proprieties and consequent certainties. On the other hand, that beautifully and unreflectingly maintained social order was one in which she herself, ultimately, could not live, and it therefore contains the threat of entrapment and suffocation.[36]

The relationship between these two attitudes and the designs they uphold and denigrate are central to her social aesthetic. Against its neatness, its architecture of behaviours and communities, the modernist sense of fragmentation is pitched as either terrifying or exhilarating, the latter most fully expressed in the novels of the 1920s, and in *Fighting France* (1915). Newland's sense of estrangement from his amniotic envelope of tradition is always figured in images of atomisation, of sundered relationships between behaviour and meaning, between thing and use, between taste and understanding. The embroidery, plants, and eighteenth-century glazed ware gathered in his mother's house, the hyper-ideation of his experience as the Archer and Welland families formally and ceremonially disentangle him from Olenska, and of course the unvisited cases of the Cesnola Antiquities in the museum are all, like the hoarded bibelots in Mrs Jones's vitrines, versions of fragmentation, collections of unrelated objects and thoughts coincidentally (and thus meaninglessly) grouped together as if to propose a coherent pattern which, on examination, proves specious (in the words of the museum curator, 'use unknown'). What Nancy Bentley has described as Wharton's technique of defamiliarisation, in which the disparity between cultural artefacts and the social circumstances which require and produce them as their expression, is repeatedly evoked and referred to.[37] Newland can dream of a beneficent social fragmentation in which adulterous transgression would have no meaning, where social categories like 'mistress' and 'wife' would cease to exist, while all around him ethnographers like Sillerton Jackson and Larry Lefferts investigate and preserve social behaviour and formal observances with 'the patience of a collector and the science of a naturalist' (*AI*32). Newland can ironise his family and social circle as primitive tribes; but he himself maintains a superstitious link between things and their names: certain words said aloud are a kind of bad magic, as in his refusal to describe Fanny Ring straightforwardly as Julius Beaufort's mistress, and his separation of her possessions from Fanny Ring herself. The same Newland who would like to live in a New York which honoured writers as avidly as dukes can unthinkingly approve the rigid social order which distinguishes between 'ordinary' dukes and dukes who are related to Old New York. Even in his intellectual pursuits Archer has no coherent focus: his accreditation as a *litterateur* consists in lists of books and authors, many of which are valued for their novelty; his sense of Olenska's exotic appeal is constructed from her pictures, some nuances of speech, and – again – her books. The picture we get of her through Newland's eyes is fragmented, incomplete, indistinct.

The central violation of the tribal boundaries represented variously by curtains and cousinages is the love affair between Olenska and Archer; but what is most extraordinary about this violation is how little actually happens. Its almost imperceptible events lurk in the fringes of their daily lives, the furtiveness almost absurdly maintained to mask a very primly conducted infatuation. It is hardly an affair at all, but more like the ghost of one, consisting of a couple of embraces and a tearful scene in which Newland lays his head on Ellen's lap. It is carried on principally in a series of uncomfortable or brief or interrupted meetings, or during journeys in carriages, where passion is bundled away, little is said, and what is mainly heard are Newland's thoughts raging against the constraints of his predicament, thoughts which even at these critical junctures he cannot express. His constraint is not only verbal: the freedom perspicaciously offered to him by May, and the proposal of a single physical liaison by Olenska, are too enfranchising and he cannot seize them. Newland is crippled by an inability to think in the present moment, to act or refrain from action *in propria persona*; by a tendency to represent his caste or family; by his preference for anticipated pleasure over pleasure at hand. His idea of happiness, like many of his thoughts about a relationship with Olenska and with the *outre-mer* which she represents, is based on fantasy, in this case of a world without social regulations, the very last place where he would thrive; but although Olenska (who has a practical knowledge of boundaries and their transgression) is right to regard that country as a delusion, it is mostly so because Newland could never travel there even if it did exist, a failure of which we are reminded even in the final scene when he cannot take opportunity by the forelock and ascend to Olenska's Paris flat. Cynthia Wolff argues that Newland's failure to reestablish contact with Olenska in the novel's last pages is a triumph of his acceptance of the life he has lived and was made for over the dream of escape which he put away in the course of his marriage to May.[38] This is *Newland's* interpretation; the ending of *The Age of Innocence* is not, I think, quite so comforting. Even at 57 Newland is the same man he was at 27 – the adventure of Olenska is one which he will defer eternally, preferring anticipation to experience. He would rather stand anonymously in a Paris square gazing up at a window than encounter the owner of that window. The young dilettante has not changed; he is merely a middle-aged dilettante. The complacency of his upbringing and conditioning are higher walls than any citadel in the world. This is the conditioning which Wharton herself escaped.

Men at work

> 'The New York view about that is rather narrow, as we know.'
> (*OM*113)

In *A Backward Glance* Wharton begins her explanation of herself with a close account of the career of Ebeneezer Stevens, the great-grandfather she referred to as, 'our Great Progenitor' (*BG*14); even in late age, after nearly three decades' residence abroad and international literary success, a Revolutionary war hero remained the primary, legitimising element in her self-description. Her plural pronoun ('*our* great progenitor') is not Veblen's 'divine assurance and imperious complaisance' of high caste;[39] it is rather the expression of family in its most corporate sense, the family which early in the autobiography she carefully locates in the American colonial bourgeois landscape from the 1630s.

Her tribe – actual and fictional – is distinctly a New York tribe, not Bostonian or Philadelphian, a tribe which 'had not come to the colonies to die for a creed but to live for a bank-account,' (*OM*4); and the Jones side of the family (unlike the Rhinelander/Stevens side) had not so far, as Wharton remarks drily of such colonisers, 'committed [themselves] as to be great' (*OM*8). They tended instead to make excellent investments, such as the parcel of land which is now the 50s and 60s east of Central Park.[40] This tribe has a strict sense of moderation. It likes 'doing things handsomely' (*OM*3), but it loathes flashy money; its members gossip incessantly about the vulgarity of the new millionaires while conspicuously enjoying their hospitality. Wharton's family was antediluvian, the *ur*-race which held sway before the deluge of money which drowned Old New York at the end of the Civil War. Some of her cousins (daringly) married Astors, whose fortunes at least antedated the Rebellion; but the New Money with names like Rockefeller, Morgan, Gould, Vanderbilt or Belmont presented difficulties for them, especially when these new names were placing 'Wall Street under obligations which only Fifth Avenue could repay' (*HM*387). Her tribe does *not* consider itself aristocratic (although it is happy for non-tribal New York to do so), modestly conceding that aristocracy is always a problematic concept in a democracy. Alexis de Tocqueville observes:

> In aristocracies, men are separated from each other by lofty stationary barriers: in democracies, they are divided by many small and almost

invisible threads which are constantly broken or moved from place to place.... Whatever may be the general endeavour of a community to render its members equal and alike, the personal pride of individuals will always seek to rise above the line, and to form somewhere an inequality to their own advantage.[41]

For Wharton the conundrum of class-consciousness in a democratic republic is beautifully opportune: when there are no convenient ranks or titles by which to differentiate those who matter from those who don't, the codes become hideously, often hilariously, complex, especially, as Paul Fussell and Lewis Lapham have demonstrated so convincingly, Americans of all categories have always *insisted* that there is no class structure in their country.[42] Although in *The Age of Innocence* she smartly musters the families of Old New York into a neat ziggurat, her stories show that so tidy a structure is likely to be deformed by money.

'Don't tell me', says one matriarch in *The Age of Innocence*,

all this modern newspaper rubbish about a New York aristocracy. If there is one, neither the Mingotts nor the Mansons belong to it; no, nor the Newlands or the Chiverses either. Our grandfathers and great-grandfathers were just respectable English or Dutch merchants, who came to the colonies to make their fortune, and stayed here because they did so well.... they have nothing to do with rank or class. New York has always been a *commercial* community, and there are not more than three families in it who can claim an aristocratic origin in the real sense. (*AI*49)

Even more interesting than the insouciance with which the speaker admits to a *declassé* trading background is the precision with which she uses the word 'aristocracy', a replication of the linguistic precision described by Wharton in her own family ('My parents' ears were wounded by an unsuitable word as those of the musical are hurt by a false note' (*BG*51)). The speaker, like Wharton's parents, is pointedly literal-minded in her definition of 'aristocracy': she seems resistant to the metaphorical use to which this term may be put, even in a nation without a peerage or a notional division between gentlemen and others. But this ostentatious modesty is tempered by a snobbery only apparent to the initiated, in the form of an ancestor-cult which solely, it would appear, determines social eligibility: Newland Archer smugly and approvingly observes, of the entertainments for a distant English cousin of noble family, that only New York could distinguish between a mere duke and the *van der Luyden's* duke (*AI*62). The organic nature of such demarcations, and the likelihood of their evolution over time, is desperately misunderstood by most of the older, and the more conservative, characters in the Old New York novels. In the 1870s Ward McAllister and Mrs Astor tried to conjure a buttressed social precinct when they dreamt up 'the Patriarchs', a self-designated set of gentlemen of the best families who were to act as custodians of Society, and to assert their authority by limiting invitations to a few select balls. Of course, no such embalming of social status can ever be achieved, and Wharton even makes fun of Patriarchal pretensions when she has Lizzie Elmsworth and Virginia St George in *The Buccaneers* attend such a function masquerading as titled English ladies with very improbable accents.[43]

One of the 'invisible threads' referred to by de Tocqueville is the choice of profession. Although, he claims, 'in democracies, nothing is more great or more brilliant than commerce,' aristocracies prevent their members from pursuing this commercial wealth.[44] Elmer Moffatt anatomises this caste division when he tells Undine Spragg that her aristocratic French husband's 'ancestors are *his* business: Wall Street's mine' (*CC*323). One of the most striking features of Wharton's tribal classifications, consequently, is the work she gives her male characters. A harmless snob like Sillerton Jackson can profess tradition, genealogy, good manners, and other kinds of socially useful arcana with nearly academic concentration, as *arbiter elegantiarum* of Old New York in *The Age of Innocence*, *The Old Maid*, and *New Year's Day*; he is an indispensable repository of semi-sacred information. Old New York's real business, as Moffatt says, is its past; other professions are given only glancing notice. The older generation, naturally, live on their inherited wealth; that leisure, and Sillerton Jackson's encyclopaedic example, have spawned at least one younger imitator in the person of Larry Lefferts, whose authority on 'the question of pumps versus patent-leather "Oxfords"' has never been disputed (*AI*8); Henry van der Luyden's vatic pronouncements on social decorum seem to exhaust his professional capacity. The younger men – Newland Archer, Ralph Marvell, Lawrence Selden – usually practise law, although never with any ferocity or application (compare this with Dexter Manford in *Twilight Sleep*, who is a highly successful divorce lawyer, and, predictably, *not* of Old New York). 'Though it was supposed to be proper for them to have an occupation', says Wharton in *The Age of Innocence*, 'the crude fact of money-making was still regarded as derogatory, and the law, being a profession, was accounted a more gentlemanly pursuit than business' (*AI*125). Ralph Marvell, a putative lawyer, has not been trained to work for the style of living he is expected to maintain, and must lose caste by going into business; Newland Archer goes to his law office mainly to read the papers. It is with weary wonderment that Kate Clephane recollects the fact of Fred Landers's office hours: 'What on earth did he do there...? Most of one's men friends...were lawyers' (*MR*46). They may not go into politics; professional literary activity is 'bohemian' and compromising; and academia is distinctly below the salt, a pursuit *wilfully* followed by men like Professor Emerson Sillerton, whom 'nothing on earth obliged...to be an archaeologist, or indeed a professor of any sort' (*AI*220). Although the unborn early-twentieth century generation in *The Age of Innocence* will, astoundingly, '[go] in for Central American archaeology, for architecture or landscape-engineering; taking a keen and learned interest in the prerevolutionary buildings of their own country, studying and adapting Georgian types, and protesting at the meaningless use of the word "Colonial"' (*AI*345), no such opportunities offer to Newland and his friends in the 1870s.[45] The best he can hope to be is the friend of Theodore Roosevelt and to act as a sagacious elder in the burgeoning New York of the new century.[46]

Early or late, however, the one thing never willingly admitted to the social precinct is 'trade'. Julius Beaufort is a banker, and Sim Rosedale is some sort of property tycoon; if they are socially suspect or ineligible it is rather on the grounds of taste and belief (they are Jews). Mrs Lemuel Struthers, however, is viewed askance by Newland Archer's family because her money does come from trade (shoe polish), even though the process of social adjustment is already in train, since 'everybody' goes to Mrs Struthers' Sunday entertainments, and nobody bothers to remember that 'her champagne was transmuted Shoe Polish' (*AI*60). Mr Raycie in *False Dawn* scorns his son's new friend Ruskin because Ruskin *père* is a wine merchant: 'he looked at his son with an expression of unutterable disgust. "Retail?" "I...believe so...." "Faugh!"' (*FD*57) It is not Mr Raycie's abhorence of trade which betrays him, but rather his willingness to name it, and moreover in the almost clinical 'retail' (and indeed, his dreary way of expressing his artistic *desiderata* resembles nothing so much as a shopping list). Mr Raycie's unvarnished vocabulary does not participate in the high-caste scruple about not calling things by their names. He is like Claude Walsingham Popple, the society portraitist of *The Custom of the Country*, a man whose gentility is doubtful precisely because he keeps insisting on it so bluntly. Old New York will admit of forebears who began in banking, the India trade, shipbuilding, and so on; but hypocritically it has closed the gates on the self-constructed and on late-comers: Delia Ralston's socially eligible husband is, by the rule of thumb laid down by Ward McAllister, only *just* a gentleman, being merely of the fourth generation of genteel Ralstons.

In novels set in later periods than *The Age of Innocence* and *The Old Maid* these professional demarcations are more occluded. The men in *The House of Mirth* are almost all bankers or some other kind of financier; there may be inherited wealth among Lily Bart's expensive set, but it is not especially noticed; and only brand-new climbers like the Gormers or Mrs Hatch create any adverse comment. The operative snobberies of this *haute bourgeoisie* include having either no serious profession, like Melville Stancy, 'a lawyer in his leisure moments' (*HM*440), or one like investment banking, which seems effortlessly to produce riches. Mabel Lipscomb, the wife of a mere stockbroker in *The Custom of the Country*, is still beyond the pale to the turn-of-the-century sensibilities of Washington Square, a locus virtually invisible in the striving culture of *The House of Mirth*. Dexter Manford, of *Twilight Sleep*, the successful divorce lawyer (itself a suspect specialisation in the remnants of Old New York), is a farmer's son from Minnesota, which is supposed to account for this anomaly; he is also married to a manufacturing heiress whose 'pioneering and motor-building' energy had been inimical to the genteel idleness of her first husband, an Old New Yorker.

Rarely do Whartonian men engage in *practical* work. Martin Boyne in *The Children* is an engineer, as are Guy Thwarte (*The Buccaneers*), Ethan Frome, and *Ethan Frome*'s narrator. The actual job of building railways or bridges, anything of everyday use, is always marginalised, even in these novels, and non-existent in the Old New York group. Old New York instead expects its men to behave like Arthurian knights, observes Jim Wyant in *Twilight Sleep*, performing only picturesque, honourable tasks, mainly chivalric, mainly towards women, tasks emblematised by Arthur Wyant's attempt to kill Dexter Manford. But as Newland Archer recognises, that decorative manner is really so much humbug: in the period of *The Age of Innocence* (the 1870s) it merely disguises necessary patterns and conventions which maintain social stasis. By the time of *Twilight Sleep* (1927) that code is no more than a quaint archaism: the knights of Old New York are old, helpless, and discarded; they are always forgetting what time it is.

Images of snow: Whartonian womanhood

> 'The conditions of action on this continent were not favourable to really superior women.'[47]

Old New York chivalry, vigorous or vestigial, is directed, like its medieval antecedant, nominally toward its women. What this code expected and constructed as its object notifies us of Old New York's social organisation. In Wharton's fiction, the woman it evolved is usually either a cause or a result of Old New York's 'dumb dramas' of disappointment. Like her most famous female protagonist, Lily Bart, Wharton was not raised to do anything except be 'suitably' married. Neither her international literary reputation nor her money, her cars, her honorary Yale doctorate and her membership of the Legion d'Honneur, and her wide correspondence and friendship with many of the leading writers of the early-twentieth-century were the likely product of an Old New York upbringing. 'Isn't marriage your vocation?' asks Selden. 'Isn't it what you're all brought up for?' (*HM*13) With no provision for her education being thought necessary, Edith Wharton was an autodidact, gathering her learning as she could, principally from her father's 'gentleman's' library, a brilliant German governess, and the guidance of an older, bookish friend.[48] No writing paper was provided for her, so her early literary productions were executed on pieces of discarded wrapping paper. Her first full-length work of fiction, a comedy of manners entitled *Fast and Loose*, was produced at the age of fourteen, at 30,000 words no mean feat. It was equipped with highly sophisticated mock-reviews from the literary weeklies, which scrupulously pointed out all its faults:

> The very title suggests something desperate. Who is fast? What is loose? Apparently the author's well-meant intention was that everybody & everything should be fast and loose.... How is it that the heroine, who, we are anxiously informed, is the fastest woman in London, does nothing that would have raised a blush on the rigid countenance of an elderly Quakeress? (*FL*113–14)

Her family's reaction to this effort is not recorded; but they were happy enough, it seems, to have a selection of her adolescent poetry privately printed, either not scouting the inauguration of a literary career, or perhaps believing that such teenage effusions could not portend much in the way of ability. The furtiveness with which the child must have had to acquire her cutting wit and astonishing fluency in the diction and style of the journals invites speculation. The Joneses were not literary, and one wonders how she got access to the loftier magazines. In addition to the paucity of current literary material in the house, she was actively discouraged from reading for some time after her recovery from a childhood bout of typhoid fever – the usual Victorian prescription to prevent the stimulated imagination from drawing blood to the brain, away from the needier convalescent organs. She describes her early pleasure in literature as 'a secret ecstasy of communion. I say "secret", for I cannot remember ever speaking to anyone of these enraptured sessions. The child knows instinctively when it will be understood, and from the first I kept my adventures with books to myself' (*BG*69–70). Early on, it seems, she was aware of the marginal, even the illicit, nature of her literary behaviour. She showed a story to her mother, written when she was about eleven, which began:

> "Oh, how do you do, Mrs Brown," said Mrs Tomkins. "If only I had known you were going to call I should have tidied up the drawing-room" (*BG*73).

Mrs Jones's only comment, that 'drawing rooms are always tidy,' 'was . . . crushing to a would-be novelist.' The remark has the usual hallmark of 'not-x', of ruling out all possible alternative conditions with a peremptory dictat. Indeed, Wharton's version of her childhood seems to consist of 'not-x': no school, no writing materials, no encouragement. The act of production by girls, beyond a few inessential decorative objects, was held to be deeply unfeminine and anti-social. Her will to write made her quintessentially 'not-nice'.

In spite of assertions to the contrary by the likes of Martha Louise Rayne (*What Can a Woman Do?* (1893))[49] that literary women need no longer attract the ridicule to which they were subject in earlier eras, still the serious, professional American woman writer might socially legitimise her output in sheer necessity only if she were producing charming or improving works of unimpeachable propriety. Although Mrs Rayne cites George Eliot, the Brontës, Mrs Gaskell, and Mrs Humphrey Ward as exemplars of female literary craft, among Americans she can summon only Rosa Hartwick Thorpe (celebrated author of 'Curfew Must Not Ring Tonight') and 'the sweet, pure, wholesome works' of Mrs A.D.T. Whitney (*We Girls* and other light classics).[50] To cite more weighty examples, Louisa May Alcott and Harriet Beecher Stowe *had* to write, the one to contribute to the meagre finances of her feckless and improvident father, the (predictably) Transcendentalist Bronson Alcott, the other to support her large family during her husband's professional vicissitudes; but then neither Alcott nor Stowe was fettered by the exceptionally rigid rules which governed Wharton's upbringing. Where Wharton's women must not work, must rely on inherited or bestowed wealth, books such as Alcott's *Little Women* and *Work* insist almost shrilly on the propriety and ethics of certain forms of female labour as against unearned income, especially that derived from loveless marriages.[51] But these women were as far from Edith Wharton's world as could be: of professional, bohemian, decently genteel stock, they wrote or worked *as* professionals; and, indeed, Wharton's two or three forays into the world of Alcott's Christy (*Bunner Sisters, The Fruit of the Tree*, and *Ethan Frome*) are extraordinary, but muted, restrained, and narratively remote, written not from experience but from inventive conjecture about people without choice. Until she abandoned Old New York altogether, Wharton's imaginative proclivity, and her willingness to publish, be paid, and be known for it, placed her firmly in a very dubious category for which her world hardly possessed terms, precisely because nothing on earth obliged her to be a writer of any sort.

Her 'tribal' connexions in New York were biographically far behind her by the time she had settled in Paris. But sometimes, as Wharton recognised, it is easier to analyse one's own country and background from afar, and her most profoundly backward-looking novels, the ones set in Old New York, or among the descendants of that world, were all products of the 1920s, written after the war (which she experienced wholly and vividly in France), after she was thoroughly expatriated.

For all its ghastliness, the war itself was not the subject of her deepest response, although, as I argue in the final chapter, it was the trigger. The theme on which she writes with the most relentless sense of horror, which seemed most to appal and fascinate her, was the education and training of the young women of her generation and class. Her evocation of the extreme vacancy and sterility of the socially determined American female character, and of female arts (dress, decoration, entertainment) at times achieves the fine strangeness of Poe and Melville, making her, at her height, most thoroughly American when farthest from America. The most sinister of these characters is May Welland.

In Edith Wharton's youthful world of post-Civil War Victoriana, it need hardly be said, girls were not educated or broadened; they were kept from anything thought to be 'improper', which tended to include books, politics, and even social experience except for the most limited and chaperoned kind. They had to be dull, pretty, well-mannered, and well-dressed; they were expected to be 'terrifying' naive young women 'who knew nothing and expected everything' (*AI*42). Even though institutions like Oberlin College and the State University of Iowa had been coeducating since 1837 and 1856 respectively,[52] higher education was virtually unheard of for girls of the upper class. Mothers were urged to stay their girls from too much study because young ladies were thought to be unequal to intellectual strain of most kinds: it would ruin their mental and physical health and make them unfit to be wives and mothers by making them too masculine.[53] They were not to cultivate artistic talents, either, beyond what would be pleasing in the home, since serious devotion to – say – music or art might distract them from their ultimate purpose, the comfort of their husbands.[54] Their profession was marriage; to work for their living by necessity was not genteel; to work by inclination was *outrée*. A young woman was to be decorative, self-effacing, complementary but never competitive, innocent and sympathetic – in short, the angel in the house. She was to cultivate *female* friendships or else be thought unladylike. She was expected to be devoted to her parents until her duty shifted to her husband. Physically restricted by her clothing and her gestures, and geographically limited to her own household or chaperoned visits to others, she could not even move about at a party on her own account; etiquette forbade the initiation of social exchange with men by a woman, either in private drawing-rooms or in public places. Even the paying of calls on other women, one of her few forms of social movement, was itself a highly regulated, ritualised kind of social interaction performed with her mother which, in its restrictiveness, seems to stand almost in parodic relation to the easy, free intercourse of the men among themselves in their clubs, their opera boxes, and in sporting activity.

Women were thought to be morally superior to men precisely because completely innocent of worldly knowledge. They chose reading for their daughters, as Wharton's mother had done for her (though she probably would have been horrified to discover that her daughter had obtained Goethe's *The Sorrows of Young Werther* at the age of 13); and the supposed guilelessness of a young woman put her in need of male muscles and logic to shelter her fascination and pathos. Newland is captivated by every article of this familiar Victorian catalogue, most of which he finds in May, who is what Lady Grenville praises in 'the old-fashioned English maiden': 'a rosebud in appearance and purity, gentle of heart, soft of speech, the denizen of our ancestral homes, a lady in soul, and mind, and manner'.[55] He believes her to be innocent and guileless in the extreme, even though she explicitly reminds him that 'you mustn't think that a girl knows as little as her parents imagine' (*AI*148), even in the face of subsequent evidence of her manoeuverings to expel Olenska, even 30 years on, when he finds she had always been aware of his emotional plight.

'Brilliance' in women referred to their complexions and social graces; girls with other – presumably pragmatic or intellectual – gifts are compassed by social arbiters like Mrs van Rensselaer in the imprecise adjective 'clever',[56] a word used of Olenska by May, and by the less respectful of 'semi-women, mental hermaphrodites.' Wharton was 'oppressed by this creation of factitious purity, so cunningly manufactured by a conspiracy of mothers and aunts and grandmothers and long-dead ancestresses' (*AI*45), a conspiracy which half a century after her own girlhood was still producing translucent, virginally dressed, insubstantial creatures like Fitzgerald's Daisy Buchanan, whose blasé summary of her privileged life – 'I've been everywhere and seen everything and done everything'[57] – suggests that it has left no impression whatever upon her. The strain of this oppression seems to leap out of a photograph of Edith Wharton, taken shortly after her marriage, which shows her in a tightly corsetted suit with two tiny dogs perched one on each shoulder; she is hemmed in by dogs and whalebone stays, and her melancholy face seems to express her condition. [Plate 4]

It is because women served important tribal functions that the rules governing their behaviour and upbringing were so exact. Women preserve the traditions of tribes, especially in new or pioneering nations;[58] they are the repositories of social value (Mrs van Rensselaer astutely observes that a woman marrying 'down' can elevate her husband to her own social rank, but a man who marries beneath him acquires the caste of his wife).[59] Another important tribal function of women illustrates Veblen's 'canon of pecuniary decency', which insists that women practise a 'ceremonial futility' as a way of advertising their husbands' merit.[60] Receptacles of social value, prized for exterior qualities such as beauty and grooming, the well-bred Old New York female becomes that quintessentially American nightmare, the blank, the white, or the transparent. From *Moby-Dick* and *The Narrative of Arthur Gordon Pym* to Stevens' 'Auroras of Autumn' and Frost's 'For Once, Then, Something' and 'Desert Places', whiteness 'with no expression, nothing to express'[61] invokes terror, despair, and helplessness:

> There yet lurks an elusive something in the innermost idea of this hue, which strikes panic to the soul . . . that ghastly mildness, even more loathsome than terrific . . . ,[62]

says Melville; and the phrases conjure May Welland. Like a Civic Virtue, she is an impersonal representation of her sex and class and background. Her character is of minimal complexity; her tastes are unerringly derivative; Newland reflects that she will never surprise him. Bourget complains of 'the innumerable Mays' one meets at Newport: even her name is generic.[63] The type is characterised by an artificially induced innocence; and the 'abysmal purity' (*AI*7) of May and her kind is always charged with unnatural images of whiteness. The recently engaged Newland marvels that he will always have 'this whiteness, radiance, goodness' (*AI*23) at his side, and proudly believes that 'she doesn't even guess what it's all about' (*AI*6) when she watches Faust woo Marguerite. May clings to her parents, and argues for a long engagement because little girls owe that much to their parents, because all her friends have practised it. But later he begins to see that May's eyes are 'too-clear' (*AI*145); transparent (*AI*189); her signature flowers are white; she is usually dressed in white, silver or blue-white (even her stage-double, Marguerite, wears white with a hint of blue beneath); she is 'a young Diana' of forbidding virginal purity, or 'an image made of snow' (*AI*45).[64] On her wedding day, consequently, May disappears from the scene: Newland is thinking instead of Olenska as May comes up the aisle; the service consists of a series of disembodied actions ('the ring was on her hand, the bishop's benediction . . . given' (*AI*186); and then the couple are being driven away. Except that she is 'radiant', we never *see* May, any more than Newland does. Narratorially she is transparent.

May and her kind share a frightening indistinction: they employ, as Bourget notices, a few universal adjectives ('lovely', 'enchanting', 'fascinating') to describe everything from paintings, landscapes, horses, music, a bonnet, a statue.[65] Beyond this, they are 'carefully trained not to possess' judgement, versatility, and experience (*AI*44), to have no opinions, no imagination. 'Experience dropped away from' May (*AI*211); and she seems to have embalming fluid, not blood, running in her veins, which preserves her from any impression which her own life might importunately make on her, a conceit which makes her almost corpse-like.[66] Her vocation, like Lily Bart's, is marriage; but she cannot be emancipated from such a fate because she 'had not the dimmest notion that she was not free' (*AI*195) (and elsewhere such women never stop to wonder why women are treated differently from men (*OM*66)). Deployed by her family like a counter on a board, May is the human embodiment of property in a society where daughters are likened to twenty-storey buildings, where each May knows her value, and speaks of herself 'as of a certificate of New York Central or Chicago Burlington and Quincy stock'.[67] May Welland is a carefully tended and protected species, bleached of colour and character like hot-house white asparagus, or like her own heavily veiled complexion, cultivated for an anodyne 'niceness' which makes her a suitable match for the Old New York male, but, significantly, not for Julius Beaufort, the flamboyant outsider who is unmoved by this kind of sterile tribal beauty.

It is a kind of spiritual foot-binding, a deformation which dehumanises her, makes her as innocent as a baby even at her death, but also – horrifyingly – as ignorant as a blind Kentucky cave fish, looking 'blankly at blankness' (*AI*82). Her life, thinks Newland, has been 'as closely girt as her figure' (*AI*349); 'what if "niceness" carried to that supreme degree were only a negation, the curtain dropped before an emptiness?' (*AI*212). (This phrase notably incorporates the force of negation, the language of 'not-x', and the favourite Whartonian image of curtains.) Newland thinks of unbandaging May's eyes once they are married, of introducing her to the world; but it is *Newland* whose eyes are to be unwrapped. Niceness is almost colourless, drained of interest or detail, terrifying in its profound emptiness.

Niceness is not, finally, adequate as a condition of being or as a linguistic construction; unendurable, a kind of monstrosity, next to it the world of not-niceness, so resolutely ignored by the ladies of the tribe, is nothing less than robustly familiar, life-enhancing, admirable. Newland suspects that 'not-x' is a realm which must be explored, not relegated to a negative, blank category. In the moment of the first stirrings of his passion for Olenska, he seems to see 'the faint white figure of May Welland – in New York' (*AI*77). The fundamental tragedy of the novel is not that he cannot have Olenska; rather, it is that he *must* have May.

Any number of Whartonian females replicate the type of 'nice' girl propagated by the tribe. Often, niceness is signalled by literary taste. Undine Spragg is not really a 'nice' girl at all, but she aspires to niceness. In spite of her rapacity on two continents, she has no flair as a *grande horizontale*, but longs merely to have what she wants while remaining 'respectable'. Sandra Gilbert and Susan Gubar wittily type her not as *une femme fatale*, but *une femme banale*.[68] She reads pulpy sentimental novels, and goes to frothy Broadway productions with gaseous names ('Oolaloo' and 'The Soda-Water Fountain'). Lily Bart reads Omar Khayam. May Welland prefers Tennyson (the 'wrong' Tennyson – *Idylls of the King*) to the pre-Raphaelite Brotherhood; and Lita Wyant only reads fashion magazines, her cultural blankness ultimately more fit for Hollywood celluloid than for any profound humanity. Charity Royall works in a library but does not read at all. Wharton notes ironically that important books from gentlemen's libraries, such as Whitman, were 'brought out, like tobacco, only in the absence of "the ladies"' (*FG*21).[69]

May Welland was not by any means Wharton's last word on the subject of female vacancy. A later novel of the 1920s, and set in that decade, shows two of May's direct descendants. The title of *Twilight Sleep* (1927) is taken from a form of obstetrical anaesthesia of the time, so-called because it supposedly made childbirth painless, translating the experience into 'one of the loveliest, most poetic things in the world...' (*TS*14). Twilight sleep is a late analogy of the Old New York fear of 'anything unpleasant', and the women of the novel devise various techniques for inducing that anaesthetic numbness: Pauline Manford can ignore her dysfunctional family by following a frenzied timetable which leaves no time for their problems. Pauline's daughter-in-law, Lita Wyant (languid, beautiful, bored, pure Daisy Buchanan in her 'milky translucence' (*TS*35)), adopts the opposite strategy with a household whose dreamlike impracticality (the chairs are like mattresses), torpid atemporality (there are no clocks, no meal schedule, no fixed hours at all), and low-level lighting (except for the spotlight trained day and night on the goldfish bowl, too dim to read by), abstract her from responsibility and engagement. Of separate generations, both Pauline and Lita are blank, empty, vacant, transparent, their personal barricades against feeling acting as a cloche to protect tender and immature plants against the elements.[70]

Visibility and solidity in women are, by contrast, notable, even odd. In the opening opera scene in *The Age of Innocence* Ellen and May are seated together. In one sense the pairing is perfectly bland: both are granddaughters of Mrs Manson Mingott, one of Old New York's grandest (and most eccentric) *doyennes*. But in every other respect Ellen is as notable, as visible, as unique, as May is colourless, transparent, and representative. It is exactly the opposite of this transparency which first attracts Newland to Olenska; she is dark, opaque, mysterious, different in her habit of doing the things that 'are not done', in her odd and unconventional background. She keeps books in her drawing room; she goes to Mrs Struthers's parties and to Sarasate's concerts with the disreputable but cultured Julius Beaufort; her English grammar has become oddly inflected by her long immersion in Francophone societies, and she uses terms of endearment apparently indiscriminately (she calls her Italian maid 'my dear' – *not done* in New York); her clothes are exotic, eccentric, and 'disturbing' to Newland; her social manners are peculiar ('It was not the custom in New York drawing-rooms for a lady to get up and walk away from one gentleman in order to seek the company of another. Etiquette required that she should wait, immovable as an idol, while the men who wished to converse with her succeeded each other at her side' (*AI*63)); she lives at the wrong address ('"What does it matter where one lives?" . . . He fancied that her New York was still completely undifferentiated, and the conjecture nettled him' (*AI*74).) Her little house is strange and interesting, and breaks every known rule of Old New York interior decoration.[71] Newland is fascinated and disconcerted by her, and is especially puzzled and mortified by Olenska's interest in Beaufort. But Beaufort is exactly the sort of man who *would* interest her – as she him – in his unique visibility. They are both 'foreign', and they speak each other's language. Newland, a complacent but not unintelligent young man, about to marry into the most complacent of Old New York families, is suddenly reminded by Olenska how much lies beyond his Old New York boundaries. Olenska, contrary to the disposition of Old New York, is active and impulsive, two traits specifically disallowed in a woman. She is also wonderfully free of any sense of embarrassment: only marginally tolerated by New York society, she is amused and puzzled by its regulations: 'Is New York such a labyrinth?' she asks. 'I thought it so straight up and down – like Fifth Avenue. And with all the cross streets numbered!' (*AI*76). Like her grandmother, the redoubtable Mrs Manson Mingott, the woman who in her widowhood had a mansion built for herself in the wilds above 34th Street, Ellen Olenska has an 'almost parvenu indifference to the subtler distinctions' (*AI*102). Ellen does not realise how generous and 'kindly' Old New York has had to be to accept her back into the fold.[72] Only tribal insistence on blood-loyalty keeps her in its good graces, and even this is accomplished only at the official behest of the high votarists of the cult, the sepulchral and lapidary van der Luydens; and the unnerving anonymity of the vacuous May Welland, her sightless, colourless eyes, her pale blonde head empty of everything but platitudes, is their exact phenotype, living proof of endogamous, non-fissiparous Old New York interbreeding.[73]

Constriction – geographical, intellectual, even physiological and genetic – is very often the abiding image of Wharton's fictions, her protagonists the (mostly failed) aspirants toward an enlivening liberty of behaviour and opinion. They include Newland Archer, Charity Royall, Lewis Raycie, and Annabel St George, as well as the heroically awful Undine Spragg. But *The Age of Innocence* seems to refract American womanhood with special power through imagined fates, possibly because Wharton was imagining herself: May Welland is the woman Wharton was designed by Old New York to be; Ellen Olenska, what she actually was, her imaginative projection of what it would have been like to return to the narrow compass of her innocence. 'Innocence' read as a terror, a monstrosity, a deformation, makes the title of the novel and its themes rather more ironic, less 'nostalgic' and sentimental.

Libraries and studies: where real things happen to men

How bizarre, then, must Wharton have seemed to her milieu! She could not – initially – justify her creative output in financial necessity.[74] Even if she had been a needy young woman, the only money-making she might with propriety have performed within her caste would have been the trimming of hats or the production of small decorative items of the kind bought by her friends at charity bazaars. The *inclination* to write was by the standards of her tribe even more peculiar in the world of nice women than writing itself.

Serious literature among her own group was naturally the province of men, and even their tolerance for it was limited. One of her distant cousins was Herman Melville, also a resident of New York, but 'deplorable Bohemian' (*BG* 68) that he was, Wharton says she never heard of him or read one of his books until she was an adult. Writers were worthwhile only if they were also gentlemen:

> in general [Old New York] liked novels about people in society, whose motives and habits were more comprehensible, spoke severely of Dickens, who 'had never drawn a gentleman', and considered Thackeray less at home in the great world than Bulwer. (*AI* 33)

'Intellect, to be praised by the old society', declares the indefatigable Mrs Van Rensselaer, 'had to be accompanied by the companion virtues of birth and breeding',[75] and cities Wharton as a prime example of this combination. But Wharton remarked retrospectively: 'In the eyes of our provincial society, authorship was still regarded as something between a black art and a form of manual labour' (*BG* 69); her own literary output was merely estranging to her family; literature:

> puzzled and embarrassed my old friends far more than it impressed them, and in my own family it created a kind of constraint which increased with the years. None of my relations ever spoke to me of my books – they simply ignored them ... the subject was avoided as if it were a kind of family disgrace ... they were felt only as a drawback and an embarrassment. (*BG* 144)

Like Mrs Astor, to whom architecture and painting were subjects for men, or really, 'chiefly for learned persons who read Ruskin' (*AI* 34–5), Wharton's tribal characters are usually worried by literary and artistic types:

> they were odd, they were uncertain, they had things one didn't know about in the background of their lives and minds ... [Old New York told] their children how much more agreeable and cultivated society had been when it included such figures as Washington Irving, Fitz-Greene Halleck, and the poet of "The Culprit Fay". The most celebrated authors ... had been 'gentlemen'; perhaps the unknown persons

who succeeded them had gentlemanly sentiments, but their origin, their appearance, their hair, their intimacy with the stage and the Opera, made any old New York criterion inapplicable to them (*AI*101).[76]

(It is immediately clear, by the way, that Washington Irving and Fitz-Greene Halleck were gentlemen because their first names are last names.) The eccentric and unusually 'visible' Medora Manson in *The Age of Innocence* is said once to have inaugurated a literary salon, but it soon died out in the arid intellectual climate of polite New York; the real-life Peter Marié, another possible historical model for Sillerton Jackson, tried to introduce 'intellectual teas' and 'poetical dinners' to Old New York, also without lasting success.[77]

With heavy irony Wharton considered the library of her parents' house, a room to which books were eventually relegated by fashionable redecoration of the old-fashioned brownstone. Known as 'the study', the room was an offhand homage to a long-declined acquaintance with culture:

[as] there was felt to be some obscure (perhaps Faustian) relation between the Middle Ages and the pursuit of culture, this sixteen foot square room in a New York side street was appropriately furnished with a huge oak mantlepiece sustained by vizored knights, who repeated themselves at the angles of a monumental writing-table, where I imagine little writing was done.... (*FG*21–2) [Plate 5]

The literary experience of Mr Raycie in *False Dawn* might have occurred in such a library: it is limited to 'drowsy after-dinner snatches from Knight's "Half-hours with the Best Authors"' (*FD*49) (a book Wharton remembered from her father's collection). Essentially lazy, but socially pretentious, Mr Raycie takes his literature in small, medicinal doses, just as he wants a painlessly acquired, ready-to-hang art collection.

Although there are a great number of libraries in Wharton's fictional houses, they are rarely used in the normal bibliophilic manner. Jack Alstrop's 'library' in *The Spark* is 'luxurious' and 'bookless' (the narrator suspects that the spines are false), the room no more than an opulent setting for cards. Pauline Manford's library in *Twilight Sleep* has real books in it, but only because she is too literal-minded to call a room a library otherwise, her honesty in the item of books in ironic relation to her self-deception.[78] The library of her husband Dexter is an index of his personal frustration: it is a collection of improving essays in science, religion, and history, but he is too shattered by socialising to get through Macaulay's complex periods. His dream of being read aloud to by Pauline is, like the books themselves, marginalised by his wife.

> She regarded the desire almost as a symptom of illness, and decided that Dexter needed 'rousing'...; and from that day, Manford's life, out of office hours, had been one of almost incessant social activity. (*TS*59)

Ralph Marvell's study is, by contrast, genuine; but perhaps its very authenticity marks it out as the setting of tragedy: late in *The Custom of the Country*, unable to supply the money Undine needs like air, Ralph shoots himself there, pathetically surrounded by his socially and financially useless books and papers and unfinished literary attempts.

Books are thought to be out of place in the fashionable New York drawing room: one of Lizzie Hazeldean's tenderest memories of her dead husband is his insistence on plenty of reading material. 'She had never before lived in a house with books in it' (*NYD*39), and their presence long after his death continues to be noticed and remarked upon. The books 'scattered about the room' in Ellen Olenska's little house in the wrong part of town are among the first indicators that she is not 'one of us'; unlike Lizzie Hazeldean, she *is* a woman who reads; and, amazingly, she keeps her books visible to guests, as if she were displaying personal secrets or unmentionable articles of clothing. The library in the Trenors' country house in *The House of Mirth* is mentioned solely because it is a place of illicit meetings (specifically between Selden and Bertha Dorset); *because* it contains books it is almost by definition sure to be safe from intrusion.[79]

This suspicion of or indifference to literature, which makes these libraries and studies peculiarly notable, is not confined to the upper crust. In the novella *Summer*, the unused village library, like that of Wharton's father, has been built with some care and even with minor grandiosity by a benefactor of North Dormer, but it is dank, and the books moulder. The library's remoteness from any practical or intellectual local need figures the remoteness of the village itself. Ethan Frome's initial interaction with the narrator is in the loan of a book about 'some recent discoveries in biochemistry' (*EF*9), but Ethan's own 'study', a poor underfurnished room where he keeps some poetry and a few technical books from his abortive engineering education, is made unusable because its stove never lit and is later appropriated to heat the room of the new hired girl. This relegation is characteristic of the frigid Frome domestic atmosphere, and of the hard household economy insisted upon by Zeena.

A few of Wharton's most interesting men read and even write, but often almost furtively, always marginally. Furtiveness is a quality connected with bookishness and literary pursuits – indeed, with almost any intellectual activity – and one of her favourite descriptive flourishes is an account of the private study of her public man, the room where, in Old New York terms, he enjoys his intimate and possibly forbidden pleasures of the mind. Newland Archer unpacks his newly arrived London shipment of books in the late evening, after work and (daringly) in preference to three dinner invitations; it includes *Middlemarch* and some of the recent pre-Raphaelite volumes. His 'homelike and welcoming' library has reproductions of his favourite paintings, 'rows and rows of books', and functional curtains and furniture. He dreams of a similar room in the future matrimonial home which will have this 'sincere' arrangement.[80] The moral burden of domestic design is clear in 'sincere': curtains and windows open and close, books are collected as literature rather than as decorative objects or costly rarities, the fireplace works and is kept burning at odd hours to accommodate the reader. It is important that such sincerity is invoked in a library, and it is a sign of Newland's ultimate surrender of this domain that in the last chapter his study has become 'the room in which most of the real things of his life had happened' (*AI*344). These 'real' things, appropriately, are nothing to do with books, but with christenings, family announcements and decisions, and meetings with Teddy Roosevelt. Newland's architect son has 'done over' the room in Chippendale, mezzotints, and a china collection (no books are mentioned in the new arrangement), making it – no doubt – pleasant and attractive, but quite unlike the more private appointments it had had in Newland's young literary manhood. Except for the battered Eastlake writing-desk, Newland's study now seems a lot like an updated version of the brownstone decoration, with its bric-a-brac and prettiness, of Wharton's mother. The study is an enclosure, moreover, into which unwelcome intrusions of the social, tribal world are made by people like Janey Archer and May, when they wish to discuss family matters – in May's case, the prospect of a first child. Newland's reading in those early days was interrupted, his solitude violated, by such intrusions, which usually compelled him to reject 'study' – the life of the spirit; daring ideas; Olenska and the wide world – in favour of the imposed interests of Old New York. By the end of the novel that rejection is complete: the study, as far as we can tell, has become a public, or at least a family, room, and there is a marked absence in it of books and papers. The interruptions which irritated him at the beginning of the story have become institutionalised in a room of their own.

The precision with which Wharton establishes Newland's literary tastes notifies us of the importance of the opposition between aesthetic inclination and social obligation. Ruskin, George Eliot, Vernon Lee's *Euphorion*, Pater's *The Renaissance*, John Addington Symonds, Swinburne's *Chastelard*, Balzac's *Contes Drolatiques*, Poe, Verne, Merimée (*Lettres à une Inconnue*), Daudet, and the Brownings are among his enthusiasms; and perhaps Wharton tries a little *too* hard to set him up as a frustrated aesthete. But if so, it is the product of genuine distress recollected 40 years on: Newland's tastes are very similar to Wharton's own; in him we have a portrait of her own early experience. To enjoy literature is to marginalise oneself, either in a remote room or a remote neighbourhood. To read is to be unsociable, the cardinal sin in Newland's world, and this is why books must be exiled.

Ralph Marvell's 'old brown room', like Newland's, is filled with comfortable furniture, college photos, and battered college bookcases; tables and chairs overflow with volumes and sketches, and on his desk is an incomplete essay entitled 'The Rhythmical Structures of Walt Whitman', and with a long poem (unfinished) called 'The Banished God'.[81] The essay's subject is surely playful, since Whitman, the rugged poet of democracy, was, as we know from Wharton's comparison of *Leaves of Grass* to tobacco, of all voices the one most likely to appal the rigid susceptibilities of Old New York; fittingly, Ralph is concerned with the relatively abstract matter of technique, perhaps unable or unwilling to get to grips with the non-gentility of Whitman's poetic themes and purposes. In Ralph's tradition:

> nothing . . . was opposed to this desultory dabbling with life. For four or five generations it had been the rule . . . that a young fellow should go to Columbia or Harvard, read law, and then lapse into more or less cultivated inaction. The only essential was that he should live "like a gentleman" – that is, with a tranquil disdain for mere money-getting, a passive openness to the finer sensations, one or two fixed principles as to the quality of wine, and an archaic probity that had not yet learned to distinguish between private and 'business' honour. (*CC*45)

In other words, the men's engagement with literature is as purely recreational and inessential as their professional activities, and somewhat more so than their sporting and social ones.

Writing is an eccentricity more peculiar than reading for men as well as women. Ralph Marvell's grandfather discusses marriage arrangements with Undine's father; it is the usual bargain – Ralph's slightly impoverished social cachet is to be traded for the 'settlement' which the much richer Mr Spragg will make on the young couple. But Mr Spragg, the hard-headed businessman, still wants to know how Ralph will support his daughter. 'He can write poetry', Ralph's grandfather replies; 'now and then he gets ten dollars from a magazine'. 'Wasn't he ever *taught* to work?' asks Mr Spragg. 'No; I really couldn't have afforded that' (*CC*72), says the grandfather, with delicate monetary allusion to the price of the loss of caste. There are two kinds of eccentricity being referred to here: to Mr Dagonet Ralph's writing is odd because it is unfashionable; to Mr Spragg, because unprofitable.

In *The House of Mirth*, Selden's study is the most important setting, bearing great symbolic and narrative weight. A marginal but attractive member of high society, Selden will not abjure the life of the mind for the blandishments of social prominence and a 'good' marriage, a principle embodied in his study, which we see through Lily's eyes. She likes its books, papers, worn furniture, old prints, and faded carpet, but especially appreciates the bindings of his books because they are 'ripe, rich, pleasurable'. Lily's first response to Selden's library is essentially philistine, her pleasure in his books sensual rather than intellectual, a response usually associated by Wharton with arriviste wealth, like Elmer Moffatt's, or with undeveloped or vacant taste. Lily likes the look and feel of the bindings, and is interested in their potential value, a curiosity which amuses Selden; and this study, culture's only outpost in the novel, is the setting for a discussion of price. She has come to him, depressingly enough, to learn about 'Americana', the only known enthusiasm of a dreary but fabulously rich young man she would like to marry. The Americana collection is kept in what is described as a mausoleum;[82] and Lily, moreover, wants to teach the rich young man to buy jewels for her as readily as he buys items for his collection. She does not begin to distinguish between the unimpassioned acquisition of Americana (probably the last thing Selden would be interested in owning) and genuine literary engagement. She cannot differentiate between 'Americana' (a rich man's hobby which has nothing to do with letters) and literary taste (which has very little to do with books, but much with texts) until it is too late to make a difference. Selden's study is not only strange and pleasantly shabby against the wealthy excesses and deadened aesthetic impulses of her regular milieu; it is strange of purpose and use. And it is specifically off limits, illicit to Lily because it is a bachelor's flat in a pointedly designated bachelors' building. In the accumulation of small errors which compound Lily's tragic decline, her completely innocent visit to Selden's study, where they talk partly of books, is the first instalment.

Another of the book's most important episodes occurs there. Shortly before her death, Lily visits Selden for the last time to admit to herself and to him that despite all her previous refusals, she is after all in love with him; to tell him that he has awakened her conscience, her less venal self; and to burn the packet of compromising letters written to him by Bertha Dorset, letters which, if she were to blackmail Bertha with them, would clear her of obloquy and financial exigency. The study is a refuge against these difficulties, and against a rainswept evening; everything it represents about Selden – his culture, his poverty, his moral security against the rich pleasures and ease which have ruined Lily – becomes symbolic of Lily's spiritual growth, her rejection of the life that 'could never satisfy' (*HM*498). The study, in this scene, becomes so thoroughly what Selden *is* to Lily – her conscience – that the room, not just its owner, has agency.

There are other Seldens. In *False Dawn* Lewis Raycie marginalises himself in his enthusiasm for Italian Primitives, not to come into fashion in New York until several decades after his death.[83] Clement Spender, the offstage character in the triangle which also includes Charlotte Lovell and Delia Ralston in *The Old Maid*, has deformed the lives of the two women by refusing to abandon his painting. Newland and Ralph, however, who share a vague inclination for 'Culture', are versions of a Selden who has taken the bait; the code of their tribe matches them unsuitably to women who do not share the life of the mind, a fate in which they essentially collude. Wharton's young literary dilettantes tend to associate marriage and its carnal vistas with literary ones, this act of substitution confessing that literature is not an end in itself but an analogy of some other, usually social, behaviour. Newland and Ralph each dream of introducing their wives to literature during their honeymoon. Lizzie Hazeldean, sympathetic at least to her husband's literary inclinations but incapable of sharing them, remembers only that he read some awful poem to her on their honeymoon about lovers struck by lightning (*NYD*44).

By contrast, the Countess Olenska reads Bourget, the Goncourt brothers, and the decadent Huysmans, writers with whom Newland Archer is less familiar; it is she who might teach *him* something about the new writing. It would hardly be 'manly', however, to be initiated into literary delight by a woman, to be the innocent in the relation, and he fantasises instead about coaching May to prefer 'Ulysses' and 'The Lotos-Eaters' to *The Idylls of the King*; his prenuptial vision of reading *Faust* to her by the Italian lakes is imagined not as an intellectual, but as a sexual activity, 'somewhat hazily confusing the scene of his projected honeymoon with the masterpieces of literature which it would be his manly privilege to reveal to his bride' (*AI*7). Reading *Faust* to the virginal May is going to be like her sexual initiation on their wedding night. She is innocent both of carnal and literary experience.

Poor Ralph Marvell takes his harpy to Italy for their honeymoon, mistakenly expecting that connubial rapture will issue in a rapturous communion of minds as they both await his parturition of a great work; but she has no eye for scenery and is completely unconscious that her beauty is prompting him 'to write a great poem' (*CC*83). The issue is instead a child, not a poem, and he learns that she is not a 'lovely rock-bound Andromeda' waiting to be whirled back into the blue by him (*CC*50). Lily Bart has already provided the model of Andromeda, manacled by her sapphire bracelet to the high life of pleasure and vacuity; and Selden, in the interest of spiritual self-preservation, has avoided the Persean task of liberating her. Neither Ralph nor Newland see that their Andromedas are willing captives, proof against any such liberation. On the other hand, neither is strong enough, talented enough, convinced enough, or adventurous enough to be an aesthetic hero like Lewis Raycie or Clem Spender. Each, in consequence, lives out a paltry, unfulfilled existence which for Newland ends in regret and a sense of futility and for Ralph in an early death.

Whartonian men are mostly dilettantes (if they have any aesthetic interests at all), or at best, guilty indulgers of their literary pleasures, as if literature were one of the milder forms of pornography. In *The Glimpses of the Moon* the hero Nick Lansing is a social marginal who, like Selden, is valued for his ornamental properties: he is useful to hostesses when they are entertaining intellectuals or feel like having a mild flirtation. Like Ralph Marvell, he 'writes a little', supposedly: but the account of his work has Whartonian disdain dripping from every syllable: 'His book was to be called *The Pageant of Alexander*... he liked writing descriptions, and vaguely felt that under the guise of fiction he could develop his theory of Oriental influences in western art at the expense of less learning than if he had tried to put his ideas into an essay' (*GM*63). He's not much good at fiction, in other words, or much of an art critic, but he passes for a writer among his own set. And in this set, the designation 'writer' is not professional or intellectual, but *social*. To be *thought* cultured is about as far as this learning will travel; thus, Selden's cultivation (which is genuine and unironised) is generally held to be 'a slight obstacle to easy intercourse' (*HM*103).

Culture as a positive impediment to propriety is the crux of the novella *The Spark*, where the conventional Hayley Delane, a poker-playing, party-giving banker and sportsman, has rigidly repressed his acquaintance with Walt Whitman in the military hospitals of Washington many years before, when the poet was dressing the wounds of the Northern army. This encounter, the 'spark' of the title, has changed Hayley Delane's life forever, although it is an effect which he but vaguely recognises and certainly has not understood or analysed. And the narrator of the story, convinced by Delane's occasional literary allusions that he was once a reader until something stopped him, is tantalised by the prospect that the 'something' was some momentous military experience (he is a veteran of Bull Run). His hunch seems about to be confirmed when he discovers that the event even more extraordinary than Bull Run was the meeting with Whitman; but his excitement is quickly disappointed when Delane querulously judges Whitman's poetry 'rubbish'. By name, profession, and inclination, there is nothing in the least distinctive about Hayley Delane *except* the coincidence which put him in contact with the most remarkable (and most 'bohemian') of American poets. If there is a tragedy in this tale, it is not that he has lost sight of that far-off wonder, but that he never realised what a wonder it was; instead, the questing curiosity of the narrator is merely irritating and inconvenient to Delane, who would rather not be quizzed about this particular episode.

Two Americans of the mid-nineteenth century might, in their anatomies of the social scene, have been instructing Edith Wharton in her own art. George Templeton Strong – man of affairs and gossipy Knickerbocker diarist – noted in 1855 with almost Whitmanian lyricism,

> The poet of AD 1855 will have his hands full with the men and women and things of 1855, and has no right to go back to other dead times. …His hand and his heart will find enough to feel and to do at his own door. There is poetry enough latent in the South Street merchant and the Wall Street financier…in the Fifth Avenue ballroom; in the Grace Church contrast of eternal vanity and new bonnets; in the dancers at Lewis Jones's and Mr Schiff's, and in the future of each and all. [84]

Strong recognises the possibility of art in the precise imagining of local milieu and geography, a perception hardly short of remarkable in a gentleman of rarefied, Europe-gazing Old New York.

At the end of the next decade, in 1869, Mrs Elizabeth Fries Ellet declared that

> where a society is so widely spread, it follows the law of fluids, and becomes the shallower the more it is diffused; also, that the intelligence, high culture, and fastidious taste that formerly marked the best circles, have of late given place to the mere love of display, pride of wealth, and sensuous apprehension.[85]

Mrs Ellet, more baldly than Edith Wharton, delineates the boundaries and enclosures of milieu with an almost empirical judgement. Both writers pre-empt the advice Henry James gave to Wharton in 1902: 'There it is round you. Don't pass it by – the immediate, the real, the only, the yours, the novelist's that it waits for . . . *Do New York!*'[86]

Whether set in the antiquated society of old money and manners, or in the austere and stony rural hinterland of western Massachussetts, or among the faubourgs of pre-war Paris, her themes are explicated with an anthropological eye for detail and nuance, a naturalist's empirical method, and a satirical wit which forbids much sympathy with the follies it discovers. This eye, method, and wit are virtually unsurpassed in modern literature. Although she is usually compared to the more ponderous James, her friend and mentor – a comparison which annoyed her intensely, since she thought most later James unreadable – she is nearer to Jane Austen: there is the same lightness of touch, the same deft wielding of the social scalpel, the same ruthlessness. She is, as a contemporary reviewer somewhat equivocally called her, the 'Fabre of the social apiary', an 'entomologist of society'.[87]

If she wrote best of the socially élite it was that this group was the one she was best placed by experience to observe, the group whose markers and codes she understood well enough to violate in fiction.[88] Although her first literary success was an ambitious historical romance set in eighteenth-century Italy, she took Henry James's advice to look closer to home and to write of what she found there. By the time of her literary maturity, after the Great War, although Wharton had been absent from home for many years, her fiction in this period is more than ever set within it. Emotional and geographical distance from her own world – as a novice and as an internationally established author – purified and clarified its lines, allowing her to *see* her subject and to translate it into plausible fictions.

2
Outcasts

If the book had been the work of an outsider, of some barbarian reduced to guessing at what went on behind the stockade, they would not so much have minded. . . . But here was a tale written by one of themselves, a tale deliberately slandering and defiling their most sacred institutions and some of the most deeply revered members of the clan!

Edith Wharton[1]

Wharton's social Darwinism

'I don't quite see why he is so down on Lamarck.'

Walter Berry[2]

An important image in *The House of Mirth* is the hot-house. Grand Central is compared to one of Mrs Van Osburgh's conservatories in the opening scene; and the romantic climax, when Lily and Selden kiss after her *tableau* performance as Reynolds's Mrs Lloyd, takes place in the deserted Bry conservatory, a sort of *in vitro* simulacrum of the world outside its panes, an environment as delicate and as improbable as Selden's 'republic of the spirit'. Lily imagines the whole social hierarchy as

the dreary limbo of dinginess . . . all around and beneath that little illuminated circle in which life reached its finest efflorescence, as the mud and sleet of a winter night enclose a hot-house filled with tropical flowers. All this was in the natural order of things, and the orchid basking in its artificially created atmosphere could round the delicate curves of its petals undisturbed by the ice on the panes. (*HM*242)

The hot-house, in some of Wharton's other novels the casual marker of country estates, servants, high fuel-consumption, and conspicuous luxury, has powerful specific meaning in *The House of Mirth*, where it stands for the fragility of individual life-forms in the natural competition and selection environment of the social ecosystem.

The explicitly Darwinian ecosystem of *The House of Mirth*, it is worth remembering, is quite distinct from that of *The Age of Innocence*: Lily's setting is Wharton's present day (about 1900), and it is not Old New York – there are no Archers or Dagonets here.[3] The men of this newer social world all work, or *have* worked; they have all made, maintain, or have actively increased, their fortunes. The climate of their social world is governed by that of the financial one, in which they are heavily involved. Instead of Old New York's van der Luydens (pale, thin, remote, and intensely private), their deities are the van Osburghs (heavy-set, smug, and socially indiscriminate in their 'vast crushes'). The van Osburghs are scarcely disguised Vanderbilts, part of the early-twentieth century multi-millionaire group whom the social arbiters of *The Age of Innocence* would have classed with the Strutherses of shoe-polish fame.

If these people have made their own way, Lily, too, must seek and make her fortune. But like the rare orchids and other exotic species whose requirements are too demanding to be sustained naturally in the cold climate of North America, Lily is not a self-supporting organism; she can only live in unnatural, ultimately insupportable conditions. Her dainty ideas of social suitability are unsustainably specialised: archaic, outmoded, they are more appropriate to an Old New York which social evolution has left behind, impossible in a New York in which 'the purely decorative mission' (*HM*487) is no longer a sufficient *modus vivendi*. Lily is, essentially, in the wrong novel, and the hot-house represents that displacement.

Up to a point she has survived parasitically on the wealth of friends and family; but these, it transpires, are unreliable or incapable hosts, and her parasitism is not opportunistic enough to maintain her by other strategies. She has luxurious scruples – she forfeits one of her chances of security because the young man is a bore – which exasperate and finally alienate those who would otherwise be perfectly willing to back her, by turning her into a luxury *they* cannot afford or do not require. The helplessness of the hot-house orchid at least justifies itself by gracing tables and buttonholes; but such aesthetic symbiosis is virtually unthinkable to Lily, and such an arrangement with Rosedale (he proposes the symbiotic pairing of her social caché and beauty with his money and power), or with Gryce, Trenor, or Dorset – the characters with whom she should have most in common – is one she repeatedly foregoes. Each finally indulges his own scruples about her reputation because none is in need of her as she is of them. Part of the severe logic of natural competition includes the ability of the more powerful to exercise choice (this is clear in the hierarchical patterns of card-leaving and call-paying discussed in Chapter 1); or, to put it in this novel's own relentless terms, freedom of indulgence is available only to those who can afford it. In that logic Lily has no choices. She can finance neither her scruples (which compel her to reject Gryce and Rosedale, and to burn Bertha Dorset's self-incriminating letters) nor her indulgences (she falls in love with Selden); she is, in short, unequipped to survive. Like the transplanted anemone to which she is compared, she possesses no adaptive abilities, but is instead burdened with vestigial spiritual organs which positively hamper her chances of survival; once outside the specialised conditions of the social hot-house, she is at the mercy of circumstances which leave her literally to wither and die.

As Gillian Beer has pointed out, the imaginatively disruptive aspect of Darwinian theory, which selected phylogeny (evolution of species) over ontogeny (evolution of the individual), was the cancellation of any primacy of will, desire, and ambition in favour of chance and accident in the narrative of human and species development, and subsequently in narrative structure itself.[4] Pre-Darwinian theorists, notably Lamarck, had proposed that the *will* to survive promoted mutation in individuals which could be transmitted to their offspring: such phylogenetic evolution imagined individual giraffes, prompted by necessity, ontogenetically stretching their necks, wading birds growing longer legs. But although Darwin recognised that need *may* be satisfied by spontaneous, fortuitous mutation, mutation is not, as in Lamarckian teleology, prompted by need. Individuals cannot evolve genetically to suit their circumstances; and so survival is wholly accidental. Darwinian randomness requires, in addition, much wastage, since most mutations will prove to be unnecessary and perhaps even non-viable; each individual is born with many or few characteristics which determine whether and how efficiently he will survive. Darwin's anti-teleological, anti-rationalist proposition demotes volition of all kinds, and with it human determinism, a demotion which, Beer argues, affects narrative practice from the mid-nineteenth century onward.

Wharton makes full use of this imaginative disruption in the plight of Lily Bart. A non-viable mutation, Lily is a unique, spontaneous development of beauty and grace (quite clearly she is a creature wholly distinct from her proud father and crude grasping mother); this beauty, like that of the lilies of the field, is thought by its owner to be self-justifying, so that, like the Polynesian chieftains noted by Thorstein Veblen who starved rather than be seen to perform the labour of feeding themselves,[5] she is helpless except in conditions wholly contrived by others for her well-being. Lily is thus dangerously exposed in the actual cut-and-thrust world of late Gilded Age New York, where such ideal conditions are only maintained with exceptional effort. She mistakenly thinks she can marry a man who is both very rich and spiritually developed, a combination unknown – indeed, genetically self-cancelling, it would seem – in her habitat, where the precondition of immense wealth is single-minded ambition at the expense of scruples and sentiment.[6] She can imagine *enjoying* bestowed luxury, but she cannot exert herself to achieve it, and instead chance, not self-determination, prepares her ruin. The incidents of chance always seem to force her away from various practical resolutions, downgrading the power of desire and volition at every turn in favour of the resistless tidal workings of random event. The only arena in which Lily has actual power and control is the Bry *tableau* of Reynolds's 'Mrs Lloyd', a remarkable contrivance which reduces life to artifice, in which the living Lily actively strives to become a famous two-dimensionally represented figure in a fake landscape of trees and foliage. This tableau is located in a room so mannered, so arranged, that the marble columns and the gilt armchairs seem like a *trompe l'oeil* effect. Having 'stepped, not out of, but into, Reynolds's canvas' (*HM*216), Lily can retreat from the disobedient Darwinian world of accidental mutation and adaptation. Within the totally governable contrivance of the *tableau* and the Bry ballroom, such effort as she is capable of producing wins the unacknowledged competition in beauty and taste.

The *tableau* at one end of the huge Bry ballroom, with its false ontology, its *mise en abyme* of receding layers of make-believe, is equivalent to the hothouse which is appended to the other end. In the flattened, evanescent, deadened world of the *tableau*, as in the steam-heated glasshouse, Lily is most at her ease, most herself, most successful. Outside these two settings wasteful nature has fashioned her as a beautiful and futile experiment. She will be discarded when she proves not to be replicable; she will be evicted from that small circle of light and life of the few built on social degradation of the many.

In her 1935 introduction to the Oxford University Press edition of *The House of Mirth*, Wharton spoke of 'the key' to the story in Darwinian metaphors:

> Nature, always apparently wasteful, and apparently compelled to create dozens of stupid people in order to produce a single genius, seems to reverse the process in manufacturing the shallow and the idle. Such

groups always rest on an underpinning of wasted human possibilities; and it seemed to me that the fate of the persons embodying these possibilities ought to redeem my subject from insignificance.[7]

The redeemed subject, Lily Bart, begins as one of the shallow and the idle, ends as part of the underpinning, the wasted element. The failure of her individual social ascent simultaneously traces her developing sense of the Darwinian ecosystem and her own insufficiency within it. Lily's circle offers her examples of how to dominate the competition in Bertha Dorset, how to abandon it in Selden, how to be spared it in Gerty Farish, how to survive it in Nettie Struther, and – her own experience – how to be overwhelmed by it, to have 'the sense of being swept like a stray uprooted growth down the heedless current of the years' (*HM* 515). To comprehend these alternatives, *The House of Mirth* is couched in the jargon and concepts of competition and natural selection, and the beginnings of a realist social conscience (some of the themes of *The Fruit of the Tree*, her next full-length novel, are emerging). But the novel is not really concerned with the working classes: as Janet Flanner unkindly remarked, Wharton's writing about this group generally has the brittleness of a banker taking his typist to dine, 'a mere excursion out of one's class',[8] and Nettie Struther is no more than a useful stereotype of plucky determination.[9] In *The House of Mirth* those depths are evoked only to demonstrate from what a height *Lily* has fallen, and to attach pathos to that regression. 'You don't know what it's like', Lily tells Selden, 'in the rubbish heap!' (*HM* 498).

A specialised creature, 'an organism as helpless out of its narrow range as a sea-anemone torn from the rock' (*HM* 486), this analogy of Lily as biological failure recurs: she is oppressed by 'the feeling of being something rootless and ephemeral, mere spin-drift of the whirling surface of existence, without anything to which the poor little tentacles of self could cling before the awful flood submerged them' (*HM* 515–16). Selden wonders presciently 'was it not possible that the material was fine, but that circumstance had fashioned it into a futile shape?' (*HM* 7). He imagines himself as amphibious and adaptable, able to exist in more than one environment; in fact, Selden is complacent, not a striver or a victor in any social, professional, or aesthetic contest. Lily's other serious suitor, Rosedale, is most adaptable of all, is 'not the man to waste his time in an ineffectual sentimental dalliance. He was too busy, too practical, and above all too much preoccupied with his own advancement, to indulge in such unprofitable asides' (*HM* 481). Almost like the old Darwinian vignette of certain proto-pulmonary fishes casting themselves ashore, there to find that they can breathe and crawl across the beach with their rudimentary lungs and legs, Rosedale is seen dragging himself through the socio-genetic ranks toward the apex of power and dominion, 'working up' his social position (*HM*412). Lily, by contrast, seems able to contemplate *only* ineffectual sentimental dalliances which cannot further her aims, and may even damage them; moreover, she believes that her being can only 'dilate' in luxury, a climate and atmosphere for which she is specially evolved. She does seem, however, to possess certain useful adaptive abilities: her moods usually reflect her surroundings like the protective coloration of certain animals; but this potentially useful modulation (Theodore Dreiser invokes it to explain Frank Cowperwood's immense success[10]) actually exposes her: she tends – dangerously – to feel rich when surrounded by wealth, to be pointlessly dispirited by ugliness, to feel adventurous in risky situations; and these emotions usually lead her into difficulty, not safety. And she lacks real survival instincts: all her effects, although they seem spontaneous, are in fact carefully premeditated; her resourcefulness is merely illusory; and 'it was characteristic of her to feel that the only problems she could not solve were those with which she was not familiar' (*HM*315). The reed-like suppleness which a precarious existence has taught her, and has allowed her to bend with the prevailing social wind to maintain her foothold in the shifting social soil, crystallises during adversity into 'one hard, brilliant substance' (*HM*307), a glassy unyielding finish which is more likely to crack and break than to bend. By her own admission bred to be ornamental rather than practical, Lily is merely 'very expensive' (*HM*14), her 'vague wealth of ... graces' (*HM*431) not even as pragmatic as the hummingbird's bright plumage. The 'purely decorative mission', she realises near the end of her life, is even harder to carry out in society than in nature. In terms of survival, she fails to attract a viable mate, she will not reproduce herself, and she cannot succeed as a breadwinner.

Edith Wharton thought about '*gens*' (*NYD*77), social and genetic groupings, almost as a scientist. She was occasionally excoriated by reviewers for being remote from her characters, for being – if they had only admitted it – ruthlessly unsentimental. When *The Glimpses of the Moon* was a bestseller in 1922 Wharton was accused of behaving like an entomologist, performing disinterested examinations of her specimens.[11] This quality is certainly familiar in the fiction (though it is hardly a weakness): her analysis of human interaction and of the society of

Old New York has an almost clinical precision about it, as if she were herself one of the biologists she admired;[12] in other moods, she is the investigating anthropologist describing the folkways of a backward and aboriginal people. Not that this is exclusively a 'scientific' frame of mind: it is above all, as I have already noted, the deeply American tone of Thoreau, Melville and Whitman, the grandparent impulse of Wharton's matchless ear for nuance and eye for gestural subtlety. Wharton's socio-biological frame of reference predicts modern social analysis, which has made precisely this useful analogy between evolution/selection theory and social development, treating the macro-social structure as 'a selection environment'.[13]

There *is* an empiricist's relation to subject which her familiarity with the leading biological and socio-anthropological theories would support. Early acquaintance with Darwinian theory in the 1880s and '90s is a central theme of a chapter of *A Backward Glance*. According to her close friend Sally Norton, Wharton recognised her reading of Darwin at the age of 22 as the most important intellectual experience of her life. It was 'a new vision' which replaced any religious beliefs she had held. 'The world was more wonderful, the problem more interesting, the moral obligation more stern and ennobling'.[14] As well as Darwin's own writing, she knew the work of Darwinists T.H. Huxley, A.R. Wallace, Herbert Spencer, George Romanes, and Ernst von Haeckel.[15] Walter Berry discussed early evolutionary theory with her in several letters of that year,[16] and recommended, as well as Huxley and Haeckel, the much earlier work of Augustin St Hilaire on botany, Georges Cuvier on comparative anatomy; and H.G. Wells for accessible scientific explanation.[17] As well as James Frazer's *The Golden Bough* (1890), he proposed the anthropologists Paul Topinard and Edvard Westermarck.[18] In 1900 she was preparing to write a poem, perhaps to be called 'Amphioxus' or 'The Missing Link'; no poem survives, but a short story of this period, 'Angel at the Grave' (1901), incorporates a discussion of amphioxus, and shows how closely she had read Haeckel on the subject.[19] In 1908 she took great pleasure in entertaining the biologist Carl Snyder of Woods Hole, author of a number of evolutionary works,[20] and under his influence extended her range to include Vernon L. Kellogg's *Darwinism Today* (1907), Charles Déperet's *Les Transformations du Monde Animal* (1907), Robert Lock's *Recent Progress in the Study of Variation, Heredity and Evolution* (1906),[21] and even Jacques Loeb's *Comparative Physiology and Psychology of the Brain* (1903). By the early 1930s, through Aldous Huxley, she was acquainted with and enthusiastic about Bronislaw Malinowski, the ethnologist and author of works on tribal life in Melanesia.[22]

The themes suggested to her by the evolutionists and by the anthropologists and nascent sociologists were not only the metaphors of social organisation such as species, clans, hereditary behaviour patterns, and so on; they also suggested to her principles of boundary and exclusion. Her interest in amphioxus is a case in point. A gill-breathing notochord (a pre-vertebrate) with embryonic forms of higher systems (skeleton, lungs, etc.), the amphioxus had been proposed as the creature, or the descendant of the creature, from which vertebrates and invertebrates diverged; amphioxus is, in evolutionary thought, not just an animal, but an *event*, the dividing moment which would lead to mammalian development, and ultimately to a small genetic group – the superior tribe of *homo sapiens* – from which all other species would forever be outcast.[23] Haeckel wrote that the amphioxus, as 'the representative of the Vertebrates, . . . form[s] the bridge which alone can span the deep gulf between these two main divisions of the animal kingdom' (ie vertebrate and invertebrate), and this sense of ineradicable 'tribal' difference between species haunted Wharton.[24] Of dogs she wrote:

> the *us*ness in their eyes, with the underlying *not-usness* which belies it, . . . is so tragic a reminder of the lost age when we human beings branched off and left them: left them to eternal inarticulateness and slavery. *Why?* their eyes seem to ask us.[25]

The preoccupying *outsiderliness* of other creatures, denied access to or intimacy with herself and her kind, was a sense of difference which invaded her own identity: she felt herself to have a particular understanding of and sympathy with animals, as if she too were, like them, an outsider. 'This feeling seemed to have its source in a curious sense of being somehow, myself, an intermediate creature between human beings and animals, and nearer, on the whole, to the furry tribes than to homo sapiens.'[26] She seems almost to imagine herself as the spiritual amphioxus, a 'missing link' as she called it.[27] This powerful sense of difference, frighteningly evident in her fiction in recurring images of human muteness, settles particularly on a conception of outsiderhood, of the prevention of some commonality of language, experience, and behaviour.

If the Lamarckian world-view accentuates determination and volition as the impetus of survival, the Darwinian counterpart dismisses those qualities by insisting that only accidents of circumstance combined with accidents of proficiency account for the survival and success of any individual. This spiritual contention is clear in Lily Bart, who is the Lamarckian victim of a Darwinian universe: no amount of wanting to adapt herself, of willed behaviour toward survival and success, can help her in her struggle with a hostile environment and adverse fortune because – and this she does not fully understand – will alone, desire without active promotion of desire, is not sufficient even in a Lamarckian universe. Every one of her practical resolutions – to live within her means, to make a living, to be kinder to the poor, to marry Rosedale, to blackmail Bertha Dorset – is diverted by chance and comes to naught. Every misfortune she endures – that Rosedale sees her emerge from Selden's flat; that Selden sees her emerge from Trenor's house; that she is the convenient stalking-horse in the war between the Dorsets – arises from coincidence or expedience. Lily's culture consists of accidents, of *trouvailles*; appropriately, her self-portrait as an Oresteian outcast is an analogy she happens upon when she comes across a copy of the *Eumenides* 'lying around' in one of the country houses she has visited. Wharton is very careful to maintain this allusion to Orestes as the novel's primary *leitmotif*, itself founded on 'cast off' literary matter, serendipitous encounter.

Lily is physically and temperamentally ill-equipped to meet the demands of her environment: she is crippled by her aversion to 'vulgarity'; she cannot even learn simple manual tasks like sewing; and her whole physique seems virtually used up in the effort of having to live in anything less than sumptuous comfort. What few choices she has she uses badly: unable to lower herself to a distasteful marriage of convenience with Rosedale or a lucrative flirtation with Trenor, she alienates them into the bargain; she has no idea how to trade on obligation and social debt to secure herself in the slippery world of fashion.[28] Only at the end of the novel does she abandon her Lamarckian idealism for Darwinian pragmatism and inevitability; in the last chapters she starts to classify herself with the large, undifferentiated mass of workers, to imagine herself as an unidentified piece of flotsam 'on the whirling surface of existence', a member of that undistinguished many on whose failure the pleasures of the successful few are erected; this realisation amounts to a phylogenetic revision of all her ontogenetic self-beliefs.

Men, on the whole, are better served by a predatory posture; if they are still aspiring to predation, like Rosedale, they have a convenient Lamarckian code of achievement which expresses and sanctions what is in fact their ruthless Darwinian behaviour; this behaviour and attitude is the subject of the money-novels of Theodore Dreiser and Frank Norris with which *The House of Mirth* has so close a relation.[29] Jack Stepney and

Gus Trenor do not like but are impressed by Rosedale because he is 'getting somewhere'; even Lily has to confess a secret admiration for a man who is perceptibly reaching his object, who is fulfilling her proposition that 'the final test of genius [is] success' (*HM*107). His object is to be able to move at will in the social circle Lily already, but only tenuously, inhabits; he speaks in the vigorous language of Lamarckian desire – he is 'working up', 'getting in', 'getting square' (*HM*412–14) – and will eventually be indistinguishable from the beefy Trenor, who is seen 'preying' on jellied plover, 'his heavy carnivorous head sunk between his shoulders' (*HM*87). Wharton's predatory businessmen are, incidentally, always corpulent: Moffatt, van Degen, Rosedale, and Trenor are red, sweating, overflowing, shiny, round. Lily wonders why rich people always grow fat, and wrongly concludes that it is because they have few worries. In fact – and this is Lily's fatal blindness – they get that way because they are constantly feeding on various kinds of financial and nutrient prey; even Undine Spragg has grown stout by the end of *The Custom of the Country*. Theodore Dreiser's Frank Cowperwood finds the inspiration for his subsequent career in an emblematic duel between a lobster and a squid in a local fishmonger's tank. The lobster, Frank observes, has better weapons and better protection, allowing it to devour its opponent at leisure and making the outcome of the battle a foregone conclusion; the squid, on the other hand, is ill-adapted to such conditions and such a foe and can only exhaust itself in fruitless avoidance of inevitable destruction. Parts of the squid are eaten over time until, at last, it dies. 'How is life organized?' Frank muses. 'Things lived on each other – that was it.'[30] Social and financial success is based on supremacy of cunning, and survival is always at some else's expense. The unsuccessful or failing – Mr Spragg, George Dorset, Ralph Marvell – are used up and unhealthy like the squid, a trait displayed latterly by Lily as she is socially dismembered by Bertha Dorset. Dorset himself used to be robust and full of life, according to Carry Fisher, but in the novel he is being cannibalised by his rapacious wife, and he specifically suffers from indigestion.

'What a miserable thing it is to be a woman!' says Lily, fully aware from the outset of the Lamarckian possibilities available to men and apparently denied to women, who cannot seem to strive without blotting their reputations (*HM*9). But Lily, once again, is wrong. If women cannot avail themselves of the paths of advancement (in the form of money-making and obviously aggressive behaviour), they are perfectly capable of an equivalent style of predatory activity which is thoroughly Lamarckian in its pattern. The functions Lily cannot fulfil are ones to which her more successful friends are by definition well adapted: Carry Fisher has a clinical

eye and a lamprey-like talent for feeding on the fattest specimens; Bertha
Dorset and Judy Trenor have made advantageous matches to men who
clearly have little but their money to recommend them, confirmation
that an over-developed sense of beauty (Lily's proud boast) could have
been positively damaging to their prospects. Instead, Bertha exercises
a particularly exemplary rapacity; she is the attenuated emblem of red-
clawed nature, figured by Wharton in shifting effects and sudden mood-
changes which allow her to prey successfully on any social condition and
on any individual who meets her immediate need.[31] As we discover
during the Monte Carlo episode, hers are especially highly developed
survival strategies. We see them first on the train to Bellomont, when
she uses the deference allowed to pretty women to *insist* on a seat next
to Lily ('...porter – you must find me a place at once. Can't some one
be put somewhere else? I want to be with my friends' (*HM*36));[32] she
expects, as if by *right*, to displace some other, anonymous fellow passen-
ger, and does so without noticing or thanking him. Bertha seems pliable,
malleable, sinuous, qualities indicating a useful adaptability, but her flexu-
osity is not Lily's reed-like pliancy; rather, with 'her small pale face...
the mere setting of a pair of dark exaggerated eyes' and her 'self-assert-
ive tone and gestures' (*HM*36), Bertha is a slinky predator with the keen,
voracious eyes and resistless appetite of the killer. Her flexion is that of
the snake: she 'sports' with innocent young men (*HM*39), wears 'ser-
pentine spangles' (*HM*38) which 'dazzle' her prey; she is an 'anaconda'
(*HM*405) who 'has [her prey] fast' in her toils (*HM*406). The predatory
images are more fully developed on the Dorset yacht, where Bertha's
ruse to convict Lily of a dalliance with her husband unfolds, with Lily
having only a 'vague sense' of the danger, 'unnerved' by Bertha's com-
posure, 'too far adrift in bewilderment to measure the other's words or
keep watch on her own' (*HM*332). 'Bertha was pursuing an object', Lily
thinks (*HM*333), little scouting that she herself is that object, mesmer-
ised by Bertha's behaviour as the mouse is fascinated by the snake.

Bertha, unlike Lily, possesses protective camouflage in order to meet
adversity. Instead of behaving as Lily expects in the fall-out of her escapade with Ned Silverton – as a 'poor creature shivering behind her fallen
defences and awaiting with suspense the moment when she could take
refuge in the first shelter that offered' – Bertha is still 'in full command'
of herself and the situation, wearing a bland look that betrays nothing
(*HM*330). Shortly thereafter, Bertha springs a staged scene in which Lily is
made to bear the blame for Bertha's transgressions, a scene during
which Bertha bides her time, gathers herself, and strikes. No one present
can aid Lily because Bertha, the richer antagonist, is too dangerous. In

Dreiser's image, Bertha is the lobster, Lily the squid. The measure of Bertha's power is Lily's misguided assumption, until the moment of crisis, that it lies within her power to help the struggling Mrs Dorset to 'pull through' (*HM329*).

An important adaptive difference between prey and predator is that the former often lacks binocular vision; its eyes are on the sides of its head in order to cover the maximum field of vision and to note lurking danger. Although, as Candace Waid argues, Lily's talent for situating herself in settings and poses in which she displays herself to advantage makes her the potent artist of her own form,[33] another way of describing this behaviour is as the self-endangering attraction of predatory (usually male) gaze. Again and again we find Lily calling attention to herself, deluded or incapable of assessing her social vulnerability, as if her eyes were monocular, non-stereoscopic. Compared to the predatory Bertha, whose huge binocular eyes are noted as the dominant feature in a small face, Lily can't see the quarter in which her danger lies. The Trenor, Hatch, and Dorset scandals engulf Lily before she realises what is coming.

Darwinian theory proposes that species exist in relation to each other, in territorial and genetic contiguity, in proximity in the food-chain. This sense of spatial, hierarchical relationship is heightened by Wharton's reading in anthropology, sociology, and ethnography, disciplines which coached her to perceive human behaviour as a set of relationships which might be biologically or ecologically determined, but which are expressed in social – in other words, formal – practices. The adaptive pressure of survival is enunciated in her fiction in the terms of social science.

Maps of exclusion

'What does it matter where one lives?' (*AI73*)

In Chapter 1, on tribes, the linguistic concept of binary, cancelling opposition – 'x' versus 'not-x' – was proposed as a central figure of impoverishment and denial in which implication stands for utterance. This is Wharton's own narrative practice, too. She proceeds by negative definition, each notion of border, demarcation, periphery, implying but not specifying an area out of bounds, an area beyond the ken or notice of tribal scrutiny. This binary system is spatial, linguistic and thematic. The principle of 'not-x' in play in 'Autre Temps', in Mrs Lidcote's inability to detect whether certain modern young women on her steamer are 'nice' or 'not nice', is the determiner of Lily's decline. Following Bertha Dorset's *coup de main* at the Monte Carlo restaurant, Lily is cut by her closest friends; and though she persists for a time in delivering cards and being seen at strategic venues, the corresponding behaviour of acknowledgement, of cards returned, of *quid pro quo*, fails to materialise. The antiphonal social intonations of call and response have turned – in Lily's mind – into an epic tragedy in which gossip is conveyed by the Eumenides, who having once engaged in polite social exchange with her reciprocate now by hunting her to death. The social conversation is silenced by Mrs Trenor, Aunt Peniston, Lawrence Selden, Carry Fisher, all of whom fail at some point to respond to Lily's overtures. Lily is not-nice, and her unanswered approaches unperson her, a cancellation ultimately mortal.

Wharton extends the binary pattern of 'x/not-x' to the imagination of place, and her local geographies tell tales of enlivening niceness or its cancelling opposite. In the inferior early story 'The Fullness of Life' Wharton writes:

> I have sometimes thought that a woman's nature is like a great house full of rooms: there is the hall, through which everyone passes in going in and out; the drawing room, where one receives formal visits; the sitting room, where the members of the family come and go as they list; but beyond that, far beyond, are other rooms, the handles of whose doors are never turned; no one knows the way to them, no one knows whither they lead; and in the innermost room, the holy of holies, the soul sits alone and waits for a footstep that never comes. (*CSSI*,14)

The farther one proceeds into the house, the more personal it becomes, starting with public and unexclusive outer rooms, leading to rooms for friends, then to those for family, and finally to rooms which are off limits to all but the owner. The psychological and social world of the individual, like the interior depicted by Johnson's 'Not at Home', is imagined as a set of ever more exclusive chambers, where only close friendship or family connexion, and finally identity, can provide entry. The principle of exclusion eventually refines the tribe to a constituency of one. The furtively fleeing young woman in the Johnson painting is following the path from the outer, public rooms to the sanctuary of innerness.

The convention of being unavailable is operated for the convenience of social participants, so that the furtiveness of the young woman is perhaps generated by the potential embarrassment of discovery, the slightly awkward dissimulation the convention entails. But in *The House of Mirth* and other dramas of banishment, Wharton translates that furtiveness darkly onto certain locations; her poetics of interiors and of outdoor and natural settings is extended to include the shameful, the unacceptable, the non-existent, the unknown. Any part of the world unfashionable or inconvenient to the tribe ceases to exist.

Old New York's strict definition of the 'nice' address differentiates Ellen Olenska, who violates the code of niceness when she settles in a neighbourhood inhabited by writers, artists, and other doubtful characters. New York streets may be consecutively numbered, but they are nonetheless labyrinthine in the tribal atlas. As a stranger lacking discrimination of place, Olenska has been fooled by the grid-iron structure of much of Manhattan, slyly adopted by the city fathers 'lest they should be thought "undemocratic" by people they secretly looked down upon' (*OM7*), and she never masters the nuance of not-nice location. Only a licensed eccentric like Mrs Manson Mingott, Ellen's grandmother, can flout geographical proprieties with impugnity, so secure is her wealth and her position in the clan; her address in the sub-arctic latitude of what is now midtown Manhattan is made good by the argument of wealth, equivalent to Bertha Dorset's ability to misbehave and refuse to accept the consequences. Bertha and Mrs Mingott have social credit based on 'impregnable bank account[s]' (*HM421*).

Mrs St George, mother of the heroines of *The Buccaneers*, like Olenska, cannot command such compliance, being an outsider; and she is disturbed that her otherwise fashionable house (it is the hastily-sold mansion of an Irish gangster) is irremediably located:

> *no one* lived in Madison Avenue... what a difference it made to a lady to be able to say 'Fifth Avenue' in giving her address... 'Madison Avenue' stood at best for a decent mediocrity [my emphasis]. (*B42*)

We note once more the absolute 'no one' (the natural opposite of 'everyone'), the 'not' phrase which signals a host of unspoken, implacable complexities of hierarchy and group membership, of pale and hinterland, in which Mrs St George is initiated too late. She aspires to this kind of propriety where Olenska remains in ignorance of it. Mrs Percy Standish in *Twilight Sleep* lives high up on the east side, a location peculiar even without the added idiosyncracy of her concrete 'Viking' house. The overt satire of that novel initially turns the poetics of location and interiors into the basis of comedy, but it is comedy which darkens in the bizarre house of Mrs Standish's niece, Lita Wyant, where rooms are painted black, and the goldfish die of sleeplessness in their over-illuminated tank. Similarly, the strange miasmic environs of Mrs Norma Hatch in

The House of Mirth (discussed later in this chapter) alarm us, as they do Selden, as clear signals of Lily's directionless spin out of her usual orbit.

In *Summer*, the orphan Charity Royall is said to have come originally 'from the Mountain', a brooding presence in the story, locale of lawless, primitive, autochthonous people with virtually no civilising influences or customs, who function as the prior, unedified race common to many mythologies. Their presence on the horizon is a lesson in what North Dormer might become if the collective grip on its fragile civility were loosened. Originally rescued from the Mountain as an infant, and likely to be evicted from the prim village when pregnant, Charity flees to this outcast anti-community, the 'not'-society which balances North Dormer. Between these two extremes of mountain and village is an old derelict house, a house with good bones on a hillside, where Charity and Lucius Harney make a domestic setting for themselves for the purposes of love-making, an ironically proposed household which Charity will never in fact be offered by Harney when he comes to make a matrimonial decision. The pregnancy which is conceived there would damage the friable culture of North Dormer; and that damage is reified in location.

Harney is visiting the district to look at early American domestic architecture. It is a precious architectural book which first draws him into conversation with Charity at the library in North Dormer (itself a notable architectural feature). Wharton always associates architectural and ethical integrity; her favourite styles were based on neo-classical principles, and it is no accident that the house on the hillside is an abandoned Federalist structure,[34] a house which seems to embody a lost propriety in its fine proportions and ornaments, a no-longer-tenable code of life which might have insisted that Harney stand by Charity. This compromised house is sited in a liminal place between a wilderness of 'people who don't give a damn for anybody' (*S*41) and a civilisation where 'the whole place' would instantly condemn her.

Like the geography of Wharton's inner life, the house of many rooms, the landscape of her outcasts is also figured in transitional or liminal settings such as hotel rooms. Hotels are not simply an index of restlessness, as in the case of Mrs Hatch and the Emporium; they are an index of relegation, their precincts filled with languishing ex-members of various tribes; they provide for these outcasts an exemplary geography of status: the name, the setting, and the site of, the view from, and the room in, the hotel must stand in place of the usual social indicators such as kinship and household. In *The Mother's Recompense*, the net gain which Kate Clephane derives from her year-long reunion with her daughter is not the restoration of the maternal bond but the upgrading of her hotel room when she returns in defeat to the Riviera. Such equivocal locations reflect the fluid constitution of this discharged population, most of whom are socially disabled (by drugs, crime, matrimonial and professional failure); hotels are the impersonal settings for their pathetic attempts to justify themselves or to re-establish their original standing within their new, liminal group. Even the Mountain in *Summer* has a more coherent and organic social disposition than the hotel, which functions as the locus of atomised social fragments but does not impose any definable pattern of existence.

Her aspirant tribal members – Mrs Hatch, the Spraggs, the St Georges – are always connected to hotels and hotel-culture, which is ostentatious but sterile; they establish themselves there, mistakenly thinking to find the social élite within their portals. These *arrivistes* are usually found fretfully wondering why they are still as distant from that enclave as ever; it is usually only when they discover that their models would never condescend to spend a night in a hotel (either staying in their own (inherited) properties, or in those of their friends) that they settle in one place. The dimmer bulbs among the aspirers, like Mrs Spragg, never do decipher the social code, and continue to live in hotels in the conviction that a return to 'housekeeping' would be a step down in the world. Even so, to purchase one's house has delicate and potentially damaging social implications: like the inveterate story about Brahmin ladies of Boston, who do not buy, but have, their hats, the acquisition of even a socially suitable house is fraught with complication and discredit. To buy or to build suggests earned, rather than inherited, wealth. Rosedale, for example, can never be fully admitted into the sacred precinct on the strength of his money and his house alone, which is why he needs someone like Lily to marry him; he is condescended to partly because he is planning to buy the newly-built house of a recently bankrupt millionaire, complete with a gallery of Old Master paintings and a veritable menu of architectural styles. The acquired mansion has the talon-marks of the predatory, successful financier on it, but, with no innate link to its new owner, and generally full of random and mixed cultural allusions, it is also profoundly liminal.

Wharton is always interested in noting and establishing such geographical boundaries and architectural characterisations in her fiction, inspired by addresses and regional appellations. In 1930, she playfully affected horror at a friend's Washington, DC address (3108 P Street NW):

> No salt and unplumbed sea was ever as estranging as that nauseating address: 3108 – hideous example of the unimaginative desire to simplify, which *always* complicates! ... Well, ... I'll make a last supreme effort in mnemonics, ... to master the charmless charm which must serve to evoke you ...[35]

For Wharton, the very nomenclature of Washington street-names is 'estranging', 'charmless', 'nauseating'. For the story 'Velvet Earpads' she wanted the American 'princess' to refer to

> 'my betrothed's ancestral estate of Staten Island', as if she had said Inverary ... Staten Island must be replaced by some state that is scorching in summer and bitter cold in winter, and sufficiently familiar to sound funny. ... What I want is something like: 'His ancestral estate of Illinois', but I don't know if Illinois is hot enough in summer. ...[36]

This is, of course, a characteristic Whartonian crack about 'the West' (a place which, in the same letter, she confesses is undifferentiated in her mind from the midwest, or indeed from anything west of the Hudson),[37] but it is also characteristically attempting to designate and delimit (if only onomastically) parts of America which are, in her frame of reference, not-nice.

Wharton's first published short story is structured on the concept of location, of borders. 'Mrs Manstey's View' (1891) concerns an old woman struggling to preserve the vista of back yards from her window. Mrs Manstey surveys these uninviting plots almost regally, and knows intimately their abandoned junkpiles, ragged fences, stray cats, and persistent flowering vegetation. The lilacs, a horse chestnut, magnolia, and wisteria interest her because, in spite of the surrounding squalor, they have a way of 'foaming over' the fences between the yards, of 'growing in spite of the countless obstacles opposed to [their] welfare' (*CSSI*,4). Building work which will destroy the trees and block her view is begun over her objections, and – astonishingly – Mrs Manstey turns midnight arsonist, but dies of pneumonia thus contracted. Wharton's attention is drawn to ideas of limit exceeded by disorder (in this case, the beautiful disorder of flowering plants which is replicated in Mrs Manstey's disorderly conduct), and by the striking details which situate the story in a shabby part of town: the buildings Mrs Manstey can see are mostly other boarding-houses like her own;

a factory's smokestack has poetry equivalent to a church spire on the horizon; Mrs Manstey's house itself testifies to some unspecified prior grandeur now lost, in the description of her window as a *bow* window at the back of the house, as if such an ornamental feature might once have looked out on extended grounds, on a view unencumbered by other people's washing and by dingy fences and walls. Mrs Manstey's own social isolation is contrasted with the democratic efflorescence in the yards: widowed, rheumatic, estranged from her daughter, her friends now dead, she is relegated, contained within a narrow shabby room in a grimy district, unknown and unnoticed. The flowers are also relict, but are not confined. The story is one in which, like 'Bunner Sisters', Wharton is able to convey the pinched existence of a class of women of whom she knew little because she is alive to ideas of space and liminality which are among the necessary conditions of such tragedies.

Wharton's degrees of rejection can usually be assessed by the violation of boundaries, where people, not plants, flow over into undemarcated areas, and *The House of Mirth* uses the spatial relationships of boundary, enclave, and hinterland to depict such rejection. Lily Bart's journey from the cushioned fortress of high society into dejection and poverty is charted more rigorously in terms of setting, household, and local geography, than any other work by Wharton; this progress of the outcast is framed as a journey through a series of significant domestic and social interiors, themselves situated in specific and meaningful locations. The streets of New York make a map of her increasing liminality. If the hot-house, the most enclosed, exclusive, environmentally 'arranged' room of very grand houses, is a metaphor of Lily's ideal place, the story takes her ever outward from that seclusion, even as the narrative extends out from the initial scene in Grand Central, which is *hotter* than a hot-house, into houses and places of increasingly muddled spatial and social order, and doubtful moral propriety.

To belong within any set of bounds, one must possess place. Lily's deracination, her essential alienation from any specific, personally elected place, facilitates her passage over borders, makes her easy to unplace. This placelessness, which amounts to a lack of privacy, is figured in publicity. In the opening scene, Selden encounters her in the undifferentiated space of the Grand Central Station,[38] where, although she stands out as superfine and exquisite, although he imagines her 'air of irresolution' to be 'the mask of a very definite purpose' (*HM*3), she is actually adrift and rootless. She is indeed, as he thinks, 'in the act of transition between one and another of the country-houses which disputed her presence' (*HM*3), between borrowed rooms full of other people's luxury where she is most at ease; but transience and impulse, not resolution, are the themes of Lily's comings and goings. Although she seems to be 'everywhere' (in the society pages, at the best parties, as well as on park benches and in bachelor apartments), and although Selden likes to think of her as having plans ('her simplest acts seemed the result of far-reaching intentions' (*HM*3)), Lily has no designs and no place; she is 'away' when she should be present (when her aunt falls ill and dies, for instance), and nearby when she should be as far away as possible (when Mrs Hatch tries to snare the van Osburgh heir). These are the accidents of the unplaced person in unmeant association with untoward events. Grand Central, place of arrival and departure but not of extended sojourn, is the reverberating emblem which initially places Lily 'nowhere', and whose image is continually reverted to in the course of the novel.

The fortuitous initial encounter there between Lily and Selden, the two principals, is like the shifting fluidity of the thousands of anonymous fellow-passengers: Selden is purposefully returning to work from a country weekend; but it is a static, accidental moment for Lily; she stands still as if waiting for someone (it is the first of the story's many accidents that Selden's sense of her deliberateness should be confirmed by his own arrival); she is stemming the human tide in the great terminus,[39] an image which will be evoked again in the metaphor of Lily as a supple and bending reed, in the scene following the Bry *tableaux*, and again, readjusted in her own idea of herself as 'uprooted' and 'swept' (*HM*515). As the important initial instalment in the novel's motif of *coincidence*, the coincidental encounter with Selden leads to the visit to his study, which in turn sets off the train of unlucky events. Lily, swayed back and forth by unforeseen incident like the encounter with Selden, will subsequently float on a tide of luxurious, impersonal interiors, severely managed conservatories, and gardens 'tutored to the last degree of rural elegance' (*HM*77), later drifting into a relatively unmanaged outdoor world consisting of Central Park, the streets of New York, and eventually anonymous benches in unattractive, unnamed parts of the city. These locations are further mapped out on the landscape grid where she subsides into ever more remote, ever dingier neighbourhoods until she is 'stranded in a great waste of disoccupation' (*HM*489).

Potential 'place', elected location, would be Lily's salvation. The cosy, inelegant flat of her friend Gerty Farish is a model for place and home; but it symbolises to Lily all that she cannot tolerate – it is small and full of 'cheap conveniences' which make the mechanics of living too obvious for Lily's fastidious sensibility (she is greatly disturbed by all evidence of domestic machinery, from the spring-cleaning in her aunt's house to the noises which come through the thin walls of her boarding-house room). Gerty's flat additionally requires a discipline of gesture which prevents her habitual 'dilation' in the form of physical 'effects' which heighten her beauty; Lily feels literally confined and stunted there. Like Lily, Gerty has a tiny income, but unlike Lily, Gerty manages to eke out a fragile though enthusiastic independence, throwing herself with energy into charitable work for the improvement of the lives of poor working girls, instead of consorting with the leisured individuals to whom she is related. Gerty is sweet-natured but plain; she is not moulded into Lily's 'futile shape' or plagued by the need of luxury; she is made by circumstances to manage her lot successfully.

Even tinier and more primitive a place of rest is the spotlessly clean household of Nettie Struther, a dwelling with 'the frail audacious permanence of a bird's nest built on the edge of a cliff' (*HM*517). Its precarious but pluckily maintained security is a revelation to Lily, who – probably for the first time in her life – is invited to sit down in a kitchen and to hold a baby. Gerty's and Nettie's households are the product of survival strategies as fiercely pursued as Bertha Dorset's or the manoeuvres of a financier; both are contrived out of little to shelter the human animal against the social meteorology of New York. Although each offers succour and relief to Lily at critical junctures, she is never once capable of imagining so plain an interpretation of domestic security. We know from Mrs Peniston that Lily doesn't 'know one end of a crotchet-needle from the other' (*HM*162); and although she is at home making and serving tea on a moving train, her boarding-house room' (the only room of her own she ever possesses) is spartan and comfortless, as if she were literally helpless to perform a single service for herself, incapable of rooting herself, of cherishing the simple amenity of a private place.

Lily's other rooms all belong unequivocally to someone else: even her quarters at her Aunt Peniston's are furnished with cast-offs which once belonged to her dead uncle, and their ugly heavy impersonality makes Lily feel 'expatriate everywhere' (*HM*240). Lily herself, an expensive accessory whose care and feeding reflect well on her aunt, has a boarding-house relation to her 'as superficial as that of chance lodgers who passed on the stairs' (*HM*240). Although the interior of the Peniston house is conventionally dull, it is comfortable and well-maintained; it is its *style* of dullness which operates as the index of Mrs Peniston's moral complacency, and gives Lily a focus for her placelessness. The hideous curtains, the bow window with a bronze displayed in it,[40] the ostentatious upholstery (Wharton loads such disdain onto the presence of *buttons* on overstuffed furniture) mark Mrs Peniston as a woman of unreflective, unformed taste. Yet Wharton is careful to establish a competing and equal culpability in Lily, who shrinks from ugliness as her mother did from dinginess, and likes to believe she would be a 'better woman' if she were allowed to redecorate her aunt's drawing room (*HM*10). The most unimpeachable operations of housekeeping become suspect and even horrifying to Lily: she 'resents' the smell of beeswax and brown soap, is offended by the cascade of suds on Mrs Peniston's staircase. She is impatient with such hygienic operations, and generally contrives to be out of town when Mrs Peniston is commiting her sacraments of house-keeping; she 'behave[s] as though she thought a house ought to keep clean of itself' (*HM*162). As if to underscore Lily's 'expatriate' relationship to place, Wharton has the charwoman on her aunt's stairs turn out to be the same baleful Mrs Haffen who washed the stairs of Selden's apartment house, the woman who sells Lily Mrs Dorset's incriminating letters, making the agent of the novel's moral dilemma an agent of those loathed domestic operations, with soapsuds on staircases a kind of objective correlative of the horrible coincidences which knit the story together.

The real difficulty here is Lily's own rejection of stability, of place. 'There was no place in the world that she loved more than any other; her memories had no roots in the soil, her wandering impulses no hearth by which to rest.'[41] Lily *would* be a better woman if she were able to establish some sort of foundation for herself (which might, as in her musings, include decorating a room of her own). But her disposition is essentially unstable, transient, drifting, much like her periodic resolutions to cut back her expenditures, so that her many perturbations in unsatisfactory surround-ings have the air of a valetudinarian incapable of discovering a comfort-able chair. Most at ease in locations whose evanescence or ephemerality is their principal feature, she delights in the sumptuous luxury of her room at Bellomont, yet she lingers on the staircase on her way to bed, unable to sustain further losses at the bridge table but unwilling to undergo 'the self-communion which awaited her in her room' (*HM*38). A brief survey of the house's rich appointments is the compromise, and we see its marble, its flowers, its carpets through the eyes of a person stranded between public and private spaces, on the fringes of one world and exiled from herself. She never *inhabits* spaces temporarily designated as hers.

Lily thinks that the 'stifling' atmosphere of her aunt's house inheres in its ugliness, but what really affects her is its overtly engineered orderli-ness, the serious attention given to the kinds of domestic proprieties – schedules and annual rites – which Lily associates with labour, dreari-ness and rootedness. Although she longs, so she thinks, for a place, for constancy and security of some sort, she cannot tolerate them when she discovers them. The stupendously undomestic Bry interior, more theatre than household, hard even to ascertain as real, seems, like the hothouse, to satisfy Lily; but every other shelter, offered or possessed, is in some way unsuitable. She is annoyed by the homely contrivances of her friend Gerty, invites Grace Stepney's enmity by disdaining her 'sincere admiration' for the Peniston curtains so that Grace does not offer to help her when she loses her inheritance (including the house) from her aunt. Selden's study seems marginally interesting to her, but she never seriously considers marrying him, which would have given her that delightful study, or one like it, forever. Only the penultimate scene in the book shows Lily, at Nettie Struther's, in touch with anything like ordinary domesticity.

Wharton discourses, late in the novel, on tradition, rootedness, belonging, and place. If 'inherited passions and loyalties' represent 'the house not made with hands', or 'the old house stored with visual memories', Lily is the inverted form of these: her house is merely her luggage, symbol of the transient; and her 'centre of early pieties' (HM516) is no more than the fortuitous encounters of perpetual travel. In what is perhaps the most telling incident in the novel, Lily recklessly gives to Gerty's charity the money intended to pay for a very elaborate new dressing case, merely because a self-congratulatory eleemosynary mood is on her for delaying the order when (coincidentally) she runs into Gerty. (Lily would require lessons in domestic account-keeping if she were ever to find a place of her own.) The luxurious valise with its many drawers and compartments is as complicated architecturally as a house, and Lily would virtually live out of it, her money, checkbook, library (a single volume of Omar), ornaments, and toilet articles all disposed in their appropriate places. [Plate 6] Gaston Bachelard notes that a casket or chest can be a dwelling-place;[42] for Lily the case would in some literal sense be 'home'. Instead it is casually converted into a place for working girls to keep them off the streets; Lily gives away her dwelling-place en passant.

These liminal settings and occasions – the train station, staircases, railway carriages, borrowed rooms – are Lily's hallmark. She stays with the Gormers in their rented country-house, and visits the unfinished one they are having built; she goes to Alaska with them in their private train, a household on wheels. She spends a season on the Sabrina, the Dorset yacht, a home in transit all over the Mediterranean which touches solid land only to visit places like Monte Carlo, the Grand Central of European wanderers. After she is disinherited by her aunt she is reduced to a shabby hotel on the edge of a fashionable New York neighbourhood, only to be rescued by Mrs Fisher and *her* rented version of domesticity. Her disastrous visit to Gus Trenor in his Fifth Avenue house takes place out of season, when all the furniture is covered and Trenor is camping out in one room before returning to Bellomont and his wife. Each of Lily's locales and each of her places of crisis is impermanent, qualified, even mobile. Homeless and rootless, she is not simply the outcast, but represents the very condition of exclusion itself. The house of mirth is, ironically, the *only* house to which Lily can lay claim.

When at last Lily finds something to do – she becomes social secretary and companion to a divorcée, the helpless, idle Mrs Norma Hatch – it is in a setting whose *tour de force* in linguistic vagueness sets alarm bells ringing. The Emporium Hotel and the life of the unmoored *nouvelle riche* who inhabits it evokes a lexis of blurred outlines: 'drift', 'float', 'flow', 'languid', 'wan', 'pallid', 'indeterminate', 'suspended', 'confused', 'indistinguishable', 'inertia', 'void', 'blur', 'indolence', 'disorder', 'haze', 'jumble', 'limbo', 'wilderness' – all these are packed into a few paragraphs; Mrs Hatch's oneiric surroundings are like Lita Wyant's in *Twilight Sleep*, as unfixed and ill-defined as the nebulous expectation that Lily teach Mrs Hatch how to be 'nice' and 'lovely'. Selden, discovering Lily in this 'vast gilded void' (*HM*445), exclaims with what might be the philosophy of the whole book, 'You don't know where you are!' (*HM*451).[43] Lily is inured, at this point, and can respond vigorously, 'there is very little real difference in being inside or out' (*HM*453), as if the vagueness of Mrs Hatch's milieu has infected her previously exact sense of propriety. Mrs Hatch's floating world is one in whose physical attributes we may read Lily's own inclination, and the acceleration of her social decline.

Lily's tenure with Mrs Hatch is short-lived, however, because she is wrongly suspected of helping to engineer a liaison and marriage between her employer and a young scion of the van Osburgh clan; again she is caught within hailing distance of something 'not-nice'; again, she is unaware of the danger until too late. The proposed crime against this powerful family summons its 'harpies', whose wrath against Lily is the greater because she seems to have forsaken her old loyalties, to have cast her lot with the outsiders, the bounders, the social climbers.

If in consorting with the Gormers Lily had been living in 'a social outskirt which [she] had always fastidiously avoided' (*HM*376), that marginal purlieu is revisited in the boarding-house, located in 'the degradation of a New York street in the last stages of decline from fashion to commerce' (*HM*464). The hard, implacable lines of 'x' – usually represented by Wharton in the ugly and uniform rows of expensive brownstones marshalled into strictly numbered categories of longitude and latitude – are scrambled in the demographic shift that converts what might once have been the kind of neighbourhood familar to Lily into 'not-x', one in which, as at Mrs Hatch's, social behaviour and atmosphere become confused. The scene is lit by 'a dreary March twilight', the borderland between day and night; in this crepuscular light, after an exhausting day in the sweat-shop, Lily feels weariness and lassitude rather than the springing and elastic health of more leisured days. She has just come away from an abortive social exchange in which another of the millinery workers, a kindly Miss Kilroy, attempts to commiserate with Lily's headache and suggests Orangeine. After the feeblest of exchanges, 'neither knew what more to say' (*HM*464). The blurred urban landscape seems to affect Lily's power of conversation, and she cannot even sustain the old, prac-tised social formalities; she is losing her sense of pattern. This indeterm-inacy finally settles on her like a pall, in a death not clearly either one thing or the other, a vagueness proposed as early as the first paragraph of the book, when Lily is discovered indecisive in the liminal and trans-itory space of Grand Central Station, between trains in a waste of disoc-cupation.

The boarding-house, Lily's final liminal locale, mirrors the marginal status of its occupant. The room subjects her to 'uncongenial promiscui-ties' (*HM*487) – servants 'thrust' meals in through the door, the 'intimate domestic noises' of other boarders and the murmur of the street penet-rate its thin walls and compromise her privacy, as if the room were per-meable and really had *no* barriers against the outside world, no boundaries between Lily and not-Lily. Sleep and waking, like the dreary March twi-light, are indistinct to her: chloral, though it brings a kind of sleep, does not leave her rested, and her dreams keep her awake. As she organises her possessions, on the evening of her death, she draws forth from her trunk the dress she had worn for the Bry *tableau*, a dress which now appears 'a heap of white drapery which fell shapelessly across her arm' (*HM*513). When she wore it at the Brys' it showed her outline distinctly and to great advantage. Like the now-shapeless dress, Lily's death itself has a wavering outline; accident or suicide, it has no definition, it lacks agency. If her death is, in the evolutionary sense, an accident, it con-firms, along with the accidental, not-nice landscape of New York, Lily's lack of power and organising purpose. If it is, on the other hand, a sui-cide, it is ironic that in the battle for survival death is her single gesture of self-determination. Lily's journey, in sum, is one which passes from the tightly bordered precincts of fashion, propriety, and tribal exclusiv-ity to a relaxed set of moral and social boundaries, and this relaxation is figured simultaneously in Lily's geographical decline from within bounds to marginal or out-of-bounds. Lily's unpersoning entails un*placing*.

Rituals of casting out

> 'It was the old New York way of taking life "without effusion of blood."' (*AI*335)

Liminality is not confined to the clear demarcations of New York City. The western Massachussetts setting of *Ethan Frome* and *Summer* is deliberately remote from the more familiar urban landscape of the eastern seaboard; but even within the out-of-the-way little communities of Starkfield and North Dormer there are degrees of remoteness: the unrelenting strictures of social geography are found even in the wilderness. Ethan's farm is set far from the village (itself often cut off by the snow), separating the protagonist doubly in his misery from the wider world and from his own locality.

> [Ethan] seemed a part of the mute melancholy landscape, an incarnation of its frozen woe, with all that was warm and sentient in him fast bound below the surface; . . . he lived in a depth of moral isolation too remote for casual access . . . his loneliness was not merely the result of his personal plight . . . but had in it . . . the profound accumulated cold of many Starkfield winters. (*EF*9)

There is nothing near the farm except the family graveyard which inscribes the land with other Ethan Fromes of earlier generations. Located on what has become, since the coming of the railroad made it superfluous, merely the road to the Frome farm, surrounded by dead Fromes (and there seems to be little difference between the live Fromes and those in the graveyard, according to Mrs Hale), grim, remote, frozen like its Frome owner, the farm is autotelic, a place without outside referents.

This segregation, social as well as spatial, is not fixed only by locale; Ethan, the personification of his landscape, brings his isolation with him. In the first episode he stands outside the church hall watching Mattie enjoy herself at a dance attended by the young courting element of the community, a dance from which he is excluded by marriage. The scene separates and situates Ethan in the snowy outdoor world beyond the range of the church lights, freezes him, as his marriage had done, in 'pure and frosty darkness', against the 'mist of heat' and motion, the overstimulation and the vibrant redness of the dance and of Mattie herself within (*EF*16). As the dancers leave the building, Ethan hides behind the open door, able to hear and see the flirtation but unable to participate, an exclusion strikingly manifest, in the narrator's Introductory Note, in 'the red gash across [his] forehead' (*EF*3), the archetypal mark of the outcast, the primal stigma.[44] Like other young Whartonian men, he is troubled by silence or inarticulation: he does not call out to notify Mattie of his presence; and throughout the novel he is repeatedly struck dumb, or is too quiet to be heard, 'by nature grave and inarticulate' (*EF*36). Speechlessness is apparently genetic: Frome women traditionally fall silent: 'the sound of [his mother's] voice was seldom heard' because she is listening (*EF*36). Ethan too is listening: 'field and sky spoke to him with a deep and powerful persuasion' (*EF*19); but these messages are troubling and unmeaning, and he cannot respond to them. The sky reminds him of 'an exhausted receiver' (*EF*15), an emptied flask, a blank, a linguistic vacuum which isolates him further.

Social, geographical, and linguistic segregation are introduced by the narrator. Nameless, an engineer come to Starkfield to perform some service at the local power station, a job which is held up by an inconvenient carpenters' strike, this narrator is professionally interested in the impersonal problems of civil engineering projects, and is specifically uninterested in the strike by the men, which he mentions only once, without elaboration. His interest in Ethan Frome is (unsurprisingly) also disinterested, analytical, slightly bloodless, scholarly. The sight of the horribly crippled man provokes his intellectual curiosity; to pass time he sets about to solve the mystery of Ethan, Zeena, and Mattie with pieced-together evidence from a number of sources. Although he has some contact with Ethan Frome, Ethan is not himself one of these sources, his taciturnity and 'bleak and unapproachable' look forbidding any such enquiry. The narratorial position is therefore complicated: the engineer speaks *in propria persona* in the prologue, shifts to partly verbatim reports by Mrs Hale and Herman Gow, and finally settles, in the first chapter, on the omniscient third person, which may or may not be his imaginative reconstruction of events; he returns to the first person in the epilogue, which leaves him on the threshold of the Frome house, where he has been invited, to observe the outcome of the story he believes he has correctly reconstructed. The confusing, refracting quality of these narrative layers sunders the story itself from the reader, a story, the narrator confesses, whose 'deeper meaning...was in the gaps' (*EF*5), in the boundaries between its various versions. His fascination with his researches and the tale it yields is reflected in the tone of his telling, a tone which meticulously examines, but remains aloof from, its subject.[45]

What we learn from this narrative is that although Ethan's marriage has been more debilitating than his accident, Zeena's *froideur* is inflected, even caused, by the landscape from which Ethan himself is almost indistinguishable; we learn that the Frome malaise has caused him to accept some of the marks and travails of the outcast, including 'the look in his face which . . . neither poverty nor physical suffering could have put there' (*EF*7). The liminal or outsiderly individual of whom his neighbours refrain from speaking fully, Ethan is the communal *pharmakos*, the figure in whom his society invests its fear of accident, illness, and failure, whom it prophylactically isolates in a precinct beyond communal bounds. Before his accident the constraints imposed by Ethan's querulous wife freeze him more efficiently than any season or snowstorm; but Zeena's very frigidity and silence are clearly caused by her marriage to Ethan and her residence on his land. Initially he seems caught in the toils of a lifeless partnership, unable to escape into the life-giving warmth of Mattie Silver. But Ethan's escape from his deadening world is impossible, not because of Zeena, but because he was born into captivity; 'there was no way out – none. He was a prisoner for life' (*EF*70). The Cain-like mark on his forehead is, we are meant initially to think along with the narrator, a sign of and punishment for his deadly sledding adventure, and the relationship with Mattie which led him to it; but in fact it stands for some more essential flaw than a sledding accident: there is a history of damaged women in the Frome family, and accordingly, Ethan and all the previous Ethans unwittingly injure the women in their lives. The accident has converted Mattie into a second Zeena. Ethan is the agent and the effect of his own tragedy, its elements all contained Oedipally within one man. This is the deeper meaning of the tragedy, which resides in its gaps.

In some respects the novel shares themes with *The Age of Innocence*, written a decade later. Newland Archer is faced with a similar dilemma, and both Ethan and Newland struggle against inarticulacy and the urge to abandon established convention – in the form of an apparently soul-destroying marriage – for a fascinating outsider newly arrived in the community. Mattie Silver's attractions are modest in comparison with Ellen Olenska's exotic allure, but in the monochrome landscape of a New England winter, such simple ornaments as a red shawl, a red ribbon, and a rosy complexion recast the world just as completely for Ethan. Cynthia Griffin Wolff has noticed the recurrence in *Ethan Frome* of the image of the threshold, a boundary often presented but not crossed by the narrator.[46] For Newland, such boundaries are socially imposed, and his failure, finally, to violate them is a voluntary submission; he attracts no punishment for testing the limits of propriety. For Ethan, however, the threshold is illusory: wherever he goes, like Mephistophiles, he brings his inner landscape, his family curse, with him. His only attempt to cross the threshold, through suicide, fails horribly, leaving the two lovers maimed and inexorably bound together with Zeena in a dreadful triangle of resentment and need. The momentary pleasure of coasting – childhood's exhilaration reduced to a poor little tragedy – is, as Robert Frost's poem 'Brown's Descent' reminds us, a way of using the unbounded winter landscape to achieve freedom, where snow buries 'lots... walls... everything',[47] as it does the walls of Ethan's fields in the narrator's first sight of them. Snow erases prison walls, but the potential freedom of coasting is pitifully converted into Ethan's perpetual imprisonment, bodily and spiritual, at the end of the story.

I have been describing literal boundaries and demarcations, the precincts to which outcasts are relegated. But outcasts have usually transgressed abstract limits, usually sexual codes; the damage to these invisible limits is reified in actual, physical ones. Male misbehaviour, as we would expect, is either charming and mildly exasperating to his family, or resolutely ignored, as if it did not exist; the Archer clan treat Newland's entanglement with Mrs Lefferts Rushworth ('the lovely widow') and with the Countess Olenska in these ways. Julius Beaufort is well known to maintain a flamboyant mistress but is apparently safe from tribal censure.

When men are outcast, it is more likely to be on intellectual grounds: a man's tastes or his politics set him apart from his caste until he renounces them, or (more interestingly) until conventional taste catches up with his. John Amherst, social reformer of *The Fruit of the Tree*, is snubbed for his political ideas by the mill-owning family of his socialite wife, only to be rehabilitated as one of them once his notions of humane working conditions have become fashionable. Until then they regard attention to the workers as 'not-nice' and faintly embarrassing. Lewis Raycie is banished to social limbo in *False Dawn* for having embraced Ruskinism and for having purchased the severe, unfashionable art of the early Italian Renaissance. These purchases compel his odious father to adjust his tongue to the enunciative pitfalls of 'Piero della Francesca' and 'Fra Angelico', the strangeness of the new words tokens of new and suspect aesthetic and social groupings; the father fears them almost as much as Newland Archer and other young men of the tribe fear to hear the words 'mistress' and 'whore' on the lips of ladies.

A woman's transgression, however, is like mortal sin; she bears an indelible stain which can almost never be washed away; and even the unsubstantiated rumour of impropriety can blacken her reputation, as it does Ellen Olenska's ('*somebody* met 'em living at Lausanne together' (*AI*41[my emphasis])). The assumption that Lily Bart has recompensed Gus Trenor's $9000 loan with sexual favours is the beginning of her descent into death; there are of course no comments about Gus Trenor's behaviour. To invoke Wharton's own recurrent Aeschylean analogy in *The House of Mirth*, the woman is always guiltier than the man for equivalent crimes. 'When "such things happened", it was undoubtedly foolish of the man, but somehow always criminal of the woman. . . .' (*AI*96).[48] Wharton's sexual transgressors, moreover, belong to a culture which acknowledges theoretically the possibility of unhappy marriage, but does not, in the case of women, admit of escape. Newland Archer argues against this custom when he declares:

> [Ellen] had the bad luck to make a wretched marriage; but I don't see that that's a reason for hiding her head as if she were the culprit . . . [she] has had an unhappy life: that doesn't make her an outcast. (*AI*40)

We like Newland Archer for daring to say this to a social arbiter like Sillerton Jackson; but there is not one Whartonian man able to sustain this view, or anything approaching it, in the face of tribal disapproval. Ellen *is* outcast, for her failed marriage, for her rumoured elopement with her husband's secretary, for her supposed affair with Newland, and – as Henry James says in *The Europeans* – because 'the conditions of action on this provincial continent [are] not favourable to really superior women'.[49] Wharton's outcast women pay the price for Newland Archer's feebly held conviction.

Punishment for abstract or suspected transgression can be carried out formally, visibly. Early in *The Age of Innocence* Ellen Olenska's rumoured but unverified impropriety causes all of Mrs Manson Mingott's family to decline her invitation to meet Olenska with ritual excuses, leaving Olenska socially stranded. Because the taboo against dining with an untouchable can only be broken or assuaged by divine intercession, it requires the intervention of the imperial, deific van der Luydens to compel her cousins to break bread with her, an intervention ceremonially solicited and given.   In the antiphonal version of this event, May's choreographed dinner-party at the end of the novel ritually enacts Olenska's casting out, and invitations are this time accepted without coercion or demur. Compared to Lily Bart's sudden ejection from the Dorset entourage, Olenska's expulsion is measured, balletic, anticipated by all participants, and executed according to a prescribed form.   It is a solemnity enacted by the injured party (May) to signal defeat and banishment of the assailant (Olenska, who participates in full understanding), and to restore amends in family harmony.   The formality, with its exacting regimen of courses and engraved invitations deployed almost like ceremonial implements, heals the tribal breach by reinstating the proper order from the potential chaos of impropriety.   The punctilio of Old New York (heretofore represented by the harmless social pedantry of Sillerton Jackson) suddenly acquires purpose and gravity in offering the sacral patterns of order by which restoration is accomplished. Sillerton Jackson is converted from doctrinaire to shaman.

Divorce and illicit sexual behaviour are the fetishised expressions of tribal irregularities; but Olenska is not even divorced at this point, and she is, moreover, firmly resisting Newland's wilder ideas of elopement. Her crime is to be ignorant of boundaries and margins, and on this account she is defamiliarised well before the final dinner-rite. She has already – at peril – crossed certain cultural boundaries: her literary inclination, for example, and the casual publicity of it in her book-strewn sitting-room in a 'bad' address, confers on her a tripartite 'not-niceness' of which the least element is the violation of Old New York decorative propriety. A greater infringement is her advanced and informed taste – so distinct from the mild circulating-library enthusiasms of her female cousins – which marks her out as unladylike; this suspicion is corroborated by the 'manliness' of her relation to literature: hers is an intellectually developed taste (we cannot imagine her browsing through Ouida); and she possesses what looks like a small library (ladies do not have libraries). Worst of all, her literary command and experience suggest dominance over less conversant sensibilities: culturally (as sexually) she is a woman of the world; she could initiate Newland and other 'advanced' young men into the unknown delights of Huysmans and the Goncourts, much as Newland hopes to initiate May in Goethe. If she had lived quietly, penitently, under the guidance of some staid female relation, without calling attention to herself in dress, taste, or behaviour, Old New York might have forgiven her for her husband's brutality and even for her suspected dalliance with Newland Archer. But Old New York is less shocked by Olenska's marital vicissitudes than by her insouciant reception of its own judgement on them. In unwittingly violating this discretionary secondary boundary of her tribe she offends its self-esteem.

Divorce, adultery, illegitimate childbirth, and incest, disruptive behaviours capable of social, as well as genetic, miscegenation and boundary-breaking are figured in terms of their remoteness from the normative married relation, the relation which stands, above all others, for tribal propriety. Marriage can disguise or redeem any of these misdemeanours. New York would be best pleased if Olenska were to return to her husband, no matter at what cost to herself. Newland's suspected relationship with her overtly threatens the dynastic union of Archers and Mingotts/Wellands, and covertly endangers the emerging familial unit represented by May's pregnancy.

Charlotte Lovell, the mis-styled 'old maid', endures punishment for one kind of tribal misbehaviour (failure to marry), but imposes on herself punishment for a worse one (bearing a child out of wedlock). She must accede to, and indeed encourage, the withering social designation of the novella's title, which categorises her by her lack of husband, because it deflects attention from the true state of affairs – that she is an unmarried mother. Charity Royall, in danger of communal expulsion, goes to the Mountain where the legitimacy of marriage or parental relation is hardly an issue; rescued from her predicament by her marriage to her guardian she is subject at least to our troubled sense of impropriety, that this 'solution' is hardly recuperative, can only barely contain the incestuous implications inscribed in her name ('Miss Royall' becomes 'Mrs Royall').

The awful genetic threat of incest, illegitimacy, and adultery is most vividly imagined in *The Children* (1928), in which a group of youngsters confusingly related to each other by marriage or through one parent recombine as a tribe whose characteristics are familial disarray, parental absence and disregard, genetic exogamy, all initiated by the practice of serial divorce. The story – horrifying in tribal terms – revolves on the children's rejection of parental claim, and on their loyalty to each other rather than to their various progenitors. Their sympathiser, Martin Boyne, acts *in loco parentis* to them, an undertaking by which he forfeits both a projected marriage and his chances of attaching the teenaged Judith Wheater. The familial pattern is so deformed in the behaviour of the parents that Boyne – forced into the parental role – is made against his will an illegitimate parent; the overt cause of his disappointment is the age difference between him and Judith, but the real stricture is the incest taboo, which he incurs without any genetic justification.

Wharton's own unsatisfactory *marriáge blanche* ended in 1913 with little of the social ostracism experienced by her divorced characters. By 1913 the rising divorce-rate had blunted the formerly delicate social sensibilities of as little as ten years before; and Wharton, long since settled in France, was immune to New York's displeasure. Her case was sympathetically judged by her family *not* because of what she had endured in the way of incompatability and, latterly, Teddy Wharton's mental illness, but because he had embezzled money from her trust fund in order to spend it on show-girls. It was a financial and social, not a sexual, infraction by Teddy that put her clearly in the role of injured party, much as Julius Beaufort's fall from grace is brought about by fraud rather than sexual impropriety. By 1919, six years after her divorce, Edith Wharton was impatiently reminding her sister-in-law that the divorcée hardly stood out: '[her] "past" is what mine is, and yours, and that of any other woman whose marriage has been a calamity'.[50] She admits, however, to being addicted to her 'normal supply of divorce proceedings' in the press.[51] In the early story 'Souls Belated' (1898), the very word 'divorce' leaps out at Lydia Tillotson from the ornate language of the divorce decree, 'an impassable barrier between her husband's name and hers' (*CSSI*,103), but by the time of *The Fruit of the Tree* (1907), divorce is almost anaesthetised: 'it has grown almost as painless as modern dentistry' (*FT*280). 'There [is] a divorce and a case of appendicitis in every family one knows', says Carry Fisher (*HM*65). 'The Other Two' (1904), a story about a thrice-married woman whose ex-husbands are not only still living, but on friendly terms with her third, notes that divorce is 'in itself a diploma of virtue', and Alice Waythorn's husband congratulates her cleverness in dealing with 'the newest social problem' (*CSSI*,393) of former spouses who remain in one's social group. The odd, even amusing, situational exigencies of divorce offer opportunities for pithy observations about modern manners, especially those which discover women either unscathed or rehabilitated, rather than cast out, by it.

Other stories, however, consider the constrictions rather than the liberations of divorce: the breaking of bounds results in imprisonment rather than freedom. 'Autres Temps' (1911) is a *Mother's Recompense*-like tale about the clash between the shockability of Mrs Lidcote, divorced and returning to New York after many years' self-exile, and her divorced daughter's more modern, pragmatic approach to the subject. Mrs Lidcote's respect for the taboo is replicated in the texture of her diction, which cannot manage to shape the word 'divorce' until the story is many pages old.[52] The delayed irony of the new attitude is that although the daughter's divorce is apparently unnoticed by 'Society', the mother has not, by retrospective grace, been granted the same reprieve, and she must be hidden away by her daughter to avoid damaging embarrassment. For certain generations and certain sins there is no statute of limitations, and Mrs Lidcote is literally incarcerated in her room over one weekend because her presence among her daughter's prospective in-laws would contaminate the atmosphere and endanger the new couple's desire to wed. By contrast, the propriety of Pauline Manford's divorce and remarriage is an unexamined *donnée* seventeen years later in *Twilight Sleep*, the crux of the story resting instead in the contest between predatory men and their defeated male antagonists. Dexter Manford, her second husband, having first acquired Pauline – Arthur Wyant's wife – invites Arthur's retribution later when he embarks on an affair with Arthur's daughter-in-law. Incest and adultery rear their heads in this predicament, but unembellished divorce no longer has power to astonish.

When a friend's son had been abandoned by his wife, Wharton noted 'that the lady left simply because she was bored. Oh, how I want to write a novel about the American bored wife!'[53] In fact, in *The Mother's Recompense* she had already done so. Kate Clephane, sensitive but thoughtless, has spent 18 years in the wilderness of third-rate hotels and fourth-rate expatriates on the Riviera, partly for abandoning her husband and child, but mainly (and this is the indelible stain) for leaving with *another man*, making her both unnatural and a brigand. The man meant nothing to Kate; her real love affair began and ended much later, in Europe, without knowledge of it ever reaching New York. Never an insider to begin with (Kate is from some unspecified southern region), she is allowed back once her former husband and his implacable mother are dead, and then only because she seems to have lived an appropriately *penitent* life since.

The story is initially about recollection: long since abandoned by her lover, Kate is reminded of her old life by a telegram, and remembers her love for her daughter, remembers to act and dress her age, remembers (indeed!) how old she really is after years and years of Lethean European existence. The original social ostracism which Kate endured for quitting marriage and motherhood is, as we might expect, something to which her relations never allude, once they have received her back into the fold, almost as if they had forgotten it. Like Mrs Lidcote, her old admirer and sympathiser Fred Landers can hardly bring himself to discuss the circumstances of her exile, informing her that Hylton Davies, with whom she fled, is 'not a man that many people remember' (*MR*51). The New York to which Kate is readmitted can contain her guilt by appearing to have lost all memory of it, a denial which makes Kate's second, hidden infraction – by coincidence, the man her daughter intends to marry is Kate's ex-lover from the European dalliance – impossible to forget or to bear, and seems to her almost palpable, like the mark on Ethan Frome's forehead. The question, therefore, 'how much does Anne know' about Kate's past, asked by Kate in all innocence, before she knows the identity of Anne's lover, is crucial, and frighteningly proleptic of the crisis which ensues. Fortunately, Anne, like the rest of tribe, 'doesn't ask questions'. But Kate is a manipulator of a 'negation' every bit as forceful as the tribe's own silence.

The other, unspoken, transgression, one of the numerous things that 'a mother couldn't confess, even to her most secret self' (*MR*16), is the one about to be committed by Chris and Anne, the ex-lover and the daughter. Because of his past affair with Kate, Chris is in effect poaching filial attachment from her; and Anne is unwittingly the transgressor against her mother, a modern Electra claiming the mother's sexual partner for herself. Revelation of this quandary would only villify *Kate*; Anne and Chris would remain blameless, a pattern of unfair, retrospective penalty similar to the one imposed on Mrs Lidcote in 'Autre Temps'.

Wharton was always fond of coincidence in her narratives. But she rightly recognises that stigmatised individuals are often subject to chance appearances or coincidental conditions which seem to convict them further. Kate's misfortune is the unhappy confluence of fates which brings her daughter and her lover together. *The House of Mirth*, as I have already suggested, consists almost wholly of coincidences (a feature which connects it all the more strongly to certain types of Greek tragedy), and Lily is even more relentlessly unfortunate in this item. Kate, like Lily and other perpetually stigmatised individuals, is one in whom accident seems to collude with public preconception: the 'error' of having dallied with a younger man is only culpable when, fortuitously, Kate's daughter is found to have taken up with the same man.

The greatest irony of *The Mother's Recompense* is that the truth of Kate's past might be perfectly clear if Old New York bothered to keep its eyes open to events outside its own domain. Despite Kate's conviction that everyone must have guessed her secret, the vigilance of Old New York is not as lyncean as it would wish: the youth of the man and his position as her daughter's betrothed makes any such history inconceivable, a form of not-niceness which never even occurs to them. This secret transgression is one which only Kate and Chris can know of; each counts on social pressure and conditioning to keep the other silent. Loss of voice within the group is a penalty of transgression; Kate is effectively silenced by the taboo she would seem to have broken retrospectively. Sexual and parental jealousy, the intolerable incestuous implications of this dilemma, are known only to Kate and Chris, a tribe of two distinct from the unsuspecting world. Even such a tiny tribe cannot endure transgression; as the female it is she who is compelled again into self-imposed exile, her fierce devotion to her child overridden by the shame of possible exposure and the humiliation of sexual defeat. Tribal propriety is more powerful than parental love.

Reconditioned malefactors

> 'She asks no questions; never has.' (*MR*48)

The ability of the tribe to redeem its malefactors is remarkable, but it depends on nothing being said. In *The Mother's Recompense* a bizarre first family dinner for Kate in New York is half-filled with refurbished violators of social norms. Kate fled America in about 1903; when she returns a few years after the war, the whole edifice of modern manners has been profoundly altered or rebuilt. Present is her cousin Lilla Gates, a divorced, jazz-talking, druggy flapper whose past and current misbehaviour have become an indulged crotchet; and spritely Nollie Tresselton, a well-meaning, twice-married cousin-in-law. Kate's own past is carefully kept out of the conversation, but she need not be hidden away like Mrs Lidcote. But the rearrangement of social norms is ironised by Lilla's mother, who 'was still [as two decades earlier] gently censorious, though with her range of criticism so deflected by the huge exception to be made for her daughter that her fault-finding had an odd remoteness' (*MR*66). Social amnesia preserves her, smooth and undamaged by memory, a weird wax-work not entirely human-seeming to Kate.

Such unfamiliar social settings present the bewildering but protean liminality of a miscreant like Lilla as a kind of estrangement, a defamiliarising which leaves returning exiles confused, alienated, or, like Gulliver, unable to rationalise what they see. Although the stigmata which exiles often bear announce their condition – Lily is wasted, Ethan is scarred, Olenska is outlandishly dressed – the alienation they experience in being unable to read or make sense of tribal insiders is as ostracising as any blemish; additionally, it confuses their own relation to normative society. Wharton emphasises such confusion by allying narratorial attitude with that of some of her exiles and outsiders (Kate Clephane, Lizzie Hazeldean, and Martin Boyne, for instance, and the narrator of *Ethan Frome*); their very perplexity is itself estranging. Kate, for example, can't work out whether or not she is to resume her duties as head of household and is agreeably surprised to be addressed as 'Aunt Kate'.

Those outside the pale characteristically have difficulty reading the insiders' social signals, signals which they either never knew, or which long absence has made them forget; they also have trouble making sense of insiders' physical presence. At the dinner in Monte Carlo, Lily (already a partial exile) fails to see that she is about to be caught in the crossfire between Mr and Mrs Dorset; the illegibility of the signals is figured in the appearance of Mrs Dorset, her chief antagonist:

> Mrs Dorset's [gown], in particular, challenged all the wealth of Mr Dabham's vocabulary: it had surprises and subtleties worthy of what he would have called 'the literary style'. At first, as Selden had noticed, it had been almost too preoccupying to its wearer; but now she was in full command of it, and was even producing her effects with unwonted freedom. Was she not, indeed, too free, too fluent, for perfect naturalness? (*HM*348)

The structure of this passage is curious: it begins with Mr Dabham's assessment, but since Mr Dabham is by all accounts a wide-eyed, impressionable, and indiscriminate society columnist for something called *Riviera Notes*, he metonymises Bertha Dorset in her dress, which fascinates him merely in its intense fashionability. Selden's more discriminating consciousness then takes over. Selden is already, we know, very worried by the Dorset crisis, especially since he correctly predicts the damage Lily will sustain. The untrustworthy Bertha and her preoccupying, unusual dress signal to him some 'unnatural' behaviour which is shortly to ensue; and in the next moments she evicts Lily summarily from her entourage, on grounds she knows to be spurious, but which will save her marriage by deflecting her husband's attention from her own misdeeds with a younger man. Dabham's and Selden's views of her turn Bertha into an inhuman, costumed mechanical figure; the one point of view, absent but crucial, is Lily's. But Lily has, as usual, no view: temporarily reconditioned and lulled by her inclusion in the Dorset party, she is off her guard and has in effect already become a stranger long since; she misreads all the Dorset signs and thus has no prenotion of the imminent disaster. She remains convinced until the penultimate moment that Bertha is desperate and requires her aid. If she is puzzled by Bertha's behaviour, she interprets it as a captious gesture of distress. Wharton signals this portentous incomprehension in the exclusion of Lily's point of view from the unfolding narrative.

Such narrative delicacy is exchanged in later works for explicit bewilderment:

> Kate had been away so long that, as yet, the few people she had seen were always on the point of being merged into a collective American Face . . . the only way to tell the Drovers from the Tresseltons was to remember that the Drovers' noses were even smaller than the Tresseltons' (but *would* that help, if one met one of either tribe alone?) . . . the sameness of the American Face encompassed her with its innocent uniformity. (*MR*65,68,90)

One young man's face is 'as inexpressive as a foot-ball; he might have been made by a manufacturer of sporting-goods' (*MR*83). Another blank countenance is that of Lilla Gates, Kate's restless, jazzing niece. Her 'dyed hair, dyed lashes, drugged eyes, and unintelligible dialect' (*MR*64) add to the impression of illegibility: large and white, with a small expressionless face, and a strange lassitude, the images suggest nothing known in nature, and it is very difficult to visualise her. She likes music and dancing, but not conversation: 'I only like noises that don't mean anything' (*MR*69), she says. Lilla is another autotelic image; seen without referents through Kate's eyes, she becomes for us an enigma, an unreadable message from an alien world.

In *New Year's Day*, the widowed Lizzie Hazeldean rejects her long-time lover when he proposes marriage because the connexion was never more than a business arrangement to her – she perpetuated their liaison for years in return for the occasional cheque as a way of financing comforts for her dying husband. This unladylike rationale and rejection is incomprehensible to the lover, who cannot at first understand what she is saying; it is as if they speak different languages. New York is about to ostracise her (but not him) as 'fallen'; the lover determines to 'save' her:

> Yes, he had really brought himself to think that he was proposing to marry her to save her reputation. At this glimpse of the old hackneyed axioms on which he actually believed that his conduct was based, she felt anew her remoteness from the life he would have drawn her back to. (*NYD*127)

Not only are they culturally, almost linguistically inaccessible to each other (like other Whartonian men, he is shocked when she describes herself straightforwardly as his whore; as we know from *The Age of Innocence*, 'ladies' do not know such words), but the lover looks physically

strange to Lizzie: 'his face, . . . perhaps because of its architectural complete-
ness, seemed to lack mobility. . . . It was so ostensibly a solid building,
and not a nomad's tent' (*NYD*111). This suggestion of homelessness,
of vagabondage and boundarilessness reinforces the woman's sense of
estrangement from tribal norms. His face works nervously; he grunts
occasionally; his rugged handsomeness passes into florid heaviness; when
he draws out his handkerchief on several occasions to dab at his lips,
the scent of cologne is increasingly repugnant. Although this is a man
well known to her, and at the height of tribal eligibility, the episode
makes his assumptions, background, and expectations extraordinary,
unperceptive and inexplicable; all this remoteness is figured in his odd,
almost inhuman person. This man becomes a piece of valuable New
York real estate, but can never become her soul's companion.[54]

Divorced women, in Wharton's world, can be countenanced if they show
'signs of penitence by being re-married to the very wealthy' (*HM*91); but
Lily Bart's friend Carry Fisher is an interesting exception to this rule.
She has not remarried, and consequently occupies a marginal position
in the society in which she brokers marriages and alliances; she acts as
a social conduit between the rich but unfashionable and the fallen fashionable, two sets of liminal characters searching for *entrée* or rehabilitation. Stigma, says Erving Goffman, is 'a language of relationships, not
attributes',[55] and Carry Fisher is fluent in that language. He notes that
certain stigmatised individuals succeed in maintaining a foothold in
'normal' society while having sympathy with and understanding of the
discredited individual who shares the stigma. Borrowing a term from
early 1960s gay culture, Goffman designates such bi-partisans as 'wise'.[56]
Carry Fisher is a 'wise' character, one who has broken the taboo on divorce
but, perhaps because *twice* divorced, twice daring, can operate with impugnity on her own terms. Like Lily a member of Judy Trenor's set, and like
Lily a borrower of Gus Trenor's money, she escapes the obloquy Lily
attracts, and can confess the hypocrisy of this double standard. Although
'she actively gleaned her own stores from the fields of affluence, her real
sympathies were on the other side – with the unlucky, the unpopular,
the unsuccessful . . .' (*HM*402). She is the only member of the New York
circle who exerts herself seriously on Lily's behalf, the only one with
any practical solution to Lily's difficulties (she suggests both husbands
and jobs). She tries to bring Lily together with Simon Rosedale, the
despised social mountaineer who has rationally proposed marriage to

Lily for the benefit of each. The 'wisdom' of Carry Fisher recognises the commonality of aim and need in Lily and Rosedale, a likeness Lily herself finds it painful to credit. Carry wields a power not unlike Undine Spragg's: sexually experienced, she does not risk her purity as Lily does when she takes financial and sexual chances. Divorce for her has a curiously enabling function: the marriage which made sexual initiation legitimate is dissolved without reversion to maidenhood, but instead shifts into social freedom. The same double standard obtains far down the social scale. Another 'wise' character, Nettie Struther, is initially 'fallen' but is reconditioned by a man's willingness to ignore her past; more powerful than Lily, though lowlier, Nettie like Carry is in a position to assist.

Men, too, may occasionally be 'wise'. Originally snubbed and excluded by tribal New York, Rosedale in transforming himself from *rentier* to plutocrat converts his outsiderliness into an unusual ability to transcend tribal boundaries with the power of his wealth. Even so marked an outcast as Lily is not beyond the recuperative power of his money and *successful* difference. A Newland Archer, with all his innate tribal authority, could not renovate Olenska, and could never refurbish Lily Bart. Even Beaufort, for all his similarity to Rosedale, cannot compel New York's civility to Fanny Ring; he, after all, has been introduced to the clan by Mrs Manson Mingott's son-in-law, and he has married into it by attaching Regina Dallas. Rosedale, out of bounds from the start, retains the freedom of the alien allied with the unassailable argument of money and the cautious acceptance of great fortunes into the tribe. The outcast, in this respect, may become ultimately powerful, because he can finance the negation of tribal scruples. Rosedale is the one character always willing to speak to Lily, and even to help her; he never cuts her because he doesn't, as Lily recognises, understand cuts; 'not-x' means virtually nothing to him, a trait which makes him both impervious to nuance and agreeably unaffected. Money in the hands of the outcast is the most efficient social surfactant.

The restorative powers of outcasts – Rosedale, Nettie Struther, Carry Fisher (who is a sort of Vergil in the lower circles of social purgatory) – are not confined to readmission to the enclave. Lily herself, in an ironic subtext to her Oresteian self-characterisation, becomes the *pharmakos* or scapegoat, the figure in whom society ritually invests its sense of its danger, its misfortunes, in order to drive them out of the community in a cleansing ceremony. Scapegoats personify the ills of a society, mainly in the form of natural catastrophes, epidemics and the like. James Frazer describes such an annual Siamese custom in which a debauched woman was carried out of the city, thrown on a dunghill, and forbidden to enter the city again; she was thought to attract all malign influences (especially pestilence) to her.[57] Just when Mrs Peniston starts to hear from Grace Stepney of Lily's compromised reputation, we are told that 'It had been a bad autumn in Wall Street. ... Even fortunes supposed to be independent of the market either betrayed a secret dependence on it, or suffered from a sympathetic affection' (*HM* 194).[58] The gathering clouds over Lily seem to be connected with this financial infirmity, and the Bry *tableau* which follows immediately after the remarks about Wall Street is a ceremonial display much like those which precede the ejection of the *pharmakos*; from the morning following the *tableau* evening, Lily's fortunes slide precipitately, beginning with Gus Trenor's duplicitous note and compromising encounter with her. At the reading of her aunt's will she notices that the other women 'scuttled off as if I had the plague' (*HM* 361), as if she literally carried social pestilence with her. Lily is driven farther and farther from the central enclosure (the *tableau* and the conservatory), carrying out of the story everything not-nice which has attached itself to her name, and by extension all that is discountenanced in her social circle. Lily purifies the New York she leaves.

Tents, railway stations, birds' nests, and hothouses are the domestic metaphors Wharton's outcast women inhabit. Frequently wanderers by nature, the transgressions they commit are as likely to be functions of this tendency as of adverse circumstance. Female vagrancy consists of indeterminacy, fluidity of place, and the condition of liminality. Lily's motto, 'Beyond', suggests this constant impulse forward to the next wayside halt; it may also ironically summarise her final position beyond the pale, beyond help. Kate Clephane and Lily Bart share a fundamental disinclination for stasis.

> [Kate] had forgotten to go to bed, she had forgotten to undress. She sat there, in her travelling dress and hat, as she had stepped from the train: it was as if this house which people called her own were itself no more than the waiting-room of a railway station where she was listening for the coming of another train that was to carry her – whither? (*MR* 178).

It is the reverse of that earlier house-like image of a woman's sensibility; the traveller's costume betokens Kate's natural inclination. Her life in

France consists of hotels, interchangeable people of little intrinsic interest, and wondering where to spend the summer. Her desperate economies in other areas are made in order to retain a maid, because 'it looked better to be able, when one arrived in new places, to say to supercilious hotel-clerks: "My maid is following with the luggage"', as if life consisted principally in arriving in new places. The transience of Kate Clephane, in other words, is innate. We are told that she is a transplanted southerner without many people of her own, a stranger by marriage in her husband's New York tribe. She left her husband not because he was cruel or deviant, but because domesticity was too oppressive; 'the thick atmosphere of self-approval ... which emanated from John Clephane like coal-gas from a leaking furnace' (*MR*16) is an image which turns him into a household implement; by extension the things of the household are demonised. Her willingness to abandon her child has long since been developed into an elaborate mental fiction which mystifies the horror of it; like Lily, she casts this mystification in Aeschylean terminology. 'She had "lost" Anne: "lost" was the euphemism she had invented (as people call the Furies The Amiable Ones), because a mother couldn't confess, even to her most secret self, that she had willingly deserted her child' (*MR*16). The euphemism explains the incident in terms of Greek tragedy; and Wharton allows it at least to nudge the boundaries of that mighty form when we are subsequently invited to judge the discovery of her ex-lover in her future son-in-law as a piece of cosmic misfortune. The ancient Phaedrean horror of matriarchal incest (for Chris is 'young enough to be Kate's son', and will become the legal equivalent of a son once he marries Anne) would be intolerable; like the Greek model for this incest dilemma, Kate is driven to distraction, if not to clinical madness, by her predicament. Her second abandonment of Anne is compelled by these same 'amiable ones' in the form of Enid Drover, Nollie Tresselton, Fred Landers, and Anne Clephane herself. But, cloak it as she will, Kate's second flight from New York is not aberrant, but typical. The euphemistic 'losing' of the infant Anne becomes literal in the course of the novel.

Lizzie Hazeldean, like Kate Clephane, is a woman recalled from exile at the beginning of the story (in Lizzie's case, the exile is inflicted on her for her father's sexual and financial disasters); her re-entry into Old New York can at best be only temporary or qualified. Like Lily Bart, she lives on the self-righteous bounty of an older woman, one of her father's former parishioners. Not born into the tribe, and in any case already expelled from it once, she re-enacts her expulsion just as Kate does, for specific sexual impropriety. Lizzie was originally punished for a sin not her own, whereas Kate was guilty as charged. Despite tribal forgiveness of this crime, Kate departs again to escape another, secret, transgression, whereas Lizzie returns to merit her punishment. Kate is a repeat offender who has internalised the tribal code, punishing herself for what the tribe will never discover; at the end of her story Lizzie is enjoying the company of naive young men who think her 'the jolliest woman in New York', but she is celibate, emotionally remote, mechanically graceful, a woman whom ladies do not visit, who operates within sight but beyond the pale. Kate exiles herself to the other side of the Atlantic; Lizzie is on the other side of town.

Perhaps the most pitiful of all Wharton's female outcasts is, like Kate Clephane, one who imposes the condition on herself for one sort of misdeed in order to conceal a still greater one. Charlotte Lovell in *The Old Maid* never had great prospects, being neither rich nor beautiful; as a young woman she yielded to impulse once, for which she paid with a secret pregnancy. Through the stratagem of looking after a group of poor orphans, she contrives to keep her own child with her, unacknowledged. When she becomes engaged to a young man of good family and is forced to choose between her child and her future husband, who insists that she give up her orphans, her well-meaning cousin Delia counsels her to break the engagement rather than tell the fiancé of her past. Delia, rich and generous, then welcomes Charlotte and the single remaining orphan (Charlotte's illegitimate child Tina) into her own family. Over the years, Tina falls into the habit of calling Delia 'mother' and her mother 'Aunt Charlotte', an arrangement which suits the two women because it camouflages the truth. It becomes evident, too, that Tina's father was Delia's own spurned suitor, an artist who had the single consoling fling with Charlotte before fleeing in disappointment to Europe. Thus it falls out that the old maid, Charlotte, has had to make do with everyone else's leavings: the single love of her life was really nursing a passion for Delia; the daughter of their union loves Delia as her mother, not Charlotte; Charlotte has had to renounce the only other chance of happiness and security she has been offered when she rejected the marriage proposal in order to protect her secret; she is reduced by poverty to living on Delia's charity; finally, in order to make Tina marriageable within Old New York society, Delia legally adopts her and settles part of her fortune on her. These circumstances have withered Charlotte; her bearing and manner are stiff, cold, unexpansive; physically and emotionally she is (like Lizzie Hazeldean) in a kind of internal exile, remote and shuttered off from life. As an 'old maid' she is outside the magic circle of the safely married, and yet the very soubriquet is the tribe's way of reconditioning her as a necessary, almost folkloric character within the social network. Set in the 1850s, this story poignantly discovers the severity of a society so strict that it can enjoin secret self-punishment on even its peripheral members. Charlotte is stigmatised by her tribe for being what she is not and can never confess to not being: an elderly virgin.

The finale of this cleverly-wrought and pathetic tale occurs on the night before Tina's wedding, when Delia and Charlotte debate which one of them should go upstairs and offer traditional 'mother's advice' to Tina. Delia generously wants Charlotte to go to Tina, although she longs to do it herself; but Charlotte bitterly admits that Delia is more fit to perform the duty, since it is she who has truly fulfilled a mother's function in Tina's life, and is officially in possession of, and permitted to impart, sexual knowledge. The climax is in effect an outcasting, the ceremonial expression – in this case through the rites of motherhood – of tribal, familial identity. Charlotte must consent to her own ritual negligibility in conceding this maternal task to Delia. Charlotte's double bind – her tribal character (old maid) in conflict with her actual experience (lover and mother) – is curiously reminiscent of Wharton's own helplessness before her wedding night, when, desperate for reassurance from her mother, she implored Mrs Jones to have just such a talk with her. Her mother's recoil and disapproval shocked her daughter: 'I had been convicted of stupidity for not knowing what I had been expressly forbidden to ask about...' (*LI*35). And the brittleness of Charlotte's thwarted motherhood sounds like Wharton's own much-reported manner (what Kenneth Clark described as 'the frozen mitt' handshake[59]). Edith Wharton never had children, perhaps as a protective measure against such impossible choices.

Self-exile and outcasthood are remarkably similar. In *Summer* the people of the Mountain are a 'sort of outlaws, a little independent kingdom ... they have nothing to do with the people of the valleys – rather look down on them, in fact' (*S*130). This description will serve equally well for Edith Wharton the expatriate in her relation to the America in which she could not find a place of her own; and the subject of the final chapter is the function of expatriatism and statelessness in her work, especially the modes of reinvention and freedom provided by exile. But before approaching the subject of Wharton's voluntary exiles, it is necessary to consider her bounders.

3
Buccaneers

'...no employment and no acquisition is morally possible to the self-respecting man...except such as proceeds on the basis of prowess – force or fraud. When the predatory habit of life as been settled upon the group by long habituation, it becomes the able-bodied man's accredited office in the social economy to kill, to destroy such competitors...as resist or elude him.... So tenaciously is this theoretical distinction between exploit and drudgery adhered to that in many hunting tribes the man must not bring home the game which he has killed, but must send his woman to perform this baser office.' (Thorstein Veblen)[1]

Product placement

'Undine Spragg – how *can* you?' (*CC*5)

'Undine Spragg' is a strange, comic, ugly name for a woman by all accounts beautiful, graceful, and 'respectable'. Writers (especially satirists) sometimes use proper names to declare social, geographical, and temporal condition, for a name can announce its bearer the way dress or physiognomy can. Jonson, Dickens, Sinclair Lewis, and Martin Amis, for example, let certain proper names carry the weight of fashion, heredity, allusion, and pretension for their bestowers (parents, novelists, manufacturers), and in their bearers (children, fictional characters, products, towns, and companies). Tribulation Wholesome, Jane Murdstone, Vergil Gunch, and Keith Talent can evoke abstract features of individuals with the striking, suggestive ellipsis.[2] Edith Wharton, however, rarely commits herself to such onomastic specificity: although her *place*-names are frequently suggestive (Aeschylus Avenue, Eureka, Bellomont, Honourslove), her personal names are less so. But 'Undine Spragg', the name of the protagonist of *The Custom of the Country*, although it would hardly surprise us in *Bleak House*, glares like a neon sign amid Wharton's more usual, organic nomenclature. And because it is the book's first phrase, it seems, like a strong perfume, to enter the fictional room ahead of its owner.

Let us examine this 'Aristabulus Bragg' of a name. The peculiar unloveliness of the ungainly syllable 'Spragg' allies itself aurally to 'slag', 'gag', and 'straggle'; its initial consonant cluster assails the ear as gracelessly as it does in 'spray', 'sprawl', 'sprat', 'sprout', and 'spree', plosively suggesting the embouchure of spitting or of disdain. On the other hand, those consonants also recall 'sprite', a word, as we shall see, particularly associated with 'Undine'.[3] An attempted pronunciation of 'sprite', it seems, has swerved disastrously off the tongue. Or 'Spragg' may stand simply for Wharton's (absurd) sense of the lumpiness of middle-western taste and refinement. But when to it she adds 'Undine' – hard to know how to pronounce, delicately feminine, probably foreign – our initial judgement is dislocated. Is she 'undeen', 'undīne', or 'oondeen', and which syllable is stressed? Her hapless mother calls her 'Undie', which may or may not be authoritative. The mystery (or unreliability) of pronunciation, the irksome yoking of the adamantine 'Spragg' with the sinuous and ethereal 'Undine', is also a feature of the girl herself.

'Undine' is, to those acquainted with European folk-lore, the name of a water-sprite, a creature without a soul who, to become human, first lives with human foster parents and then marries and bears a child to a human husband.[4] To Ralph Marvell her name suggests the motion of waves and an improbable allusion by the Spragg parents to Montaigne;[5] and this, too, occurs to Wharton, who describes her irritating rippling effects and ceaseless posing. Mr and Mrs Spragg, however, commemorate in her christening the successful hair-waving formula invented by her father and patented in the week of her birth, a substance so-called because – as Mrs Spragg explains – of '*un*doolay . . . the French for crimping' (*CC*48). The product is not named for sprites or for aqueous disturbances, but for a hairdressing technique so the daughter, who is named for the product. She could as well be called Marcelle, or Blondine, or Clairol. By name and by nature, Undine is a product, genetic and commercial, a roaming brand-name. A brilliant self-promoter and self-merchandiser, Undine bears a name which is an exact account of all that she is. Her name appears as the first two words of the novel, an advertisement of its commercial theme.

In 1907, as Edith Wharton set to work on *The Custom of the Country*, the President of Harvard announced the foundation of his university's new School of Business Studies. The shared nativity of Wharton's magisterial money-novel and Harvard's capitulation to the study of money is not fortuitous; her contemporaries were already fictionalising the stratospheric entrepreneurs like Vanderbilt, Morgan, Yerkes, Rockefeller, Frick, Belmont, Gould, and Cooke. Mark Twain's *The Gilded Age* (1873) and William Dean Howells' *The Rise of Silas Lapham* (1885) and *A Hazard of New Fortunes* (1890) had already established the subject; Upton Sinclair was writing *The Metropolis* (1908) and *The Money Changers* (1909), muck-raking satires of the super-rich; Booth Tarkington's *The Plutocrat* (1927) would show the business titan at play; Frank Norris's *The Octopus* (1901), and *The Pit* (1902) charted railroad battles and wheat wars; and Theodore Dreiser in the Frank Cowperwood trilogy – the so-called Trilogy of Desire (*The Financier* (1912), *The Titan* (1914), and *The Stoic* (1947)) – was establishing the poetics of upward mobility.[6] Slightly later, but in the same vein, Sinclair Lewis's *Babbitt* (1922; dedicated to Wharton)[7] satirised boosterism and salesmanship, and Dos Passos' *USA* trilogy (including the *The Big Money* (1936)) acknowledged the part played by high finance, personified in the figures of John Pierpont Morgan and his son Jack, in the conduct of the Great War; and by manufacturing in Henry Ford, the visionary industrialist who put all America on the road. Fitzgerald's *The Great Gatsby* (1926), at the end of the primary money-novel era, exemplified the potential tragedy of the self-made man. At the very moment when American writers were immortalising the art of money, in short, Harvard gave its imprimatur to the science of profit.

The money-novel (of which the 'business' novel is a sub-category) takes getting and spending as its primary theme, with close attention to the social conditions which govern these activities. Dreiser's *The Financier* abandons itself with undisguised pleasure to the minutiae of transaction in the descriptions of Cowperwood's complex and arcane share dealings, loan hypothecations, his cunning, his companies, holding companies, sinking funds, and deposit accounts are as salaciousness and as relentlessly monotonous as pornography. Norris's *The Pit* pitches a different kind of fervent transactional energy in the electrifying activity of the trading floor and the tidal immensity of wheat, the commodity itself. Upton Sinclair discovers tragic poetry in Wall Street: 'Here was where they fought out the battle of their lives . . . the cruel waste and ruin of it, the wreckage of the blind, haphazard strife.'[8] The physical laws of greed, which best demonstrate themselves in financial activity, create the remoteness, the curiously detached, degree-zero style typical of money-narratives.

If money-novels are, generally, about getting rich, and business-novels are specifically about the *mechanics* of getting rich, both are subsumed in a larger category which might be described as the 'economic novel', which comprehends the whole range of such topics, and often situates itself in the milieus of labour, finance, commerce, consumption, and (because it is American) social mobility, class, and caste. *Sister Carrie*, for instance, is less about business than about upward mobility (its heroine could be the direct ancestor of Undine); but *The Rise of Silas Lapham* is a story of business *and* social misfortune.[9]

Another kind of the economic-novel in the period is what we might call 'woman-on-the-make' narratives – a genre well- known since Defoe, but suddenly appearing with renewed flourish and vigour at the beginning of the century. Among these are Dreiser's *Sister Carrie* (1900) and *Jenny Gerhardt* (1911); Frances Hodgson Burnett's *The Shuttle* (1907); Robert Herrick's *One Woman's Life* (1913); Louis Joseph Vance's *Joan Thursday* (1913); Winston Churchill's *A Modern Chronicle* (1910); Anita Loos's *Gentlemen Prefer Blondes* (1926); and Robert Grant's *The Orchid* (1905), and *Unleavened Bread* (1900), perhaps the single most important influence on *The Custom of the Country*.[10] These novels translate the energetic socio-economic impulses of the upwardly mobile, greedy, and financially cunning (traditionally male) money-figure onto the equally ambitious but economically fettered female protagonist, whose wheeling and dealing must be displaced or reinvented as forms of personal, sexual, or aesthetic transaction. The female money-novel tends to propose this woman as psychologically equivalent to male money-characters; but without commerce, or finance to convey this equivalence, she instead becomes interested in and symbolic of pure personal power, rather than of specific financial power.

Henry James, Wharton notes in her autobiography,

> often bewailed to me his total inability to use the 'material', financial and industrial, of modern American life. Wall Street, and everything connected with the big business world, remained an impenetrable mystery to him . . . James would have found . . . [it difficult] to depict the American money-maker in action. (*BG* 176)

Although it has been argued that she too was similarly incapable,[11] money is in fact her ideal subject. Among her surviving papers from the period 1910–1914, she left the outline of a money-story which attests to her interest in the uses of finance and material accumulation as a subject of fiction. An important financier is suddenly taken ill during a period of economic instability, and this is predicted to produce panic in the markets. A distant cousin happens to be his double, and is sent to some great event in place of the financier; but, timid and unnerved amid the champagne and the publicity, the cousin suffers a heart attack. To avert the panic, the real financier has to be wheeled out from his sickbed and shown abroad. The public, however, now believe *him* to be the impostor, and the cousin (now dead or dying) the real specimen, and so the threatened panic ensues. Wharton ends this note on the tantalising question, '*Apres?*'[12] It is a pity this tale remained undeveloped; it proposes as its central conceit an act of substitution which mimics the transactions of commerce, the transaction which Undine herself promotes in her career of upward trading. And '*Apres?*' might be the motto of the financial psyche. Although Wharton never produced a traditional male-centred business-novel, instead, in *The Custom of the Country* she converted the transactional principles of that genre to a narrative of female aggrandisement, and found therein the source of her most vigorous social anatomy.

Wharton exploits the money-theme in various ways. Money casts an efficient and uncompromising searchlight into the tribal and caste distinctions in which she is adept, and these distinctions are never so well-lit as when they are being violated by money's invasive energy. And the vigour of money-making and spending, the vigour of the money-protagonist, are Wharton's own, energies she is especially – perhaps uniquely among American writers of the period – qualified to describe. For the moralist and formalist of *The Fruit of the Tree* and *The House of Mirth*, the value-free, transactional vacancy of money and its manipulators is deeply alluring, the ground of the satire (a mode toward which she is always tending) which riotously dilates in *The Custom of the Country*. When she allows her incipient fascination with the archetypal money-character, the buccaneer, full rein, she licenses what is most distinctively her own voice.

She was already interested in money-subjects and the peculiar hubris of the suddenly rich.[13] In a letter of 1905 she writes:

> Social conditions as they are just now in our new world, where the sudden possession of money has come without inherited obligations, or any traditional sense of solidarity between the classes, is a vast & absorbing field for the novelist, & I wish a great master could arise to deal with it.....[14]

This class of rich is invariably linked, in her writing, with ideas of dissociation, caesura, discontinuity, disruptive themes which are figured, for example, in their supererogatory architecture, 'a muddle of misapplied ornament over a thin steel shell of utility' (*CC*44)). *The House of Mirth* (1905) interests itself in the energetic and self-making of Simon Rosedale, who tries to acquire the society belle as if he were negotiating an expedient company merger; the languid Mrs Hatch has bought into a society with 'no more real existence than the poet's shades in limbo' (*HM*442). *The Custom of the Country*, where self-making is apotheosised, comes midway between *The House of Mirth* (1905) and *The Age of Innocence* (1921) as the middle term in this great triad of novels, each of which considers the social expressions of money in a distinctive way.

The Age of Innocence recollects tranquilly and nostalgically from across the ocean the long-perished world of her childhood, and catalogues the select Old New York society with lapidary precision and stillness; only the presence of the super-rich bounder Julius Beaufort relieves its restrained monochromatic palette. Its mode is the cut-glass aphorism on the behavioural affect of class, which is merely coincidental with money. *The House of Mirth*, however, was written in the midst of her subject, set in the present of 1903–4, at a time when she had not yet left New York for good, when she herself was reaching the height of her own earnings (and expenditure), and entertaining in her palatial house in Massachusetts. The novel's admixture of very old money and very new, with all the registers between these extremes, creates a prismatic richness, an energetic instability of personality, habit, assumption, and setting. By contrast with *The Age of Innocence*, money and the attitudes governing *The House of Mirth* are febrile, oblique, equivocal, ambiguous.

Were it not for the bittersweet love affair at its centre, *The Age of Innocence* would be a witty but mild and affectionate essay on the effete society of Old New York which Wharton remembered from her childhood; if Newland Archer's world represents the territory an Undine can invade, everything that she can expend, it is nonetheless a world preserved at least in fictional amber from such assaults. But Wharton's perceptions of class, tribe, and boundary are at their most acute when they are threatened rather than when they are remembered as innocently secure, and *The House of Mirth* is thus the obvious thematic precursor of, and *The Custom of the Country*, also set in the recent past of the *The House of Mirth*.[15] Wharton herself, morever, was in personal and geographical transition in these years, and Undine and Lily (both, essentially, homeless) share these transitional qualities. *The Custom of the Country* celebrates the destructive success of an Undine Spragg precisely because Wharton is so scathing about that social lassitude, that 'innocence' she was still observing first-hand in her own and her husband's family. Her extraordinary ambivalence about Undine and her *modus operandi* is only possible for an author still struggling in the toils of a highly wrought social propriety which not only refused to acknowledge divorce, but tended to lump it with the higher affronts such as the production of literature by ladies. Although *she* reckoned that the writing of *The House of Mirth* represented betrayal from within the citadel (see the epigraph on p. 49), *The Custom of the Country* is in fact Wharton's revenge against her class.

Buccaneers

> 'The display of wealth has here to take the place and perform the office of the heraldic display in monarchical countries.' (Edgar Allan Poe)[16]

The vehicle of that revenge is the social invader or buccaneer. The entire history of American settlement is the history of incursion from elsewhere, and Wharton's social invaders follow this pattern. If the buccaneer has identifiable roots, they are usually indistinct, onomastically western – places with names like Opake, or Euphoria, or Deposit. Unlike his historical predecessors on the American continent, the social invader relies only metaphorically on armies or endurance or navigational skill; invested instead with the transcendental, almost mystical, power of money over tradition, he navigates new worlds and lays them low with his commercial cunning, or through arcane, often abstract, operations in the fiscal arena. The buccaneer begins his career as a late version of Coopers's or Parkman's frontiersman, that valiant, self-reliant, wily conqueror of the howling American wilderness who arrives in unsettled territory, subdues wild beasts and hostile aboriginals to his will, and establishes a state or a city or a family fortune by destroying what he finds in the name of profit and glory.[17] Once brute nature is conquered (in the form of mining, land-development, railroad-building, and agricultural improvement), the late frontier-figure heads *east*, not west, to subjugate the social landscape of the major metropolises. In Wharton's Old New York, this invasion occurred after the end of the Civil War, when the number of American millionaires quickly soared ten-fold.[18] War-profiteers everywhere converted their earnings – from war-loans and government bond issues, supply-transport in railroads and ships, food and clothing manufacture for the Northern army, and the fundamental development of oil and iron production which made the war effort possible – into houses, parties, wardrobes, yachts, art collections, and social prestige. If earlier proponents of the old order of seemly taste and expenditure like Mrs Elizabeth

Fries Ellet[19] had reviled the vulgar excesses of the Gilded Age, Wharton's contemporaries Upton Sinclair and Frank Norris were gleefully loading their prose with descriptions and lists of those vulgarities – rooms full of pictures, the interiors of massive steam yachts, incredible sums being rung up as tidal waves of wheat and other commodities roll onto the market and their profits into the pockets of the protagonists. Sinclair's *The Metropolis* (1908) enumerates the seemingly infinite enthusiasms of the rich, each evanescent, each merely the current season's manner of disburdening oneself of surplus cash;[20] in it is a Wall Street titan whose 'house on Fifth Avenue . . . was said to be the finest Italian palace in the world. Over three millions had been spent decorating it; all the ceilings had been brought intact from palaces abroad, which he had then bought and demolished'.[21] The profiteers' 'rule was for plunder; all the streams of profit ran into their coffers',[22] and even their architecture entails the ravaging of primary cultural landscapes and civilisations. However stoutly the old arbiters and the brash young realists resisted or satirised this invasion, it was not, in the long run, a difficult conquest: Louis Auchincloss has rightly observed that the Old New York families were themselves nothing more than highly successful bourgeois stock – merchants and tradesmen of England and Holland, mainly – and 'it never takes one class of capitalists very long to amalgamate with another'.[23] The social sanctuary which had to be breached was itself neither of long standing (in aristocratic terms, anyway), nor innate in the sense that land-owning aristocracies develop organically and propagate hereditarily over long periods. The Knickerbocker society to which Wharton's own family belonged had, in fairly short order, erected hurdles, concocted taboos, and established shibboleths virtually *ex nihilo*, in flimsy imitation of the European territorial élites.

This flimsiness makes the elegiac tone of Mrs John K. van Rensselaer's *The Social Ladder* (1924), a 'history' of American (especially New York) Society, more pathetic than authoritative. She records with relish the derogatory names given to the wealthy new invaders ('bouncers', because of their 'fast and erratic behaviour'; 'silver-gilts'; 'climbers'; and 'rodents', because they multiplied so quickly), and piously but erroneously announces that hierarchies of birth and wealth can never be permanently mingled, since wealth will always 'sink to its own level'.[24] On every count, Mrs van Rensselaer is quite mistaken. By 1924, after all, Wharton's *The Age of Innocence* already eulogised post-Civil War élite society with which *The Social Ladder* aligns itself;[25] the barbarians at the gate had long since taken possession of the citadel. As Wharton was discovering in the barbarians a fruitful subject for fiction, Mrs van Rensselaer was performing an earnest rearguard action in the manner of her Knickerbocker predecessors Washington Irving, George Templeton Strong, and Philip Hone. Her attempts to maintain this fossilised set of distinctions is as out of date in the middle of the Jazz Age as the minuet-like behaviour of the characters of Old New York.

'Social prominence', says Mrs van Rensselaer despairingly, '... [is] to be expressed... in terms of millions rather than of lineage.'[26] 'Idolatry and Mammon-worship', expostulates George Templeton Strong in disgust after seeing a new gilded civic statue of Commodore Vanderbilt;[27] 'He strips the brass from the Hudson River locomotives, and erects a brazen monument of his grandeur upon the flat ugliness of a freight depot', says James Medbery.[28] The exploiters embody the direst warnings of the established arbiters. What Mrs van Rensselaer failed to understand, what Edith Wharton did, was that New Money always trumps Old; rich Americans ride rough-shod over cultured Europeans; the bought defeats the inherited; instant gratification makes tradition yield; expedience defeats scruples; vulgarity wins out over taste. This is the central pattern of American cultural development, and in each of those contests, Undine Spragg represents – apparently resistlessly – the victorious side.

Money overwhelms the social aboriginals; as in the realist fiction of Dreiser, Norris, and Sinclair, money in Wharton's stories invariably evaporates class and hereditary distinction by mesmerising the very people who profess to scorn it, even though it is initially resisted by those whom it invades. Money allows its possessors to ignore or transcend social boundaries, to establish themselves at the centre of the tribe, like Julius Beaufort; money has alchemical properties which can convert the dreariest human material into gold, a transformation wrought on the unprepossessing Percy Gryce and Gwen van Osburgh; money has a solvency to destroy the most rigid social structures, a solvency commanded by Elmer Moffatt and Undine Spragg. And the introduction of new elements into a system inevitably alters it; the tribe, once invaded and colonised by moneyed outsiders, is no longer quite what it was. The spectacle of *ancien régime* given over to cash-worship, like modern images of Amazonian indians drinking Coca Cola, is an anthropological conceit favoured by both Newland Archer and Ralph Marvell, who cannot resist observing their own species as if they were conducting a field study.[29]

Undine Spragg and the financiers are buccaneers. The term 'buccaneer' is peculiarly resonant – from a Franco-Brazilian word for a hunter of wild cattle, later used of piratical privateers, it sounds of the adventurous, the heroic, the glamorously illegal, the predatory, and the unscrupulous. Wharton's buccaneer novels (*The Custom of the Country* and *The Buccaneers*) as well as all her buccaneer characters (who also appear in *The House of Mirth*, *The Age of Innocence*, *The Glimpses of the Moon*, *Twilight Sleep*, and *The Children*) follow the path of heroic narrative: buccaneers in these stories storm their way through social worlds – countries and continents, families and neighbourhoods – never satisfied, always, like their originals, looking for new domains to conquer.

The financial and social buccaneer as heroic, even Homeric, is a common theme in American money-novels. For Sinclair, the contentions of the financial titans rock New York: 'Swift, imperious, terrible, trampling over all opposition . . . Wall Street had reeled in the shock of the conflicts.'[30] Mr Tinker, protagonist of Booth Tarkington's *The Plutocrat* (1927), rides through a North African landscape of Roman ruins 'like some great scarlet-robed Carthaginian . . . Hamilcar or his gorgeous son Hannibal';[31] he is 'like a passage in Homer, or in some Gothic poem'.[32] In *The Great Gatsby* (1926) Nick Carraway studies books on banking and credit which promise 'to unfold the shining secrets that only Midas and Morgan and Maecenas knew'.[33] Dreiser's Cowperwood is imagined being greeted by the three witches from *Macbeth* ('Hail to you, Frank Cowperwood . . . possessor of endless riches!'[34]); of Curtis Jadwin in *The Pit* (1913), Frank Norris writes:

> Everything stopped when he raised a finger; everything leaped to life with the fury of obsession when he nodded his head. His wealth increased with such stupefying rapidity, that at no time was he able to even approximate the gains. . . . Nor were the everlasting hills more secure than he from the attack of any human enemy . . . no Czar, no satrap, no Caesar ever wielded power more resistless.[35]

In a drawing room, Elmer Moffatt retails even his own unsuccessful battle with Harmon B. Driscoll with 'Homeric volume' (*CC*145). The 'epic effrontery' (*CC*146) of buccaneers is again personified in Undine Spragg, the summary figure of this piratical socialite and business operator.[36] But there are – perhaps oddly – no such similes for Undine. Instead, she attracts two other kinds of image: of the fluid and liquid (she has the name of a water-sprite; she ripples and glitters; she is launched into New York society on the profits of the Pure Water Move), and of the adversarial, the umbrageous, the bellicose (she thinks always in terms of 'getting even', of dominating, of 'being able to "run the thing"' (*CC*53–4)).

The newspaper report of Undine's record-breaking twenty-minute divorce from her third husband and remarriage to Moffatt chronicles the characteristic buccaneer expedience and leverage overpowering restraint and decency with incursion even into the precincts of disinterested legal practice. A private train conveys them to Reno; the judge who presides over the divorce hearing does so after normal court hours, and having granted the divorce serves as Moffatt's best man a few minutes later. Moffatt's second courtship of Undine has also consisted of incursions into exclusive places and subsequent conquest in the form of purchase. At this point in his career, Moffatt's spending power, for art objects or divorces, is virtually unrestricted. It is a mode of behaviour and expectation with which we are, by this time, well acquainted. This second courtship, very near the end of the novel, is interestingly blended with a retrospective account of the first one, when Moffatt managed to carry Undine away to an earlier, illicit marriage in another state, a primitive version of the more rarefied financial combat and wealth-grabbing in which he later specialises. Moffatt's truly inconceivable wealth defies the principles of exclusion and restraint because it, and he, are predatory: there is no art, no property safe from his purchasing ability, just as there is, apparently, no social ethos safe from Undine's destructive desires, or any man safe from her predations. Like the Morgans of US Steel, of famous and scurrilous battles for railroads, banks, and insurance empires, and of peerless collections of art, books, and manuscripts, Moffatt is a collector so powerful he only goes after things that aren't for sale at any price. 'I don't suppose I could stop you if you really wanted [the tapestries]', says Undine; 'Nobody can stop me now if I want anything', Moffatt replies in complete candour (*CC*301); 'the vision of the things he could have unrolled itself before her like the long triumph of an Asiatic conqueror' (*CC*303). This man, whose career is subordinate to hers in the novel, but is in fact on a far grander scale, is, like his first and second wife, always looking for the 'next thing', always asking the question '*Apres?*'; to him, as to her, ascent is even more thrilling than arrival.

The ruthlessly self-seeking are antagonistic in all their ways to the tribal groupings and practices of the aboriginal aristocracies. They overgo all proprieties of consumption, matrimony, business practice, even elementary social and linguistic transaction. In *A Backward Glance* Wharton recalls the high standards of spoken English insisted upon by her own parents and their friends; but it is precisely this articulation which buccaneers lack: of Moffatt, Undine thinks, 'Here was some one who spoke her language, who knew her meanings, who understood instinctively all the deep-seated wants for which her acquired vocabulary had *no terms*' (*CC*302) [my italics]. Throughout the novel, the eloquent, articulate sensibility of the old tribes has been pitted against the mute, action-rich communications of the buccaneers. Undine's family do not really speak to each other in ways that someone like Ralph Marvell can understand (it was, he realises 'the result of an extremely simplified social code. . . . words of greeting seemed almost unknown to their domestic vocabulary' (*CC*88)). Undine herself has nothing to say about anything, beyond a few conventional exclamations of amazement and consternation; when she speaks, she seems to disappear. But she recognises a native speaker in Moffatt:

> It was of no consequence that the details and technicalities [of Wall Street] escaped her: she knew their meaningless syllables stood for success, and what that meant was clear as day to her. Every Wall Street term had its equivalent in the language of Fifth Avenue. . . . (*CC*303)

By their compelling money-power, Whartonian buccaneers intrude in previously closed social categories: Old New York and the aristocracies of England and France attract them and finally capitulate to them, and the realms they conquer are forever altered by the act of conquest. Buccaneers are essentially destroyers, devourers of worlds. The principles of family, heredity, land, culture, or achievement which have determined the nature of these élite populations are obliterated by the power of cash, a cancellation clearly figured in the marriages of Clare Dagonet to Peter van Degen, and of Ralph Marvell to Undine Spragg; Clare and Ralph are each 'seized' by new, brash money. Armed with cash, buccaneers can grab whatever they like; and the weaknesses of the old élites are brutally exposed by their susceptibility to buccaneer blandishments. The old money ultimately conspires, willy nilly, with the new.

Wharton's financiers are characterised by their extraordinary appetites: Simon Rosedale is first seen at the margins of *The House of Mirth* working his way up from canny property investor to extravagant millionaire whose pictures, house, and buying-power are incomplete only because he has not yet acquired the socially elegant wife who will wear his jewels and host his parties. With frank interest, Rosedale gives a fabulous diamond as a wedding present to the daughter of a socialite and potential business associate; as frankly, he recognises that Lily is also 'some superfine human merchandise' (*HM*412), requisite to his social ambitions; business and social advantage is in his sights. Julius Beaufort has the gentry of *The Age of Innocence* gasping at his taste for Bouguereau nudes and endlessly enfiladed drawing rooms. Moffatt, as billionaire railroad emperor, has driven up prices on the international art markets with the volume of his buying.

If epic similes are one descriptive category very appropriately reserved for buccaneers, this is not their only trope. Few American money-novelists, from Twain and Howells to Fitzgerald and Sinclair, have been proof against the descriptive and emblematic properties of the buccaneer house, that territorial marker and index of the socially ambitious, of thrusting *arriviste* culture. The buccaneer house is a megalomaniac's text, loaded with architectural references and arguments which are incoherent, defiant of any developed rationale of style or purpose, adverting only to the exhaustless bank account which funds it and the overwhelming desire to attract notice to that single splendid feature of the owner. After the Civil War, the enormous new fortunes, some of them seemingly magicked up out of the cauldron of the stock-market, were soon converted into real estate. First came the palatial houses of elaborate design in Fifth Avenue, where the new citizen-princes mimicked the powerful families of the Florentine *quattrocento* in their displays of purchasing power and patronage; in the next phase, their children built fantastic 'cottages' in Newport and Bar Harbor, or country estates on Long Island. Finally, they aspired to feudal power, or a pretend version of it, a move most astonishingly represented by George Washington Vanderbilt II, grandson of the Commodore, who bought 203 square miles of North Carolina surrounding Biltmore, his house of 250 rooms with its library of a quarter of a million volumes.

Henry James wrote of 'strange, colossal, heartbreaking' Biltmore in a somewhat baleful posture of bewildered incomprehension.[37] The 'impenitent madness' of such dwellings, he said, whether on Fifth Avenue, in the country in carefully disposed pastoral settings, or in the mock-feudal splendour of Biltmore, was 'utterly unaddressed to any possible arrangement of life or state of society. . . . The material pitch [of such houses] was so high that it carried with it no social sequence, no application . . . as a tribute to the ideal, to the exquisite, it wanted company, support, some sort of consecration' such as 'a great court *function*' to 'go on to'.[38] The futility of producing the *style* but not the substance of a landed hierarchy is inscribed in overweening ambition of architecture and appointment: George Vanderbilt's brother William's house in Fifth Avenue had a moat and a drawbridge; but in Biltmore George Vanderbilt built more than all the rest of his family, and indeed all of America.

As soon as he has the money, Sim Rosedale's first major purchase in *The House of Mirth* is the Greiner house on Fifth Avenue, being sold by some failed millionaire who may have been defeated in a war on the

Stock Exchange by the very man who buys it. An Old New Yorker remarks that the house is

> a typical rung in the social ladder! The man who built it came from a *milieu* where all the dishes are put on the table at once. His façade is a complete architectural meal; if he had omitted a style his friends might have thought the money had given out. Not a bad purchase for Rosedale, though: attracts attention, and awes the Western sight-seer. By and bye he'll get out of that phase, and want something that the crowd will pass and the few pause before. (*HM*257–8)

As entrenched and reactionary as they are, the more cautious brownstone élite of *The Age of Innocence* may be allowed credit for maintaining themselves in dwellings which bear some relation to their original burgherly status. The new money knows of no such analogy, and blatantly announces itself in architectural terms which, in their own past and in America's, have no antecedent. The Moffatt *hôtel* in Paris (to be discussed more fully below) exemplifies the tendency: by convention a word attached to ancestral city habitations, a word resonant with the idea of the past, '*hôtel*' as designation for Moffatt's newly erected 'ancestral home' is pure paranomasia. Likewise, the Wellington Brys' mansion in *The House of Mirth* is 'so recent, so rapidly-evoked . . . that one had to touch the marble columns to learn they were not of cardboard, to seat one's self in one of the damask-and-gold arm-chairs to be sure it was not painted against the wall' (*HM*212). Social and historical reality are confronted and dismissed by the cunning of buccaneer *trompe l'oeil*.

Exploit and industry: the Elmer epic

> 'Cotton is good, corn is good, real estate is very good; but none of these have the beautiful qualities of 3 per cent British Consols or United States 5–20s.'[39]

In his analysis of the modes of wealth, Thorstein Veblen makes a distinction between 'worthy' and 'unworthy' employments which he calls, respectively, 'exploit' and 'industry'.[40] The distinction is essential for understanding the buccaneer mentality. Industry is necessary but 'unworthy' activity which creates new things out of brute material; it is associated, in primitive form, with agriculture or manufacture, but could in a more modern form include certain services, too, such as medicine, business management, and teaching, professions not abstract enough, remote enough, from basic human materials, occupations a little too much like toil. Industry comprises work and effort of all descriptions. Exploit, by contrast, is removed from sources or means of production; it is the *seizing* of others' goods or energies for self-aggrandisement. The exercise of force over others, says Veblen, is an activity higher than industry's force over raw materials.[41]

This remoteness or nearness to the raw material of products which distinguishes honourable or 'worthy' exploit from laborious, 'unworthy' industry is a dichotomy taken to both absurd and emblematic extremes by Old New York. Men may not engage in industry of any kind; either they do nothing beyond keeping an eye on their money or sitting on the boards of charitable foundations, or they dabble in a desultory fashion in some suitably 'honourable' profession such as the law. To engage in toilsome employment is to descend the social ladder: thus Ralph Marvell, who practises a little honourable law until Undine's reckless spending creates financial crisis, loses caste by consenting to work in the dreary offices of a real estate broker, where he becomes the pawn of the arch-exploiter, Elmer Moffatt, in a shady deal. The women, of course, can do nothing but live ornamentally and direct their servants (and even this may be suspect: Wharton clearly acknowledges the sly anthropological humour developed by Veblen in her description of Mrs Julius Beaufort in *The Age of Innocence*, who ostentatiously demonstrates her freedom from even this task when she attends the opera each year on the night of her ball). The young women in that novel perform feats of archery, a sport apparently preferred because of its reference to hunting, the Veblenesque paradigm of exploit.

The financiers who populate Wharton's fiction, however, are hard to contain within these definitions. If the most honourable kind of wealth in Old New York is that which is passively acquired – does not have to be laboured for – in the form of inherited money, it is a subtlety which has no hold on buccaneers. Undine at first thinks she is seeking inherited gentility along with wealth, but she discovers after her marriage to Ralph that his family wealth is paltry compared to the plunder available to the buccaneer; she soon transfers her allegiance and dreams to the new money. Buccaneers are a hybrid species of exploiter. Having no inherited funds to exploit passively, they commit great energy to the acquisition of money as if they were industrious, and yet their means of acquisition are not only non-productive in the classic sense (they manufacture nothing, usually provide no goods or services); they specialise – mainly in Wall Street – in exploit in the form of the financial killing. Exploit is defined by Veblen as 'takings' (as distinct from 'earnings', a morally loaded word); and the vocabulary of finance appropriately reflects this combative, exploitative ethic in words like 'killing', 'hit', 'take-over', and the 'big steal'. Veblen comments that 'in the life of the barbarian, prowess manifests itself in . . . force and fraud',[42] and exploit in its most refined form is financial deception, the exemplary behaviour which seizes the possessions of others with least cost to the predator. It is clear that at least two of Wharton's buccaneer financiers (Beaufort and Moffatt) have been deeply involved in such activity; Beaufort is at last actually caught and disgraced.[43] Beaufort's background and *modus operandi* are never perfectly clear; but Moffatt is obviously industrious *and* exploitative, since he is born without hereditary wealth and is energetic in the pursuit of money; his exploits, like Beaufort's, are rarefied in numbers and pure cash, away from goods and chattels. 'Everything in Wall Street is stolen', says Upton Sinclair;[44] the history of Moffatt's business practice is a tale of steals as much as of deals.

'Jove, I wish I could put him in a book!' (*CC* 146), says Ralph Marvell of Elmer Moffatt. Perhaps Moffatt (rhymes with 'profit') is too elusive, or his dealings too vast, to be contained by narrative. In any case, like Ralph's other literary ventures, his ambition to write about Moffatt is never realised. However, Wharton is careful to weave the full and coherent story of Moffatt's epic finance into the woof of the novel, an obbligato story which moves like the 'shadowy destructive monsters beneath the darting small fry of the surface' to which Ralph compares the business titans.[45] The story of Moffatt's career is the mighty underpinning to the superficial and frivolous tale of Undine, and one which is interesting to piece together, not least because, contrary to critical opinion, it shows Wharton fully immersed in the financial subject.

Elmer Moffatt first appears in Apex City during Undine's teenage years, where he filches her from Millard Binch, her fiancé, at a picnic. He has had various desultory jobs in Apex, is now praised for his business savvy, now derided for his irresponsibilty and unreliability; eventually he is found (emblematically) in the powerhouse of the Apex water-works. The water-works is controlled at that point by Undine's father and his partner, Congressman James J. Rolliver, who have engineered a self-enriching scheme in Apex cleverly marketed as 'The Pure Water Move', a scheme to supply safe drinking water to the growing town. Moffatt scandalises Apex by walking down Main Street on Sunday morning with a local whore, and he is ostracised for this; but a little later he meets up with Undine, who defiantly joins him on another walk along Main Street, during which their real courtship begins; it ends eight days later with their elopement to Nebraska. After Undine is disentangled from this escapade by her father, Moffatt is sent packing to Alaska, and later turns up at the famous Eubaw mine in some other unspecified western state. On the proceeds of Mr Spragg's sale of his interest in Apex water, meanwhile, the Spraggs move to New York two or three years before the novel opens, either because the Pure Water Move in Apex was shady or to escape the notoriety of Undine's elopement and divorce. By the time of Undine's engagement to Ralph Marvell in New York, Moffatt has surfaced again as private secretary to Harmon B. Driscoll, a great financier and head of the Ararat Trust, who employs him because of his inside information on the Eubaw mine, which has enabled Driscoll to take it over. Since he already owns the street-railways in Apex, Driscoll would like to move in on the Apex water company against James Rolliver; Moffatt tips off Mr Spragg about this move by Driscoll because he wants him to sell Driscoll information on Rolliver and the original shady dealings of the water company for $100,000, which Moffatt and Mr Spragg will split. In a typical deal, Moffatt trades his silence about their marriage and divorce for Undine's promise to introduce him to useful members of her new set; Moffatt's thinly veiled threat to reveal her past also persuades Mr Spragg, to inform on Rolliver because he needs money to finance his daughter's marriage to Ralph Marvell. The two of them get their money from Driscoll. Moffatt hints at plans for his $50,000; and Mr Spragg fixes everything for Undine and Ralph with his share, but thereafter he is 'embarrassed' in Wall Street by the enmity of Rolliver, his betrayed former partner. Moffatt then proceeds almost to ruin Driscoll in the so-called Ararat investigation into financial irregularities in the Driscoll empire, clearly through judicious deployment of dangerous information about Driscoll's street-railway operations and his bribery of Moffatt and Spragg; but Driscoll is unexpectedly cleared, and Moffatt is generally considered to be finished, although he is by this time also 'half-ridiculed, yet already half-redoubtable' (*CC*114). Bloody but unbowed, Moffatt tries to interest Mr Spragg in a new real estate deal (presumably also connected with Apex), but Mr Spragg will have none of it. Moffatt then approaches Ralph through Undine, since Ralph's real estate firm is concerned in the transaction. It appears that Moffatt's scheme is the (characteristically) secret acquisition of a crucial piece of land which two major parties are angling for (possibly his old friends and enemies Driscoll and Rolliver); and with Ralph's help he gets the land. Thereafter we hear that the Ararat investigation is being reopened, and that Moffatt is required as state's witness; when he meets Undine in Paris, he claims to be 'all played out' in New York and is avoiding the witness box. When we next see him, however, he has apparently returned to America to testify, but will reveal nothing, paid off by Driscoll for his silence. The proceeds of *this* 'deal' are put to investments in Apex, and now, working again with Rolliver, Moffatt invests his own and Ralph's money in a move to be chartered to buy up all of Apex's public utilities (the Apex Consolidation Scheme). Although it fails at first to get its charter, and causes Ralph's suicide, the new Apex Consolidation Company receives its charter in the end, and Rolliver and Moffatt drive Driscoll out of Apex.

After that we see Moffatt as Olympian collector and as one of the six wealthiest men east of the Rockies. His money doesn't appear to derive from commodities or services such as transport, power-generation, steel, oil, technology, or even real estate (except in transfer, in passing). This story is neither exact nor public: Ralph and Undine, who have most dealings with Moffatt, do not understand his activities and can only report the vaguest impressions of them. Nor is it a story told consecutively: its earliest instalment is retailed in one of the last chapters of the novel, and Moffatt himself, who surfaces intermittently in the plot, tends to offer laconic accounts of himself from which we must piece out the history of his doings. Yet these doings are completely realised, coherent, and consistent; for all her attention to the frothy surface of Undine's metaphorical money-race, Wharton brilliantly works into it this realistic account of a corrupt financier.

In Moffatt, pure acquisition is united with non-industrial wealth; he seems to conjure money and power by various means, on the stock exchange, certainly, but also through insider trading and commerce in illicit information (in both of which we see him engaged), and possibly the formation of bubbles to attract capital investment (for it seems likely that the Apex Consolidation Scheme is something of this sort), holding companies, liquidation purchases (this may be the way in which he and Rolliver drive Driscoll and the Ararat Trust out of Apex), and the leveraged buy-out (this is probably how he acquired railroads). Although Moffatt owns railroads late in the novel, it is unlikely that he has *founded* railroads; more probably he has taken them over. The kinds of productive activity in which we see him more typically engaged seem to involve strategic 'booming' of new towns and companies, and other mostly abstract schemes which seem to rely on numerical ledgerdemain, hype, and low cunning, more than on any solid investment or production.

The model for these activities might be any one of a number of legendary financial magicians. The incessant booming of ex-urban locales all over America by real estate capitalists was big news in the period between 1880 and the Great War. The van Sweringen brothers who developed and boomed Shaker Heights outside Cleveland had to build private trolley lines to support their investment; A.B. Miller and William Mulholland (motto: 'Take it') were hydroelectric and water titans of early modern Los Angeles.[46] But it is Jay Gould whom Moffatt most clearly resembles in his operations. Gould, the so-called 'Mephistophiles of Wall Street', the kind of financier who wrecks companies and leaves only 'financially lifeless bodies',[47] was the railroad baron at the head of the Erie ring who in his long and highly lucrative career never once stooped to repay stockholders, improve business, or create beneficial social or commercial conditions for the nation through his vast schemes and deals. Instead, he played on the speculation fever of the small investor and the government alike to manipulate capital raised on worthless railroads, and invented or improved only dubious financial techniques (the watering of stock, corporate raiding, the generation of false rumour in the markets, the profligate issue of worthless bonds, and ruthless asset-stripping) to cheat his way, unimpeded, to an enormous fortune. Like Sinclair Lewis's Babbitt, 'he made nothing in particular, neither butter nor shoes nor poetry, but was nimble in selling ... for more than people could afford to pay.'[48] Gould was as far as can be from any traditional notion of industry.

Moffatt appears with disturbing frequency in the life of Undine, first as a minor player, eventually as the biggest fish of all in Wall Street. Undine thinks of money as being like a river which occasionally flows underground, to surface at unexpected points. Moffatt is like that river in her life, the embodiment of money. His creative unpredictability reflects the unreliability of his medium, the stock market. His character seems to epitomise the supple cunning, the flexibility and protean potential of male financiers, whose very livelihood depends on their ability to take creative advantage of market opportunities. Like Undine, he makes and forfeits several fortunes; hers are in the marriage market, his in the stock market. After their first scandalous union and hasty divorce in the midwest, they trace nearly parallel careers of boom and bust, only occasionally intersecting. At the end of the book, they merge once more. Moffatt is simply a more traditional money-figure than Undine; they are uncannily alike. Undine, too, is capable of instant adjustments to opportune circumstances, and is likewise unpredictable in her temperament and appetite. Because there are only two or three elements in her success (principally her beauty, her naïveté, and her blankness, her readiness to accept the imprint of projected idealising by deceived men), she is a simpler character, one who lacks the complex wit, the wily glamour, and the aesthetic intensity of Moffatt. She is entirely predictable in her tedious self-absorption. But there is no telling what Moffatt will do next, or where he will surface; his presence in the story seems arranged to remind us how unoriginal Undine really is.

The collision between older and newer money in Wharton, between the careful industry of the former and the sensational exploit of the latter, is essentially one of *attitude* toward money: old money has its roots in shopkeeping, trading, and other unimpeachable, industrious, entrepreneurial behaviour; it is characterised by the cautious laying-up of savings, careful investment and expenditure, relatively unostentatious living conditions (brownstones, ancestral portraits, inheritable silver). All this speaks of 'industry' in Veblen's sense, of earning by duty and some sort of labour (even if the labour eventually is no greater than the making of wise investments) the competence to support a certain splendid ease, security, and leisure. The exploiting buccaneers, by contrast, have adventures on the stock exchange, or in sudden land-deals and corporate takeovers, or mineral discoveries, which are combative and risky; their takings are sudden and enormous, and acquired at someone else's expense. Buccaneers are instantaneously in possession of large amounts of surplus cash which they spend nearly as quickly, and very showily.

The more industrious, older-money New Yorkers have virtually no adventures, not financial ones, anyway, and none that can be referred to in polite society (buccaneers can be encouraged to boast of their exploits on the exchanges); they have had generations to develop taste and the ambition to indulge it; they have tribally determined patterns of expenditure, inculcated by training and by the habit of usually having somewhat less ready money than will satisfy their educated tastes. Wharton catalogues with great specificity, for example, the immaculately tended and displayed collections of lace, painted fans, and china bibelots so proudly cultivated by her mother's generation. These assemblages undoubtedly have heredity-value, but are essentially simple and relatively modest in comparison with the collections of the buccaneers. The exploiters, with the opposite problem, are burdened with cash which they have not learned how to squander. They are untrained in the specific culture of superfluous expenditure. In *The Glimpses of the Moon* Mrs Hicks recalls the first house her husband bought after his initial success in business – also in Apex – whose abundance of windows immediately filled her with despair as she considered trying to wash them all. At the time of this reminiscence, Mrs Hicks has long since found out how to enjoy her millions and not worry about window-cleaning. Like Mrs Hicks, the exploiters are by definition very quick learners, and – as in business – do not fear extravagance. Exploiters have to get their money and their objects from out of the blue (which accounts for their indiscriminate architectural preferences), and it is this faculty of being able to invent requirements at speed which makes their acquisitive energy so potent. Undine Spragg, again, is the avatar of the breed: lorgnettes, writing-paper, pearls, men – Undine only knows what she wants the moment she sees it. Another textbook version of this type is Lorelei Lee, in Anita Loos's *Gentlemen Prefer Blondes* (1925), a book described by Wharton as '*the* great American novel'.[49] She needs only to hear that someone at a party has a diamond tiara for sale to discover an instant need to own it, and in another instant has found the sugar-daddy whom she will induce to buy it for her. This accomplished, she departs suddenly for Paris, where her sense of tradition, of transmitted cultural values, is summed up by her awe of 'all the famous names . . . like Coty and Cartier'.[50]

But Undine and Lorelei have inchoate appetites: they don't know what they want until they are confronted with it; they are unimaginative, merely appetitive. Elmer Moffatt, like the Morgans and some of the later Vanderbilts, is also the most astonishing of consumers;[51] but he is the embodiment of the *inventive* acquisitive imagination. Having been visibly enriched in the form of new clothes and new office appointments, he is first seen in this mode enthusiastic about a kind of carved crystal vase, a taste at this point relatively unformed, being principally for raw (though precious), lightly carved materials, not valued so much for workmanship as for brute substance. At first, this bibelot is casually noticed as a 'trinket'; later, another such vase's tracery is 'as frail as the shadow of grass-blades on water' (*CC*260), as if Moffatt's own sensibility were expanding over time. Later still, he has developed as a connoisseur of the higher arts: on his desk Undine notices a delicate piece of Phoenician glass 'like a bit of rainbow caught in cobwebs' (*CC*319), and he values the de Chelles tapestries ('old and faded' according to Undine) for their 'ineffable minglings of blue and rose' (*CC*298).[52] Although Moffatt never loses the crudeness of the exploiter in the *volume* of his buying, and although he remains elusive and essentially 'incalculable' (*CC*143) in his methods, throughout the novel his rapidly developing taste and discernment are almost as carefully charted as his business exploits. His personal and ethical grossness coupled with the subtle delicacy of such descriptions produce a fascinating counterpoint typical of the man. When he is first beginning to be noticed in Wall Street, his sophistication as a collector, reputed for his Persian carpets and Chinese porcelain, is acknowledged in the same breath as his financial skill. Moffatt in this guise is a classic exploiter in the mould of Henry Frick, who said that 'railroads are the Rembrandts of investment',[53] whose initially drossy

1 Eastman Johnson, *Not at Home* (1870s).

2 Pencraig, hallway, with 'Not at home' card, bottom right.

3 H. J. Montague and Ada Dyas, Wallack's Theater, New York, 1874, in Dion Boucicault's *The Shaugraun*.

4 Edith Wharton in her late twenties.

5 Library, Edward N. Dickerson's house, c.1882.

6. Lady's dressing-case (*London Illustrated News*, 1898)

7 The Mount, Lenox, Massachusetts, *c*.1910.

8 William A. Clark's house (Fifth Ave and Seventy-Seventh St, New York), *c*.1907.

9 View of shattered house at Nieuport, 1915.

art collection became more refined over the years as he learned discrimination equivalent to his wallet.

The steep of disenchantment

> '...she left her hands in Van Degen's. So Mr Spragg might have felt at the tensest hour of the Pure Water Move'. (*CC*168)

Annoyed with Count Raymond de Chelles, her French (third) husband, for his incomprehensible refusal to indulge her with money he hasn't got, Undine truculently reflects that he and his kind are devoted to an abstract and immaterial concept. The women of the de Chelles cousinage work at embroidery and other needlework with which to decorate St Desert, the ancestral chateau; to Undine it is a curious labour, since the house will never belong to them.

> But then that was only a part of their whole incomprehensible way of regarding themselves...as minor members of a powerful and indivisible whole, the huge voracious fetish they called The Family. (*CC*289)

Their 'industrious' behaviour and their familial solidarity – faintly dishonourable, and certainly stupid, because not self-serving – attract only her scorn. This is the reaction of the exploiting individual to toil in the service of remote, disembodied, and possibly selfless ideas like 'heritage'.[54]

Undine thinks that the perennial penny-pinching to support St Desert and the honour of the family might easily be ended if the chateau, or at least its world-famous Boucher tapestries, were sold. Her attempt to have them appraised (these Louis Quinze relics form the chief hereditary treasure of her husband's family) is a signal clash between exploit and industry, expedience and tradition. It is a piece of that very craft, the colossal needlework of the tapestries, that Undine tries to seize and convert to cash. The tapestries function as a symbol of inherited obligation, of labour or 'industry', *and* as the exemplary buccaneer *coup*. Characteristically, she seeks to put a price-tag on what is priceless, invaluable to de Chelles. She wants to know what the tapestries might be converted into (cash or dresses or central heating); and this is the act of an exploiter. But it is an act of appetite rather than of imagination. Undine has no capacity for imaginative relocation in the values of others, because she has none herself. She is outraged, bewildered, or ignorant of everything not already hers or within her horizon of wants. She is constantly said to lack vocabulary, to be puzzled by the enthusiasms of others. She tends to forget 'that other people's lives went on when they were out of her range of vision' (*CC*234). She fails, in other words, to live up to buccaneer inventiveness in her imaginative poverty; as a buccaneer she qualifies only in the ruthlessness of her acquisition. She is not original enough to have the tastes of a Moffatt because she is merely 'passionately imitative': where Moffatt would like to convert his cash into the tapestries, Undine can only imagine converting them into cash. Undine's highest respect is reserved not for the things money can buy (for these she soon tires of, or regards as merely 'the appropriate setting of a pretty woman' (*CC*309)), but for money *itself*; in this sense she is more pure a financial specimen than Moffatt, who is, after all, also interested in particular things, such as art objects, which money buys.

Undine's attitude to her own family neatly draws this same distinction between sympathy and self-interest, between imagination and vacancy. It is her parents' function to supply her with money, and she piously hopes that they remain in good health only that they may continue to have the pleasure of doing so. Her unwanted son is left to their care in New York; but when she sends for him from Paris, her parents' devotion to their grandson makes no part of her deliberations, and she pulls him out of their grasp without thought, much as she has the Marvell jewels reset. She exploits her parents in the exact Veblenian sense by seizing the child because she *can*; it is outside her philosophy to calculate him as, in a family sense, theirs, too, a family treasure selflessly nurtured by the grandparents in the way that St Desert is tended and preserved for the future by ancillary members of the de Chelles family.

Undine's ability to exploit her parents is apparently inherited, the nearest thing to 'tradition' in the Spragg family: Mr Spragg is a man who himself has made a fortune by exploit. His Pure Water Move in Apex, we are told retrospectively, was a muddy scheme to sell worthless land of his own to the town for the building of a reservoir, disguised and promoted as an act of philanthropy after a typhoid epidemic which killed, among many, Undine's two siblings. The dodginess of this deal is only alluded to, but we are told that the Spraggs had to leave Apex 'precipitately', possibly on this account. By the time the novel opens, Mr Spragg, a quondam buccaneer who was not above profiting by the death of his children, is being efficiently despoiled in turn by his even more ruthless surviving daughter, whose genetic inheritance seems to include not only his active business sense but also his taste and talent for 'steals'. In one of her self-serving romantic manoeuvres, Undine is said to manipulate her chances exactly as her father had done in his Apex dealings, as if her truest self were the one most like her shrewd parent. Everything about Undine is blatant and overstated. Even her celebrated beauty is resistant to an overlit hotel room, where she looks in her element:

> So untempered a glare would have been destructive to all half-tones and subtleties of modelling; but Undine's beauty was as vivid, and almost as crude, as the brightness suffusing it. Her black brows, her reddish-tawny hair and the pure red and white of her complexion defied the searching and decomposing radiance. (*CC*15)

Undine's very physiognomy and complexion are cast in the same impervious stuff as her personality, a substance so adamantine and inflexible that it is a wonder her admirers fail to detect it. Compare this with the 'half-lights, half-tones, eliminations and abbreviations' of Old New York, where

> all was blurred and puzzling to the girl...she felt a violent longing to brush away the cobwebs and assert herself as the dominant figure of the scene. (*CC*24)

This is a violent, aggressive, competitive beauty whose end is to destroy rather than to enhance and inspire.

The first assessment Undine always makes in her social gambits is of the female competition; she always needs to establish that her own product will outsell all others. Older women are virtually invisible to her, and she invariably finds that of her own generation she is 'easily first' (*CC*34); she is only disconcerted in this calculation when she meets a young woman, 'longfaced and supercilious', who uses her plainness at least as well as Undine uses her beauty. With Lily Bart, who regards her beauty as the raw material of success, a stuff requiring maintenance and shrewd marketing to translate it into material and social conquest, Undine shares this operational principle: she too imagines herself as a collectible object, chiefly of interest to very rich men likely to say, impersonally, of a beautiful woman: 'Gad! Where did he find any*thing* as good as *that*?' (*CC*58[my italics]).[55] This strategy works up to a point. Late in the novel, Undine is forced to admit that in the Parisian milieu of ideas (which is also a fashionable one) she has little value because she is a bore; she has nothing to say because she hasn't thought about anything except herself. 'As soon as people began to talk they ceased to see her'. 'People here don't go on looking at each other forever ... you don't work hard enough – you don't keep up' (*CC*305), she is told. We already know this about her: during her engagement dinner-party in the Washington Square house of her in-laws-to-be, the skillful manner in which the hostess weaves all the guests into the general conversation, which lingers on topics such as literature, art exhibitions, and the theatre, Undine is disconcerted, insulted, and bewildered. She has no interest in or knowledge of any of this; for her, the 'latest' fiction is sentimental romance, and she has seen a play called 'Oolaloo' 14 times; and although she has seen 'Leglong' (Rostand's *L'Aiglon*) and 'Fade' (Racine's *Phédre*), she can't remember what they were about; she can't pronounce their titles comprehensibly; she merely thinks 'Burnhard' too old; and assumes that they are being deliberately rude in not asking her about herself.[56] Her idea of conversation is restricted to the personal; anything else is fuzzy and indistinct to her. Her primitive tastes are culturally unrecognisable (*When the Kissing Had to Stop*, her favourite novel, is an invented title) beside Moffatt's informed ones, which move 'him in a way she could not understand' (*CC*317).

This conceptual absence, this total lack of mental development, this utter inability to imagine merit in the objective or the invisible, dooms her marriages, and by implication any marriage she might make. An immediate and characteristic solution to her Parisian social problem is to go to a few lectures, but – far more in keeping with her philosophy – she soon gives this up in order to undergo a course of beauty treatments. (Significantly, the choric figure of Mrs Heeny, the only character in this otherwise picaresque narrative to appear consistently, is the masseuse and manicurist who attends to Undine's toning and buffing.) Self-constructed as a commodity, Undine is only concerned with surface value in the form of jewels, clothes, and a well-honed 'gracefulness' perfected in front of the mirror. Because intellectual or sentimental development is not saleable, it is not worth anything in her social market.

Robert Grant told Wharton that his only criticism of *The Custom of the Country* was 'The difficulty of seeing sometimes in spite of her beauty why they all succumbed to her.'[57] Stephen Orgel admires the narrative distance which Wharton preserves between herself and Undine, leaving us to puzzle out or trust the plausibility of her success in her various social incarnations.[58] The strange and alienating case is that *nothing* can make us understand Undine's attractiveness to deluded Old New York or faubourg Paris, nor are we meant to attempt to understand. Since we are entirely privy to her horrifying self-absorption, and because her beauty

and vivacity are rendered bizarre and inhuman, it is impossible to imagine in what her attractions consist. Our admiration is instead reserved
for a fictional art which can keep us enthralled in the adventures of so
repellent a heroine. When de Chelles looks 'at her coldly and curiously,
as though she were some alien apparition his eyes had never before
beheld' (*CC*307), he finally recognises her as incomprehensible, a recognition we have made long since. Herein lies one of the novel's most
impressive features: its *tour de force* is spent on a creature we can hardly
believe, can almost not recognise as of our own kind. Undine and the
novel itself are constructions not unlike the madly assembled houses of
the buccaneers; the book's avalanche of things and descriptions mirrors
Undine's appetite and her imitative faculty, which prompts her to
acquire and to model herself as extravagantly, as recklessly, and ultimately
as unrecognisably, as the buccaneer architects heaped together transcul-
tural motifs.

Moll Flanders, Carrie Meeber, and Laura Dearborn are her ancestors;
Lorelei Lee, Daisy Buchanan, and Aurelie Momoro are her descendants,
as are Wharton's own Lansings and Ellie Vanderlyn of *The Glimpses of
the Moon* (1922) and Joy Wheater of *The Children* (1928). Undine herself
remains the most monstrous of them, the result of an American society
which disables its women with financial bribery, makes itself subject to
the machinations of these beautiful bribe-takers. The philosophic (and single) Bowen explains that they must be bought off and occupied instead
with the fruits of the transactions (houses, clothes, cars, jewels, and seasons in Paris) which are really central to men's interest. Indeed, Veblen
confirms and extends this function: the Undine-type is 'permitted, or even
required, to consume largely and conspicuously – vicariously for her
husband. . . . ';[59] it is part of the 'deal'. But while the men are busy fighting each other in the markets, the women have developed their own
economic network. The American male may be more interested in wrecking railroads than wrecking homes, says Bowen; and if Undine doesn't
wreck railroads, she wrecks homes in the way that railroads are wrecked.
She makes pre-emptive strikes by preventing more credible marriages
(between, say, Ralph and Harriet Ray, or between de Chelles and some
resident of the faubourg). She loots marriages as Moffatt might loot a
corporation. She is an asset-stripper; she leaves the lifeless corpses of
disillusioned men scattered about the social landscape as Jay Gould left
the carcasses of ruined companies.

This female economic behaviour is summed up by Lorelei Lee: 'When
a girl looks at Mrs Nash and realises what Mrs Nash has got out of gentlemen, it really makes a girl hold her breath.'[60] Lorelei and Undine are

gold-diggers in almost the literal sense of the word: they are excavating to see what can be 'got out of' men. Undine deploys her personal capital with the shrewdness of an investor; but her radical dissatisfaction does not allow her to enjoy the achievement of wealth, position, or acquisitions; she is compelled to trade up for ever and ever, to put her latest hit on the social stock exchange behind her as she looks forward to the next deal. In her person, Undine combines at once the financier and the funds he wields, agent and medium. In *The Buccaneers*, Wharton celebrates '"the American girl", the world's highest achievement' (*B*24); but that novel merely recognises young women as expendable commodity. Those young status-hunters are the pawns of two mutually beneficial systems (of capital and of honours); in *The Custom of the Country* both systems are at the mercy of Undine.

When Moffatt declares with the inexorability of the successful financier that he can have whatever he wants, this might as well be Undine speaking. Undine cannot for the moment, however, get what she wants from Raymond de Chelles, namely, two million francs from the sale of the famous family tapestries. This money would relieve her of her various social miseries (these are principally the dearness of new gowns and of keeping the family house in Paris open during the season), but 'it was impossible for Undine to understand a social organization which did not regard the indulging of woman as its first purpose' (*CC*306). Her constitutional inability to understand this or anything else about money is a recurring theme in the book; difficult moments are overcome by flying into a passion or simulating nervous collapse, and extracting a bigger allowance from her rapidly sinking but terrorised parents or husbands.

> [Budgetary responsibility] was a proficiency no one had ever expected her to acquire, and the lack of which she had even been encouraged to regard as a grace and to use as a pretext. During the interval between her divorce and her remarriage she had learned what things cost, but not how to do without them. (*CC*279)

But Undine, although she is an exemplary American woman in this depressing sense, is not the passive recipient of bribes as described by Bowen. She has her own initiative, her own energy, acquisitive strategies very like those of the male money protagonists, strategies only distinct from theirs because hers are not technically specific, do not operate in the commercial marketplace. Undine is, in other words, much more alarming than Bowen's American woman, or the display-object described by Veblen.

'Beyond'

> On the first of May the city of New York has the appearance of
> sending off a population flying from the plague.... Every one
> ...complained of this custom as most annoying, but all
> assured me it was unavoidable, if you inhabit a rented house.
> (Frances Trollope)[61]

Undine is an essential American literary figure: like Francis Parkman,
Huckleberry Finn, and Dean Moriarty, American protagonists perpetually on their way to somewhere else, Undine can never 'arrive', just as
she has no real place of origin or of rest, a quality signalled even in her
bearing.

> She was always doubling and twisting on herself, and every move-
> ment she made seemed to start at the nape of her neck, ... and flow
> without a break through her whole slim length to the tips of her fin-
> gers and the points of her slender restless feet. (*CC*7)

She is always tormented by the next thing, the better deal she may find
in the next place, the 'peep through another door' giving 'glimpses of a
more delicate kind of pleasure' (*CC*34).

Although Undine originates in the dismal boom-town of Apex City,[62]
and although she always invokes its social standards as an American
benchmark, to say she is *from* anywhere in particular is too sentimental
a reading of her origins, just as it is sentimental to imagine that her name
has any traditional or intended spiritual significance. Apex is nowhere,
or anywhere, its name as opportunistic as 'Undine'; it is an unmeant
booster joke (like the real place in Illinois suggestively called 'Hometown'), a place being invented every day by shady boomers like Undine's
father even as Undine reinvents herself. But Undine's placelessness is as
necessary as it is typical: like the financier, she can only aggregate by
ceaseless motion. Stasis is fatal to the stock-market, where fortunes are
made from transaction on movement in either direction; so Undine is
never at rest. Compelled by an obsessive, restless dissatisfaction with
the status quo, at first she leads her weary parents around the nation in
search of social standing and fashion until, in New York, she breaches
the ramparts by marrying Ralph Marvell, and achieves, so she thinks
momentarily, social apotheosis. Her whole existence has been devoted
to the futile pursuit of fulfilment in an odyssey around ever-more-
fashionable watering holes of the eastern United States, given over to

the prodding ambition for the thing around the corner, in the next resort. Undine almost never goes back to the places she has been; she seems to use up each place she visits. She uses up a good half the American continent in her peregrinations before she marries Ralph Marvell in New York and briefly imagines that she has 'arrived'. By the end of the novel she has penetrated as far west as 'Dakota'[63] and Nevada in search of divorce and remarriage,[64] as well as the inner circles of New York and Parisian society.

Her nomadic, rootless existence, a consequence of unsatisfied appetite, of constant divination of 'the next thing', is always, in Wharton, opposed to the prevailing hierarchy. In *The Custom of the Country* such nomadism is made to seem an American national characteristic. We first notice it as early as *The House of Mirth*, where Lily wanders among her friends and their houses, unfixed except in her guiding need for luxury. It recurs in *The Reef*, a year before *The Custom of the Country*, in Sophy Viner, who in her wanderings has lost her angular Americanness and become 'fluid' (*R*12). But where deracination entails Lily's tragedy and Sophy's misfortune, in Undine it is the source of her triumph. Lily's is ultimately a tragedy of homelessness, in which identity is cancelled with the dislocation of social identity and place. Lily's downfall arrives in the form of a hot tip on the market, critical to her finances, which is given in expectation of sexual favours which are not delivered. But Undine derives her strength where Lily loses hers; she is an opportunist whose chances are born in the tumult of financial derring-do on the stock-exchange by adventuring men; Undine is a portrait of the lady as adept social vagrant and parasite. Her social and psychological vacancy, her placelessness, makes her invulnerable, victoriously protean.

Although Apex is imagined spatially, historically, and socially, mainly through Moffatt's doings, it is nevertheless a place which yields only the placeless. Those who seem to come from Apex never stay there because they do not belong there or anywhere. Two other characters from the novel follow Undine out of Apex – Indiana Frusk, the plumber's daughter, now Indiana Frusk Binch Rolliver; and Moffatt himself, even more rootless than Undine, who appeared one day in Apex, whose origins are unknown, and whose meteoric career allows him to keep surfacing in every part of the globe. Moffatt's history, as we have seen, is a narrative lurking beneath the surface of the Undine story, and his first 'steal' is Undine herself. This is a piece of inside information which would rock the New York social world as much as the Ararat investigation disrupts the financial world. But nomadism provides protective camouflage: Old New York, like Wharton herself, isn't very clear about the geography of 'the West', and no New Yorker can know of Undine's peccadilloes there. It also transpires that Undine was even earlier engaged to Millard Binch, son of a local Apex merchant; that she jilted him for Moffatt; and that once jilted, he married Indiana Frusk, who by the time she enters the story *in propria persona* has divorced him in order to marry Congressman James J. Rolliver. Rolliver, in turn, is betrayed by Moffatt, who testifies about irregular land deals in Apex, but later becomes his partner against Driscoll. In Wharton's notes for the original ending of the novel, Undine marries Rolliver after divorcing Moffatt.[65] If Undine's absurd name confounds any normative standard of belonging – being as fortuitous as the hereditary, traditional names of the Old New York and Old Parisian families are deliberate, as whimsical as the current chase after the latest thing – the insouciant marital and romantic bonds of the Apex characters seem to create their own interbred, intermarried clique, a social tribe, a vigorous, midwestern parody of the labyrinthine cousinages and interfamilial alliances of Old New York.

This parodic buccaneer attitude to tribal structures is noted again in *The Children*, Wharton's 1928 novel of the itinerant American rich in Europe. When the protagonist, Martin Boyne, tries to explain their behaviour, he reverts to Wharton's favourite anthropological conceit, first advanced in *The Custom of the Country*:

In that crowd, no man is another man's enemy for more than a few minutes, and no woman is any other woman's rival. Either they forget they've quarelled, or some social necessity . . . forces them together. . . . But generally it's a simple case of forgetting. Their memories are as short as a savage's, and the feuds that savages remember have dropped out. They recall only the other primitive needs – food, finery, dancing. I suppose we *are* relapsing into a kind of bloodless savagery. (C174–5)

These new aphasic savages (and Undine is nothing if not forgetful, as Debra MacComb has pointed out[66]), are almost completely devoid of any of the civilising influences of culture, genuine social interaction, or even conviviality in the truest sense. The parties in the endless 'luxe' hotels consist of loud, animated uproar, of rushing about, of 'going round', Undine's expression of a right as inalienable as free speech; and Wharton's late New York novels, *The Mother's Recompense* (1925) and *Twilight Sleep* (1927) feature other vacant young women of her type whose senseless lives 'consist in going somewhere else in order to do exactly the same thing' (MR102).

Undine has 'pioneer blood' (*CC*35) which prompts her to move on; but as a buccaneer, she moves east. The Spraggs' geographical progression from a summer resort on one of the Great Lakes, to Potash Springs, Virginia, to Skog Harbor, Maine, to New York City, and eventually to Paris, charts the progression of Undine's never-satiated pioneer impulse. In each location, she feels she has arrived until some more experienced voice informs her by implication of deficiency. Thus, a plain but supercilious Miss Wincher, overheard by Undine on the veranda of the Potash Springs hotel, disdains the resort as she waits to dash to Europe, where the *beau monde* disports itself. Other buccaneers hear the cold voice of 'beyond' in hotels – even the unacute Mrs St George in *The Buccaneers* hears such a voice in a showy hotel veranda in Saratoga Springs. But Mrs St George sips furtively from the cup of ambition, a timid woman who can be distracted by a bauble. Undine is a huge maw, emptying the cup at a single draught and immediately looking for more.

The voice on the veranda functions as a narrative will o' the wisp in *The Custom of the Country*, murmuring of an ever-deferred 'arrival'. In New York Undine learns that the best people do live in houses after all, not hotels; in Paris, as a habitué of the great *luxe* 'Palace' hotels, she discovers that her loud rich American friends have no entree whatever into the aristocratic Left Bank enclave of Old Paris. She has been given

> glimpses of another, still more brilliant existence, that life of the inaccessible 'Faubourg' of which the first tantalizing hints had but lately reached her. Hitherto she had assumed that Paris existed for the stranger . . . for the dazzling superstructure of hotels and restaurants in which her compatriots disported themselves. But lately she had begun to hear about other American women, the women who had married into the French aristocracy, and who led, in the high-walled houses beyond the Seine which she had once thought so dull and dingy, a life that made her own seemed . . . undistinguished. (*CC*164)

One of these 'other American women' turns out to be the same Miss Wincher who spoke so disparagingly on the veranda in Potash Springs, now ennobled as the Marquise de Trezac. Miss Wincher has arrived; Undine will also become a Marquise, but she will never arrive. Undine's buccaneer pattern of desire-satisfaction-disenchantment reminds us that the joke-name 'Apex' is perfectly serious: Apex is everywhere; the social mountaineer scales the pinnacle in view only to survey a yet loftier eminence in the distance. 'Apex' is the word for everything Undine wants, achieves, and immediately puts behind her. It is a kind of Faustian ubiquism: this is Apex, nor is she out of it.

The narrative impulse of the novel is not simply Undine's insatiability, but the corresponding condition that such an appetite can ever be satisfied. The sense of a fugitive repleteness keeps Undine hungry; even when she has everything, there is always something missing, if only the sense of the righteousness of her acquisitions. In the last paragraph of the book, now remarried to Elmer Moffatt the billionaire railroad king, Undine surveys her extravagant new house in Paris, puts on a necklace of rubies which once belonged to Marie Antoinette, gazes approvingly at herself in the mirror, and awaits her guests for a glittering dinner. She learns that an American friend has been appointed ambassador to England and is told that her divorces debar her husband from an embassy:

> She had learned that there was something she could never get, something that neither beauty nor influence nor millions could ever buy for her. She could never be an Ambassador's wife; and as she advanced to welcome her guests she said to herself that it was the one part she was really made for. (*CC*335)[67]

'She had everything she wanted, but she still felt, at times, that there were other things she might want if she knew about them'(*CC*333). This, the most terrifying sentence in the book, is also its most typical.

Without family loyalty, tribal instinct, or any geographical place, Americans (Undine's French in-laws think) 'had no homes, . . . were born and died in hotels' (*CC*289). Of Undine, this is virtually true. In their first flush of financial success the Spraggs move into an Apex hotel improbably called the Mealy House. Later they migrate around expensive New York hotels in search of ultimate fashionability; even in financial decline the elder Spraggs remain transient, installed in a large, dreary establishment where the silver isn't always clean. No matter how pointless and uncomfortable hotel-life may be, Mrs Spragg resists any move back to 'housekeeping', as she calls it; yet the enforced leisure and inactivity of her ferociously overlit, pink-upholstered suite has apparently induced neuraesthenia.

The elder Spraggs dislike almost everything about Europe *except* its hotels, which are:

> the only European institutions that really interested Mr Spragg. He considered them manifestly inferior to those at home; but he was

haunted by a statistical curiosity as to their size, their number, their cost and their capacity for housing and feeding the incalculable hordes of his countrymen. He went through galleries, churches, and museums in a stolid silence like his daughter's; but in the hotels he never ceased to inquire and investigate.... (*CC*216)

The obsession with hotels is partly childlike, the response of a simple provincial bringing with him intimate knowledge of that most American invention, the extravagant luxury hotel, as a barrier against the cultural overload of the Old World;[68] but it is mainly an index of his own nomadic, rootless life that he reckons it up in hotel statistics, that his America, the one to which he compares Europe, *is* an America of hotels, not of houses.[69]

In the heat of his disillusionment with Undine, Raymond de Chelles refers scathingly to such a life. If this were another sort of novel, the outburst would be merely hyperbolic; but here it is absolutely accurate:

"You're all alike, every one of you.... You come among us from a country we don't know, and can't imagine, a country you care for so little that before you've been a day in ours you've forgotten the very house you were born in – if it wasn't torn down before you knew it!... you come from hotels as big as towns, and from towns as flimsy as paper, where the streets haven't had time to be named, and the buildings are demolished before they're dry, and the people are as proud of changing as we are of holding to what we have...." (*CC*307).

His wife, raised in hotels, drifting between houses as between marriages, cannot fathom concepts like home or family. 'Home' is defined as the right address; and children offer at most picturesque photo-opportunities for pretty women, or bargaining tokens in divorce settlements. Her little son Paul would refurbish her social reputation among the children-loving French; to put it as vulgarly as she deserves, she 'accessorizes' herself with her son. Paul comes to represent the competing anti-buccaneer standard of civility and familiality in the novel, as adored child and grandchild to Ralph and the older Spraggs, as cherished stepson to Raymond de Chelles and to Elmer Moffatt. But Paul is really no more than another of Undine's possessions, a useful token of social respectability and of a factitious maternal bond. Paul is a mirror of various parental and step-parental needs, a narrative lens through which we are to see an unmediated vision of buccaneer life.

In the heartbreaking penultimate scene, nine-year-old Paul has returned from school for the holidays to the spanking new Moffatt mansion in Paris, a mansion (ironically) called a *hôtel*; and here the developing play on hotel and *hôtel* finally comes to rest, with the first scene of the novel set in the one, the final scene in the other. Paul has never been in this house before – the speed at which his mother acquires and discards things like homes and husbands makes any continuity impossible – and although he manages to work out which of the many splendid rooms is to be his, he finds there are no toys, no books to read, none of 'his dear battered relics' (*CC*325). Since they exist in the concepts of history and memory, the notion of 'relics' can have no purchase in his mother's world; but Paul has not yet worked this out. Only the servants are there to receive him; new ones (naturally), they have no idea where his things are. His bedroom 'seemed the loneliest spot in the whole house'. And no wonder: it looks like a particularly sumptuous hotel room, with all the expensive impersonality of the Nouveau Luxe. There is no one to talk to except the archivally inclined Mrs Heeny, the novel's only true historian, whose chronicle of Undine exists in a satchel full of press-clippings, who can give an account of Moffatt's latest art acquisitions.

But Paul wants 'to hear about his mother and Mr Moffatt, and not about their things; and he didn't quite know how to frame this question' (*CC*329); and, with Undine achieving her identity only through her effects, it is impossible that he *should* know how to frame it. Although the question is unasked and unanswered, we have already been treated to a tour of the 'things' through the boy's uncritical eyes. He has already drifted around the new house unsupervised, and we see him gazing at Van Dyck's 'Grey Boy' hanging in Moffatt's bedroom, a boy who looks as lonesome as Paul feels. His mother's boudoir is as big as a drawing room; the library bookcases are all locked. The signals given off by the Moffatt household are disturbing: there are master paintings which are relegated to bedrooms, a relegation which suggests an indiscriminate plenty of such items; an enormous dressing room; a library full of inter-esting books caged behind gold grille-work, too valuable to handle and not for reading. These rooms indicate a house indisposed for social, familial, or cultural encounter: the publicity and conviviality of drawing rooms is forgotten in favour of *size* in the boudoir comparison; libraries are not transmitters of heritage; and famous pictures are only privately savoured (if at all) in bedrooms.

This strange, inverted house is, moreover, still partly under construc-tion even as its staff prepares for a banquet. The sound of hammering is heard in the ballroom, with the intimation that things aren't ready yet, bearing out Raymond de Chelles' premonitory outburst about American houses, as instantly built as American hotels. De Chelles' diatribe against Americans begins to sound positively scientific, or prophetic, for the hammering signifies Elmer Moffatt's ultimate exploit – he has finally got his hands on the priceless de Chelles tapestries, forfeited in the crash of a younger de Chelles' bankrolling (American) father-in-law, who is no longer able to finance the cadet branch of the de Chelles family. Undine's failed attempt to plunder the chateau of its tapestries is successfully concluded by the piratical Moffatt, an exploit which he describes earlier as 'chipping off an heirloom' for the market, as if ancestral treasures were like undifferentiated mineral substance prised from the earth. He reveres them for their quality, of course, but he never forgets that they are convertible into cash: in them he also sees 'a good many Paris seasons hanging right here on this wall' (*CC*302). When, during her marriage to de Chelles, she had invited a dealer to assess the tapestries, Undine behaved according to type: every buccaneer disregards goods as specific expressions of history, culture, or personal sentiment. She valued the tapestries at their market rate but never as a connoisseur; she was their unwilling and impatient chatelaine because she was wife of their somewhat impoverished inheritor, and would rather have converted them into other luxuries. Now, rich enough as Mrs Moffatt not to notice or resent the outlay by her buccaneer husband, she is content to own them outright, and to value the exploitative glamour their acquisition bestows upon her.

In the last scene, little Paul Marvell finally sees the newly-hung tapestries in the ballroom. Moffatt tells him with satisfaction that 'It was like drawing teeth for [de Chelles] to let them go' (*CC*332); when Paul bursts into tears, Moffatt is at a loss. Paul, of course, remembers the tapestries from his life with his 'French father' (his favourite father to date); de Chelles, moreover, has sold them to a dealer only on condition that they never fall into the hands of Elmer Moffatt, the man who stole his wife. That Moffatt and Undine should have them after all, that they should value them *especially* because of the anguish caused to de Chelles, is indicative of the cruel buccaneer temperament. Paul Marvell's tears are the expression of every damaged and despoiled victim in the book, from aboriginal New York to *la France profonde*.

It is the symbolic defeat of the old world and of tradition by the ruthless new world of money, schemes, and deals. The buccaneers, true to their name, regard Europe as a weakly fortified treasure-house ripe for plundering. Wharton's friend Paul Bourget wrote of this phenomenon, which he observed at Newport: 'For the last thirty or forty years, thanks to their full purses, [Americans] have laid hands upon the finest pictures, tapestries, carvings, medals. . . .'[70] The construction 'to lay hands on' is apt; the same locution is used by de Chelles in his accusation against Undine (*CC*307). Bourget comments on 'this love of Americans for surrounding themselves with things around which there is an idea of time and of stability. In this country where everything is of yesterday, they hunger and thirst for the long ago.'[71] The tapestries, irreplaceable symbols of family history and social continuity, may not have any such aura for Moffatt and Undine; instead, they are just another piece in the jigsaw of his fabulous collection which add the glamour of old things to his very new palace; they are no more or less to Undine than the decorating coup which makes her ballroom the most elegant in Paris.

Epic effrontery

> "All objects that we want to possess are expected to achieve something for us once we own them. The often tragic, often humorous incommensurability between wish and fulfilment is due to the inadequate anticipation of this achievement." (Georg Simmel)[72]

Bourget says: 'In America all men in society have been and still are business men. They were not born to social status; they have achieved it.'[73] Known by the chroniclers of wealth as 'nature's noblemen', these self-made tycoons generated an astonishing appetite and energy for acquisition and conquest, an energy which fascinated Theodore Dreiser and others as the subjects of their money-novels. Self-aggrandizement, says Dreiser, is a natural – indeed, a peculiarly – American phenomenon, and Frank Cowperwood's motto, 'I satisfy myself', identifies him as the natural American protagonist.[74]

'The leisure of the leisure class', says Veblen, 'is still in great measure a predatory activity, an active assertion of mastery'.[75] And every Wall Street wizard needs first to capture his succubus, a woman like Bertha Dorset, Lily Bart, or Undine Spragg, or later, Daisy Buchanan, in whom to invest his spoils. This woman is, either by beauty or birth, herself a trophy, part of the spoils, the woman described by Veblen or by Sinclair in his Veblenesque mode, the strongest social expression of marauding success:

> the woman who could consume wealth most conspicuously . . . was the most effective instrument for the destroying of the labour and the lives of other people. . . .[76]

Undine, like a hostage from an enemy tribe, was herself first seized as a teenager by Moffatt; she was his first 'effrontery' or exploit. He is remembered by Undine as having 'taken instant possession' of her, against the will of Millard Binch, at the country picnic where they first met, later 'driving off with her at a two-forty gait while Millard and the others took their dust' (*CC* 309). Such masterful exploit is Moffatt's attraction for Undine; he has no personal beauties. This mastery is the quality least evident in Ralph Marvell and Raymond de Chelles, both slim, good-looking, and contemplative, or even the offstage character Millard Binch, a man destined always to have his women stolen. Peter van Degen, though scornfully 'masterful', attempts a more ordinary predation when he expects Undine to become his mistress merely for the pleasure of spending his money. Moffatt performs something altogether more extraordinary when he insists on doing things in the 'Apex' way, in securing Undine's divorce and marrying her in the teeth of French, American, and Papal opposition.

Undine, Moffatt, and other fictional financiers have many similarities; they share a Faustian brilliance of ambition and ascendency. Dreiser's Cowperwood, the son of a lowly bank clerk, follows a seemingly inexorable upward trajectory in Philadelphia financial circles, trying his hand at a variety of businesses, incessantly moving on to a newer and better thing, until, having established himself in the purest, most lucrative forms of finance, he is ruined by the far-reaching consequences of the Chicago fire of 1871. Bankrupt and in prison for financial improprieties involving city funds, and friendless for having 'laid hands on' the daughter of Philadelphia's most powerful machine politician, he nevertheless contrives to keep a covert hand in the market; when he is pardoned and released, he quickly recoups and outstrips his old prosperity through cool-headed trading in the panic which follows the failure of Jay Cooke and the Northern Pacific Railroad in 1873. In the next novel, *The Titan*, he goes to Chicago and founds street-railways, becoming one of the richest men in the United States. Cowperwood's amoral inexorability is never reprehended. 'What were you going to do about the so-called morals and precepts of the world?' Cowperwood muses. 'There were people who believed in some esoteric standard of right...they were never significant, practical men who clung to these fatuous ideals.'[77] Cowperwood's pragmatism is not the invention of novelists; they have always been a feature of such titanic historical operators. One is reminded in modern times of Robert Moses, city-planner, financial manipulator, urban creator and shaper, a modern Faust. It is Moses who remarked with horrifying, Cowperwoodian insouciance that the only difference between building roads in the city and roads in the suburbs is that 'there are more houses in the way...more people in the way – that's all'.[78] Financiers are never interested in the social consequences of their exploits.

Wharton, like Dreiser, recognises the extreme moral blankness or vacancy which characterises financiers; and Cowperwood, Undine, and Moffatt are scruple-free self-aggrandizers whose ethical emptiness makes the way clear for a narrative driven entirely by transaction and profit, by event and process; greed or desire becomes their signal and defining trait. Even though she is barred as a woman from professional financial activity, and prevented by caste, law, and custom from exercising her own finances, Undine's insatiability and egotism are exactly like Cowperwood's.[79] But Wharton, unlike Dreiser, is writing satire, and is appalled by Undine and scornful of her ignorant power, even as she is beguiled by the poetry inherent in unalloyed greed; the narrative voice of *The Custom of the Country* is accordingly rich and intrusive, whereas Dreiser's severe naturalism maintains a scientific, reportorial neutrality which mimics Cowperwood's personality.

In *The Custom of the Country* Wharton produces, in effect, a female money-novel. With her financier's temperament and desire, Undine achieves by equivalent but not identical means the material prosperity of her male counterpart. Constitutionally in transit and full of fluctuations, she is like Curtis Jadwin of *The Pit*, the man unable to sit out the contention in grain, or Frank Cowperwood, who cannot take his eyes off the market even in prison, or in love. Undine thinks Ralph is rich, just as Ralph thinks Undine is adorably naïve. The misapprehension of Ralph's wealth causes only temporary inconvenience to her, and her divorce corrects it without difficulty; Ralph, lacking the robust buccaneer temperament, finds this disillusionment mortal. Undine's next marriage to de Chelles, the French aristocrat, effectively ruins – although it does not kill – him. Finally she remarries Moffatt, one of the world's richest men, her first husband, the only husband to survive her narratively, and, indeed, to take his inspiration from her. Undine Spragg Moffatt Marvell de Chelles Moffatt, as she is at the end of the novel, collects husbands and patronymics the way Moffatt collects art, the way Tamburlaine collects kingdoms; and like Tamburlaine, she leaves a trail of social and financial wreckage behind her. The accumulation of marriages suggests her voracious acquisitiveness, makes a nonsense of the very notion of social designation or tribe in the variety of her surnames. Undine, although she makes no money, possesses instead an almost sympathetic attraction which gathers it to her; money is a thing she expects to have by right, or by nature. Her gigantic and exhaustless appetites prompt Ralph to say, 'If I were only sure of knowing what you expect!' Undine replies with the utmost simplicity and candour, 'Why, *everything!*' (CC57). *The Custom of the Country* is the heroic account of getting it.

Like other financial and social buccaneers, Undine and Frank Cowperwood possess an unreflecting boldness, a casual disregard for the incomprehensible social structures and obligations which stand in their way, and an epic appetite for the world elsewhere, their desires never sated, their imaginations always leading them into their next position, inventing their next need. The similarity of Undine and Cowperwood is even clearer if we compare Undine to Cowperwood's lover, Aileen Butler, or to Jadwin's wife, Laura Dearborn Jadwin (in *The Pit*), both – like Undine – standard versions of the trophy woman who represents one of the best acquisitions a successful financier can achieve. Laura Jadwin, in particular, is a woman wooed by money; she abandoned her Ralph Marvell – in this case a highly cultured and sensitive artist – for Jadwin's raw financial power. Although Laura has pronounced cultural enthusiasms (and though Jadwin's taste can be summarised by his colossal, mechanically operated pipe-organ), her first raptures about her prospective marriage linger Undine-like on the things she will be able to have. *The Pit* intimates that money and sexual attraction are much the same thing, and this is the only way to account for Laura's choice of husband.

Undine, without romantic or ethical or aesthetic commitments to anyone or anything, bears no resemblance whatever either to Aileen or Laura, except perhaps in her devotion to smart clothes and connexion with rich men; and unlike Laura, she never loved Ralph or his culture in the first place; nor does she equate Moffatt's (or anyone's) money with sexual allure. Laura and Aileen have minor qualities of their own which we study in *relation* to the money-energy of their men but which they maintain quite distinctly from their financiers, and as foils to their brilliance; but the pragmatic Undine, impervious to romance, indifferent to sex, children, and husbands, is a woman without qualities, her magic even harder to fathom than Moffatt's. Her arid sensibilities respond only to his crude power. Laura and Aileen are subject to disappointment, despair, and elation; in short, they are human beings. Undine arises, like a force of nature, out of the soil of the middle west, a creature without history or tradition, autochthonous, autonomous, relentless, humourless, pitiless. Like the Whartonian financiers who invariably ride into the social citadel on the tidal wave of their vast capital, she has the same inevitability, the inexorability, the inhumanity which bears all before it.

'The bareness of a small half-lit place' (*CC*86)

> It seemed suddenly plebeian and promiscuous to look at the
> world with a naked eye, and all her floating desires were merged
> in the wish for a jewelled eye-glass and chain. (*CC*30)

Undine's inner vacancy commits her to outward show; in her triumphal New York passage she consorts with light-weights like Claud
Walsingham Popple, the society painter whose full-length portraits of
rich women notably depict their jewels to great effect. His portrait of
Undine, like so much in *The Custom of the Country*, objectifies her as a
covetable object, whose value is advertised by the size and lustre of her
pearls, the elegance of her dress, her beauty, and the pricetag attached
to her picture.[80] John Singer Sargent once said: 'I paint what I see...
I don't dig beneath the surface for things that don't appear before my
eyes;'[81] for painter and subject, surface is paramount. Undine's lovers
also take this view, which guarantees their destruction. The reptilian
Peter van Degen, Undine's first super-rich conquest, opens his cam-
paign to capture her by having Popple paint her; nobody, he concludes,
does pearls like 'old Popp'. From the first, Undine feels the pull of van
Degen's money, the only measure in her scale of values. 'She felt the
strength of Van Degen's contempt for everything he did not understand or could not buy: that was the only kind of "exclusiveness" that
impressed her' (*CC*111). Van Degen's physical repulsiveness (he is always
referred to as 'saurian' and 'batrachian') seems not to exist for Undine,
who will twice marry the unlovely Moffatt. Undine is never touched by
physical beauty in men any more than in art; she only desires everything they can have. The almost equally pragmatic Susy Lansing of *The
Glimpses of the Moon* looks at the man she will marry and says 'I'd rather
have a husband like that than a steam-yacht' (*GM*6). To Undine a husband *is* a steam-yacht; a marriage a vista of perpetually new and better
steam-yachts.

Because she is all surface, all external attribute, she has no core, no
innerness, no identity beyond what may be expressed in appearance,
and even this is adaptable. Seeing Raymond de Chelles across a crowded
hotel restaurant for the first time, she immediately alters her manner to
conform to his restrained, muted faubourg bearing, as if to distinguish
herself from her noisy American party. A terrific imitator, without ori-
ginality or integrity of personality, 'she could not help modelling herself
on the last person she met' (*CC*14). Her mimicry is a way of converting
the phenomenal world from object to subject, an infantile projection of

reality. De Chelles, 'the last person she met', impels her to adjust her beauty to meet his taste. Undine's vacancy is of the same frightful species as May Welland's.

In the first chapter, I noticed the interdictions of Wharton's mother, who reprimanded her daughter with imprecations of 'not-nice'-ness, a category which applied equally to questions about the origin of babies and Wharton's own extraordinary habit of making up stories. That opposing concepts were not formulated beyond the binary relation of 'x' and 'not-x' represented to the young Edith Wharton the height of the inscrutability which characterised her mother's elevated social existence, the mysterious efficacy of '*the*' in her mother's imperious self-designation as '*the* Mrs Jones'; to Wharton the novelist that binary opposition of 'x' and 'not-x' stands for a deep and depressing impoverishment of vocabulary and idea.

This almost completely abstracted, attenuated code, in which the range of adjectives which govern behaviour, taste, and thought is radically restricted, in which qualities lack their own existence but function merely as the absence of their opposites, is typical of money-novels, too. Frank Algernon Cowperwood, although we are privy to specificities such as his middle name, the layout of his house, and the richness of his silk underwear, whom we recognise in the guises of 'ambitious young speculator', 'collector of art objects', 'dealer in city loan', 'owner of street-railways', or 'bankrupt felon', remains, like the notion of price itself, a cipher, a man who has no more moral substance than his current value on the stock exchange. Frank Cowperwood is enigmatic, the construction of his money, the physical representation of its abstract and unstable value. Cowperwood is an embodiment of crude desire perhaps, but beyond that a character of whom we can infer almost nothing, except his current worth, which is either substantial, or not; he is either rich, or not-rich. Other financiers – all of them self-made – are powerfully unaccountable. When Nick Carraway asks 'Who is he?' about Gatsby, he is told 'He's just a man named Gatsby'.[82] Elmer Moffatt is also a cipher, a man known by his schemes, tastes, possessions and exploits, but ultimately mysterious and unaccountable, never viewed from anything but a great distance. Financiers are, like Gatsby, 'platonic conceptions of themselves'.[83]

But it is Undine who possesses this blankness and unaccountability in highest measure: she is vacant but for her trimmings, unpredictable to others because, governed by her instantaneous and insatiable needs, she herself cannot imagine such a thing as the future. Like Frank Cowperwood, she too is a cipher: although her beauty is painted out in bold strong colours, a beauty too blatant for the half-tones of Old New York or faubourg interiors, yet like Cowperwood she has no *innate* qualities. When her divorce from Ralph Marvell temporarily relegates her to the society of the unfashionable, 'her one desire was to get back an equivalent of the precise value she had lost in ceasing to be [his] wife. Her new visiting-card, bearing her Christian name in place of her husband's, was like the coin of a debased currency testifying to her diminished trading capacity' (*CC*205). Her beauty is her wealth, the currency in which she buys up. Like the false-fronted buildings in the main streets of many midwestern towns to this day, Undine's image masks a terrifying blankness behind.

Many of the images associated with Undine suggest only surface and vacancy. In an early scene in New York, we see her in the privacy of her bedroom sitting in front of her glass with her best clothes on, practising looking beautiful during imaginary conversations, tossing her head this way and that, flicking her fan and inventing graceful arm movements. Mirrors and mirroring images abound in the novel. When Undine looks at art she sees herself: at her engagement party in New York, the old family portraits of the Dagonet house seem to be 'doing homage' to her beauty from the walls. At an exhibition she enjoys 'the image of her own charm mirrored in the general admiration' (*CC*91), and is struck by the use of a lorgnette by an older woman, 'by the opportunities which this toy presented for graceful wrist movements and supercilious turns of the head' (*CC*30). To visit an art exhibition, in other words, suggests an opportunity to exhibit herself; and it is here that she meets the odious van Degen, commissioner of the Popple portrait. The scene at the portrait-painter's studio also uses this curious mirroring effect: Undine receives guests there in the gown and jewels in which she has been painted; the full-length picture dominates the other end of the room, reflecting her own image back at her. (This practice was a trade mark of Mrs John Jacob Astor, who received the Four Hundred under her likeness by Carolus Duran.) Like everything else about her, it is a circular, self-referring relation to the world, her reflexive admiration is a sort of auto-eroticism, so that she can gaze at the de Chelles tapestries, with their 'ineffable minglings of blue and rose, as complacently as though they had been mirrors reflecting her own image' (*CC*298). That complacency, the same she derives from looking at herself in mirrors, has nothing to do with great art. She and they are, in her mind, commodity, each 'fetching' high prices; she and they will end up in Moffatt's collection. This link is made again when Undine orders a gown copied from the Prudhon portrait of the Empress

Josephine in the Louvre: her imitative instinct prompts us to ask ourselves which imperial financier she will couple with (it *won't* be Ralph Marvell, this dress tells us). Throughout the novel, her lost well-being is instantly restored by a glance in the looking-glass. The mirrors or mirror-like images associated with her remind us that Undine understands the world only in terms of herself; anything beyond her reckoning is simply the binary opposite, 'not-Undine'. Undine standing in the same room as her full-length portrait and wearing the same dress, studying the de Chelles tapestries and seeing herself in them, visiting an art exhibition and finding that it is more amusing to be the exhibit than to look at pictures – in this relation to it, the world is merely self-reflective; and because Undine creates herself out of the promptings she receives from the world, she essentially assimilates or digests the world, which becomes Undine.

Such intense preoccupation with self, and moreover, a reflected self, is essentially infantile, specifically the imaginary period in which the developing infant sensibility is still incapable of distinguishing itself from the objective world. Out of this imaginary stage the child develops a sense of specularity: it begins to understand the objective world as not the same, quite, as itself, but nevertheless attempts to identify elements within it which are familiar and which can become assimilated into its developing ego. This is a stage before the emergent personality can be said to be in any sense civilised or socialised.[84] 'If only everyone about her would do as she wished', Undine thinks with petulant logic of the child, 'she would never be unreasonable' (*CC*153). The world as it presents itself to her is imaginary and specular, a version of herself; it is incapable of proposing to her anything not already native to her; the world of Undine is an enclosed system.

The trajectory of her matrimonial career reiterates this increasingly native attitude: her first husband from Apex is also her last, a remarriage which confirms Undine's initial assumptions and outlook; her second husband is in effect killed by Apex (it is the story of Undine's early marriage there together with the delayed charter for the Apex Consolidation Scheme – both exploits engineered and described by Moffatt – which drive him to suicide); her third husband is forced to sell the family treasures after the failure of an American in-law from a 'divorce state'. Each event seems to refer back to Apex; and events Undine's life are always circular. This circularity is present even in the smallest details: the fashionable pigeon-blood writing-paper purchased by Undine at the beginning of the novel becomes the necklace of pigeon-blood rubies which she wears in the last scene.[85] The novel begins in an American hotel, in the 'Looey suite', and ends in a *hôtel* decorated in Looey Quinze.

Ralph Marvell is attracted to Undine's blankness, and likes to imagine himself in a Pygmalion-like relation to her unformed Galatea. But Ralph is in the wrong myth: Undine is both creator and creature, a self-enclosed personality system. There is no evolution in *The Custom of the Country*, no adjustment to certain unalterable circumstances, because there is almost no circumstance that is completely proof against Undine's ambition. At the end of the novel, 'She knew her wants so much better now, and was so much more worthy of the things she wanted' (CC316); if this is development, it is simply development of appetite: she has grown into the vastness of her needs. By the end of the novel she has merely become much richer, merely more like herself. She is monolithically the embodiment of self-will and possesses none of that 'modelling' or nuance of character that makes even Moffatt seem almost Jamesian by comparison.

What she thinks she discovers in Moffatt, however, is the ultimate and replete image of herself: the image of world-devouring Tamburlaine is her image as well as his. Discovering that he understands her language intuitively, she discovers him as the part of herself that can supply her inexhaustible material apppetite. He 'spoke her language, ... knew her meanings, ... understood instinctively all the deep-seated wants for which her acquired vocabulary had no terms' (CC302). The reduction of social transaction and communication to speechlessness or 'meaningless syllables', the portrayal of voracity as a thing for which there are 'no terms', is the extreme to which *The Custom of the Country* inclines. Apex has, in Ralph's estimate, a reduced and primitive linguistic tradition. Moffatt, for example, responds to beautiful things which '[touch] the spring of some choked-up sensibility for which he had no language' (CC235), a reaction that may be genuine speechlessness in him, or may be Undine's uncomprehending observation of 'enjoyments ... beyond her range' (CC317). Either way, his speechlessness tends to conflate him with her; 'he used life exactly as she would have used it in his place' (CC317). Eloping in the ironically named *Semantic*, it is clear that for them language is supererogatory; the power of this speechless desire bears all before it. The Old World of culture, family, and tradition can only propose philosophy; such gibberish is completely extinguished in the implacable demands of appetite. Together, Moffatt and Undine are the bipartite monster buccaneer – the financial alchemist yoked with the heroic disposer of wealth.

The Firebird and the Water-Sprite

> 'Edith Wharton... liked and repeated the remark, that she was a "self-made man".'[86]

Henry James detected a Spraggian appetite in Edith Wharton, and his insight may locate some of the inventive power which Wharton put to the creation of Undine. In about this period he took to dramatising her extraordinary *modus vivendi* in hilariously apocalyptic language. After a visit from her in 1912 he wrote to a friend:

> The fire-bird perches on my shoulder... she held us... this pair of hours, by her admirable talk. She was never more wound up and going, or more ready, it would appear, for new worlds to conquer, eating up one for her luncheon and one for her dinner... she uses up everything and everyone by the extremity of strain or the extremity of neglect.... She rode the whirlwind, she played with the storm, she laid waste whatever of the land the other raging elements had spared, she consumed in 15 days what would serve to support an ordinary Christian community... for about ten years. Her powers of devastation are ineffable, her repudiation of repose absolutely tragic, and she was never more brilliant and able and interesting.[87]

By the end of this visit, James claimed that he and his other guests were 'ground to powder, reduced to pulp, consumed utterly'. Breathless with a genial horror of her vigorous social tourism, he found her in her ten-days visit committing 'exactly 9000 separate and mutually inconsistent things....'[88] He described another of her visits as a 'Reign of Terror',[89] and imagined being carried off in the talons of this 'angel of devastation',[90] 'hurried by her to my doom'.[91] Her name, like Bonaparte's, Attila's, or Tamburlaine's, is one with which to frighten children.[92] Although these remarks are essentially playful, his dismay is elsewhere genuine: '*What* an incoherent life!' he exclaims.[93] His epic similes resemble the heroic analogies of the money-novelists, whose protagonists invariably bestride and command worlds like gods.

Even as James confessed to Wharton his ignorance of business and of modern American life, Wharton herself was personally invigorated and liberated by all that her money could buy for her in the way of experience, technology and progress; more important, she was creatively stimulated by money as a fictional subject. Omissions of telephone, electricity, and motor-car were horrifying to her.[94] She loved the telephone, patronised the fastest steamships (she crossed the Atlantic sixty or seventy times).[95] She was an early, serial car-owner. She was delighted with and obsessed by speed. Her letters bubble with gleeful reports of especially fast trips, with the brand-names of cars and their special virtues of velocity, with verbs like 'gallop', 'zip', 'fly', 'skim', 'race', and 'rush', and a graphic account of a near-fatal accident suffered by a friend, in which her profoundest horror is reserved for the destruction of 'the beautiful car'.[96] Her travel book *A Motor-Flight Through France* (1908) conveys this sense of urgency: these 'flights' are not escape; *her* motors are virtually aeronautical, and they fly her *through* every nook and cranny of the Old World in a kind of territorial conquest. Her expeditions were exhausting and exhilarating, of an almost supernatural quality which transfixed James, which he called 'her dazzling, her incessant braveries of far excursionism'.[97] Percy Lubbock analyses her motor-mania more coolly than his friend James: 'Edith had fallen upon a new plaything as though it had been invented for her ... she claimed its service, its blind obedience to her command, and it was her slave from the first....' She understood 'the opportunity of its power'.[98]

Here is her own account of the various services entailed in such a 'flight' in Italy, to visit the mountaintop monastery where St Francis received the stigmata:

> We started about 10 o'clock, and were to 'do' La Verna and dine at Camaldoli. Ye Gods! At 11 pm we were hanging over dizzy precipices in the Appenines, unable to turn back, and almost unable (but for Cook's coolness and skill) to go on. Our luggage was all taken off and hauled behind us on a cart by a wild peasant, others escorted us with big stones to put behind the wheels at the worst ascent, and thus, at 11.30, *fourbus*, we reached the gates of La Verna, where it took us a good half hour to rouse the Frati ... [she digresses to complain about the food prepared by the monks]; the furies had only taken their aperitif! The next day the car had to be let down by ropes to a point about 3/4 of a mile below the monastery, Cook steering down the vertical ascent, and twenty men hanging on to a rope, that, thank the Lord, didn't break.[99]

She declared that 'the motorcar has restored the romance of travel';[100] but huge armies of manpower were commandeered and immense trouble taken to get this rich woman and her friends up a mountain track in a vehicle never designed for the task. It is a pity that her cars could not, after all, fly. This conspicuous consumption seems to bear out James's hyperbole.[101] Having her car let down an Italian mountain on ropes by local peasants, the wagon-loads of packing-cases stuffed with the spoils of Italy and France destined for her latest house or flat, the characteristic 'dash' from Paris to Barcelona to the Balearics to England, Scotland and Wales, all between the news of Archduke Ferdinand's assassination in late June and the beginning of the Great War in early August, are amazing and terrifying. Wharton led a hectic, often transatlantic, life, rarely with fewer than two households to run, sometimes with three,[102] equivalent sets of servants, motors, social circles, and her ubiquitous dogs. Her restlessness and insatiability are qualities on the same heroic scale as Undine's. She may have admitted the resemblance: Moffatt's nickname for Undine is 'Puss' (*CC*68); 'Pussy' was her own childhood soubriquet. Like Undine, 'her amusement at any cost and in any quantity that suits her she will have, let who will pay'.[103] What James described as 'a nightmare of perpetually renewable choice and decision' serves as well for Undine's life as for Wharton's. For all her insistence on tradition and cultural continuity, her preference for the conservative French over the buccaneer Americans, she was nevertheless highly American in her acquisition and improvement of houses, and even in her abrupt abandonment of her publishing house, Scribner's, with whom she had been associated since the beginning of her career, for Appleton, a far less distinguished, less 'literary' house with deeper pockets.[104] Undine always insists on a clean slate, on the possibility of discarding the present in favour of a better offer; Wharton's dynamism is only less forgetful than Undine's.

Wharton's inherited and earned wealth was highly visible to James and others because a significant part of it was converted into the latest form of transport. Because she could pay for her Panhard with the proceeds of her first novel, James groused that he would be able to buy an unpainted go-cart with the earnings of *The Golden Bowl*.[105] James can be forgiven his sour grapes: by 1919 Wharton was one of the leading money-earners of her literary generation, with $40,000 a year (a sum equivalent today to nearly 400,000 pounds). RWB Lewis estimates that her earnings between 1920 and 1924 must have netted about $250,000, nearly 2.3 million pounds today, and this was in addition to her annual private income of the equivalent of 275,000 pounds.[106] She was energetic in promoting her own contractual arrangements, and frankly relished her ability to extract favourable terms from her various publishers. She kept a close eye on her sales figures. As early as 1899, with only one book of short stories before the public, we find her berating her editor at Scribner's for stingy publicity:

> I find that Messrs McMillan [sic], Dodd and Mead, McClure, Harper, etc., advertise almost continuously in the daily papers every new book they publish.... Certainly in these days of energetic and emphatic advertising, Mr Scribner's methods do not tempt one to offer him one's wares a second time.[107]

Elsewhere, she urges him to add to the jacket blurbs 'that undefinable Wanamaker touch that seems essential to the booming of fiction nowadays'.[108] Wharton had a product to sell, and, immersed in the mechanics of commodification, she was as hard-nosed and uncompromising as any tradesman or financier.

A surprising number of critics have objected to Wharton's fiction on the grounds that her wealth disqualified her as a novelist.[109] But Wharton's interest in money was, of course, practical. Although her style of living was undeniably grand, she financed it herself, and maintained – as her correspondence shows – a very exact notion of incomings and outgoings. Like much poorer writers (for example, Alcott and Stowe), she had an incapacitated family member to support, whose mental illness found its most intense expression in the need to spend her money recklessly. She had to pension off her servants and she kept several friends and relations in funds. She was, in other words, not merely the transmitter of inherited income but also the provider of earnings. Although her own spending was not a clinical expression of malady, it was even more extreme and extraordinary than her husband's, and also more interesting. In the tradition of the best buccaneers, her highly developed imagination proposed uses for her money which the relatively simple Teddy in health could not have invented. Although Teddy claimed always to carry with him a $1000 bill, 'in case Pussy wanted anything',[110] the main income, as well as the creative spending of income, was all *hers*. When to Bernard Berenson she admitted in 1911 that her current work in progress was a novel so long that 'it is piling up the words as if publishers paid by the syllable',[111] fantastic amounts of money were clearly on her mind; this great pile-of-money novel was of course *The Custom of the Country*. James wrote to Wharton enthusiastically a number of times during the serialisation of the novel, which he cryptically approved as 'a full-orbed muchness,'[112] 'immense & epic & terrible, as if all about Gods & Goddesses...'. He affectionately compares her to Undine, 'you and She unsurpassed in the ranks...of the latter,[113] and calls her a buccaneer.[114] Wharton does not altogether censure Undine and her other buccaneers; indeed, what makes these characters so fascinating is her own ambivalence: she is appalled *and* impressed by the energy with which buccaneers devote themselves to their objects. If Wharton occasionally seems to write versions of her life, or a life that might have been, in various novels – May Welland is the girl she was destined by her background to become; Ellen Olenska, a version of the woman she actually became – then the pitch and fervour of *The Custom of the Country* may arise from all-too-intimate knowledge of Spragghood; in the buccaneer Wharton may also have figured herself.

The Custom of the Country is Wharton's most energetic, febrile novel. Her best stories usually achieve a carefully constructed, measured, architectural pattern in the rigorous control of detail and episode; rarely is anything extraneous introduced to her exposition; design governs all. A less convincing work like *The Gods Arrive*, for instance, feels baggy and structurally loose against the stricter pattern of stories like *The House of Mirth* and *The Age of Innocence*, which are like the seventeenth- and eighteenth-century buildings she so admired, with their Vitruvian, Palladian cadences and stately rhythms. But *The Custom of the Country*, undoubtedly a work to stand comparison with these, is nevertheless quite unlike them: its structure simulates an upward trajectory which has no hint of gravity in it, no corresponding downward path; architecturally it is more like a skyscraper than an Italian villa.

In other features, too, the novel is distinctive. As a rule, Wharton is the master of the single metonym or apparently Delphic remark which bears a complicated but unspoken set of ideas – Percy Gryce's costly collection of 'Americana', May Welland's civic-virtue face, for example. In *The Custom of the Country*, however, the descriptions are recklessly overburdened with notice of the objects of wealth – dresses, decor, motors, meals, jewels, pictures, bibelots. The sheer *stuff* of *The Custom of the Country*, the avalanche of detail, is an analogue of Undine's appetite, whose possessions and desires, in the words of Edmund Wilson, 'seem to glitter and clank with the coin that has gone to buy them'.[115] Kenneth Clark claims, although with unclear authority, that the novel's cynicism disqualified Wharton for the 1927 Nobel Prize.[116] About Undine, Wharton is partly disparaging, because Undine possesses no understanding of her gains. But about the nature of the gains themselves – dresses, houses, tapestries – she is *not* cynical: the book is the author's joyful paean to acquisition.

The Custom of the Country is in a sense an unfinished, and unfinishable, novel: in the last page, Undine querulously rages against the rule which prevents her being an ambassador's wife; but there is an inevitability here: by the logic of buccaneer narrative patterning, Undine *will* become an ambassador's wife. We can virtually predict that she will either find a way around the rule, or she will leave Moffatt for an ambassador (with a huge settlement to back her). But the open-endedness with which Wharton eventually chose to conclude the novel is more frightening; it is an eternity of conquest which other writers found in industry, commerce, money-markets, and above all, the first war, a war which, like the buccaneers, seemed to be devouring all of civilisation. If, among its many tendencies, modernist literature abandons the accumulated and conventional notions of taste, morality, and tradition which grounded the novels of the nineteenth century from Austen to James, and if, in addition, the modernist sensibility works against or breaks down conventional linguistic patterns and community, the *The Custom of the Country* may be read as an early modernist novel, and Undine the first truly modernist female protagonist. In a final flourish on her name we might conclude that Undine is the inexorable wave of the future.

'Few people have the sense of financial individuality strongly developed', says Dreiser.

> They do not know what it means to be a controller of wealth, to have that which releases the sources of social action – its medium of exchange. They want money, but not for money's sake. They want it for what it will buy in the way of simple comforts, whereas the financier wants it for what it will control – for what it will represent in the way of dignity, force, power. Cowperwood wanted money in that way.[116]

Whatever her Spraggian qualities may have been, Edith Wharton *was* interested in the social action described by Dreiser. Her remarkable war-work in France was a heroic and in some ways maternal undertaking to feed, clothe, house, cure, employ, and educate the children of, many thousands of refugees from the Franco-Belgian borderlands. The source of her amazing ability to promote significant social action was her fame, her wealth and her ambition to increase it. The charitable activities she founded and funded during the war 'stagger the mind', in the words of R.W.B. Lewis.[117] She wheedled from friends and donated her own royalties, pulled strings shamelessly and relentlessly among her acquaintance in the American plutocracy, pressed her many contacts in the art and literary worlds to contribute to books and exhibitions on behalf of her refugee work. Although it must have satisfied her deeply, even in war-time, to be buying houses and hospitals and renovating them for her Belgians, Wharton wanted money the way Cowperwood wants money. Like the truest kind of financier, Wharton was *not* a corporation, but a private limited company with a single shareholder.

4
Expatriates

'Her withdrawal from America was her most American act.'
(Janet Flanner)[1]

The lesson of the Master: Wharton and James *outre-mer*

'...unless travellers are willing to leave national prejudices
behind them, and ready to see whatever is characteristic and
excellent in a foreign country, without finding fault because it
is unfamiliar, they had better remain at home. Americans are
amongst the worst offenders...'. (Mary Cadwalader Jones)[2]

Henry James, Wharton said in 1934,

was never really happy or at home [in America]....[He] was essentially a novelist of manners, and the manners he was qualified by
nature and situation to observe were those of the little vanishing
group of people among whom he had grown up, or their more picturesque prototypes in older societies.... (*BG*176)

As a young man he evoked his native New England as cold, thin, blank,
like a bare parlour with snowdrifts piled up outside the windows;[3] over
time he succumbed to his own 'superstitious valuation of Europe', and
made himself incapable of living in, or even of temperately observing,
his native land.[4] But later he declared: 'If I had my life to live over again
it would be as an American...the mixture of Europe and America you
see in me has proved disastrous;' he cautioned Wharton about the dan-
gers of living abroad, urging her to seek 'homeliness, a Country of your
own', and at the same time shocking her by taking British citizenship

himself in 1915.[5] James was pre-modern[6] at a time when his natural subjects were faltering or had disappeared altogether in America. His Europe is in a sense his refuge from an America too poor in subjects. Although Wharton 'never felt otherwise in America than as an exile',[7] she seems, unlike James, to have found her Americanness in Europe. Most of her work of the 1920s presents exclusively American subjects in fine, severe observations of her countrymen in Europe, and of an America and its people from whom she had long been separated, whom she knew only anecdotally. In her writing about Americans abroad, as in much else, she has been linked to James in theme and outlook. But the analogy is no more just in this respect than in any of the others which tend to make her James's shadow or acolyte. Although she seems to have convinced herself – as superstitiously as James – of the universal sureness of French taste (*FW* 40) and the rightness of French tradition, she was not seeking James's 'picturesque prototypes', and if they appear it is mainly as foils for her American characters. She is signally attentive to American subjects and American personalities, which are thrown into relief by their (or her) foreign setting.

Like James she was deeply interested in cultural opportunities which only Europe offered, but she neither forgot nor evaded her Americanness or the new century; and she never recanted her position of transatlantic detachment. Wharton was an American 'modern'. Millicent Bell has rightly suggested that she 'became not less but more intensely her native self the longer she lived abroad'.[8] Indeed, she resembles *Madame de Treymes*'s Mrs Boykin in her dedication to the then very American amenities of motor, telephone, and excellent plumbing, a dedication which waxed over the years. Her accent remained distinctively American at the height of the Jamesian period – Percy Lubbock described the 'transatlantic turn' she gave to Gaillard Lapsley's first name[9] – even if she also possessed protective colouration in functional bilingualism.[10] Of her completed full-length novels, only *The Valley of Decision* (1902) and *The Age of Innocence* (1920) take a period other than her own present day as their subjects; the former she was by conviction never to duplicate, and in the latter she performs her backward glance through a detached modern lens. Only *The Valley of Decision* was written on a purely 'European' subject; *The Reef* (1912), the novel James described as 'Racinian' in situation, has not a single non-American character in it.[11]

Her American novels from 1911 onward, moreover, move away from the nineteenth-century naturalism of *The House of Mirth* (1905) and *Madame de Treymes* (1907), and into the realm of brilliant characterisation and satiric caricature, modes more typical of the modernist impulse, or at any rate more capable of seizing on modernist preoccupations. In these modes she could situate her remote, snapshot views of an America she could no longer write about at first hand, an America increasingly foreign, chaotic, meaningless to her. From 1911, the year of *Ethan Frome*, through the scathing tragi-comedies of the 1920s, her work often exhibits vigorous, almost diagrammatic design – in *Ethan Frome*'s stark patterning, in the gleeful one-way narrative of *The Custom of the Country*, and in the satiric reproof of *Twilight Sleep*. Not every novel, of course, can be categorised thus: *Summer*, *The Age of Innocence*, and the two war novels are softer, more 'genteel' (to invoke the old, outworn dichotomy) in style, though not necessarily in subject.

The shift from naturalism to caricature, where it occurs, has often been judged a declension by some critics, who accuse her of having lost touch with America, of having, especially by the 1920s, 'let her irritation get out of hand'.[12] This is a misreading of Wharton. She did not write about an actual, experienced America in *Ethan Frome*, *The Custom of the Country*, or *Twilight Sleep*, any more than she had written about an existing faubourg society in *Madame de Treymes*;[13] expatriatism had freed her to invent an America which served her fictional purposes; in its extreme versions it leads eventually to Ginsberg's Moloch. Her distance from home freed her to pursue a different, more explicitly diagnostic pattern, to engage with modernist themes and even, on occasion, modernist stylistics through which the alienness, the unintelligibility of America could be expressed. Part of the aim of this chapter will be to place Wharton against, but also *within*, the modernist era, by proposing that the theme of expatriation was in essence her own estranging modernist mode.

Let us allow, therefore, that irritation is by tradition the prerogative of the satirist. Her reading and cultural enthusiasms during the post-1907 period (the year she moved to France) are a better index of her connexion with America, and reveal a diversity of taste. The friend of Cocteau, and enthusiast of Stravinsky and Diaghilev, she saw 'Firebird' and 'Petrouschka' when they were first performed in Paris in 1910 and 1911; she heard (perhaps at its scandalous premiere) 'Le Sacre du Printemps' in 1913, which she pronounced 'extraordinary'.[14] She owned a Cezanne (given to her by Walter Berry), and liked Gauguin and other 'primitives'. She recommended to friends, as we know, Anita Loos's *Gentlemen Prefer Blondes*, as well as Fitzgerald's *The Great Gatsby*, Lewis's *Main Street* and *Babbitt* (but not *Elmer Gantry*), Huxley's *Brave New World*, Edgar Lee Masters's *Spoon River Anthology*, and Santayana's poetry. She seems to have been at least familiar with Freudian theory (although, as Dale M.

Bauer points out, she seems to dismiss psychoanalytic *practice* by attaching it to Pauline Manford in *Twilight Sleep*).[15] She disliked *Ulysses* (for the same reasons that Virginia Woolf did), *The Waste Land* (although she admired *Prufrock*), Katherine Mansfield, *Mrs Dalloway*, Faulkner, and Hemingway (and the success of these last two, in spite of their 'strong' subjects, puzzled her, when even as late as 1934 the *Ladies' Home Companion* was disturbed by the impropriety of the elopement at the end of *The Buccaneers*).[16] She approved some of the criticism of the so-called New Humanists (Irving Babbitt was a guest at Lenox[17]) and of the conservative Van Wyck Brooks, but also of the young Edmund Wilson, who paid her the compliment of calling her a satirist in 1921.[18] She was also reading other, perhaps more sensational literature – Stella Benson's *The Poor Man* (1922), a 'fatiguing' 'jazz novel';[19] a 'clever but depressing' novel by Edna Ferber (probably *Cheerful By Request* (1918));[20] and observational essays such as Agnes Repplier's *Americans and Others* (1923),[21] something called *The American Procession* (1934),[22] an article called 'Americans',[23] and Charles Merz's 'Bigger and Better Murders' in *The American Bandwagon* (1928).[24] In the period when she surrounded herself with Louis Quinze and Seize, she also seems to have admired contemporary engineering and technology. She was excited by the sound of the big guns of the Marne, audible in Paris; the supernal motor-car was her household god. Her culture, in other words, was wide, various, catholic, curious, a careful mixture of the conventional and the experimental.

Edith Wharton, self-designated exile, spoke French and German before her tenth birthday and spent a significant part of her childhood in Paris and Rome; her early European experience disqualified her, she thought, as American, or to 'think as Americans do'.[25] The 'curse' of having been raised there doomed her to the fate of 'wretched exotic',[26] only 'nourished and consoled by . . . old countries.'[27] She imagined this discontent to be fostered by European exposure, by travel and experience as a kind of microbe in the blood. But Wharton's deracination also has specific and unquestionable origin in her American background. Unlike James, nurtured in one of the most intellectually distinguished of American *milieus*, Wharton had few peers in the New York–Newport circuit of which she was part. Mentors like Egerton Winthrop and Walter Berry, and friends like Sarah Norton and her sister-in-law Mary Cadwalader Jones would offer her a community of like minds, but her early writing career in America was carried out in solitude within her family, as if it were a disgrace. The planning and building of The Mount, her glorious house in Lenox, Massachussetts [Plate 7(a)] in the years 1901–1911, with its gardens, views and interiors, moved her out of her native environment;

but after she had been spending regular periods abroad she felt that even The Mount looked well only to un-Europeanised eyes,[28] and could not help noticing 'the wild disshevelled backwoods look' of everything.[29] Even its Wren-inspired architecture and her Parisian-style entertainment of *literati* could not replicate Europe in New England. She was, as if emblematically, on the Atlantic headed for France when the sale of the property took place. She would come to America again only twice, and briefly.

The relocation was one toward which she had been moving ever since she and Teddy bought themselves, in 1893, a Newport cottage at the other end of town from her mother. The abdication from ownership of American domestic property was, for this accomplished householder, the most significant act of renunciation she could make, liberating herself to ply the shoreless waters of Expatria, to be perpetually rusticated, isolated in the haunts of the ironist and the satirist. Over the years her fiction moved away from the hybrid specimens represented by Fanny de Malrive and Sophy Viner, and toward exemplary and undiluted American types in Europe. Obliquely she indicates and approves a new cultural locus, an Americanised Europe in which good plumbing and heating and justifiable divorce from unreasonable husbands are not at odds with cultural and familial heritage. Constitutionally alien both to France and America, she claimed that freedom of observation and expression vouchsafed to those who write about countries not their own.[30]

Switzerland, she says in *Italian Backgrounds* (1905), is a didactic land of 'scenic platitudes' (*IB*14); Swiss border villages – 'stolidly, immovably Swiss' (*IB*18) – are exasperating; she accuses them of neglecting their Italianate opportunities. The Swiss landscape is not, like Italy's, 'moulded by the passions and imaginings of man' (*IB*3); Swiss hills and mountains are *merely* 'blunt' and 'weatherbeaten', in contrast to Italian hills, which consist of 'subtle contours, wrinkled as by meditation' (*IB*6). Is it, 'in short, ever well to be elsewhere when one might be in Italy?' (*IB*19). The insufficiencies of Switzerland present her with troubling affinities with America: every valley has its cataract and its cowbells; and Swiss landscape piles on its effects simultaneously, rather than serially as Italy does, like a dinner where all the courses are served at once (*IB*6); this image appears again in the same year, applied to American buccaneer architecture in *The House of Mirth*, whose ornament and allusion are indiscriminately and meaninglessly aggregated. The Swiss views remind her of 'a sanatorium prospectus' (*IB*17);[31] America in later years conjured the image of a 'huge hygienic nursery'.[32] The American mind, she said in a formulation of which she was proud, has no background, and the American landscape no foreground;[33] the Swiss landscape is explicitly Americanised by Wharton when she invokes Whitman: 'it is a scene in which *nothing has ever happened*: the haunting adjective is that which Whitman applies to the American landscape – "the large *unconscious* scenery of my native land"' (*IB*6). Switzerland is the America of Wharton's European daemonology, the obvious destination of choice for heedlessly destructive Americans like Undine Spragg and Ellie Vanderlyn, who prefer the sameness of people like themselves and the predictable luxury of resort hotels to the difference of haunted, memory-laden Italy. In her gardening and interior decorating, in her attitude to language and narrative, this duality is clear. Her images of horror range from Lilla Gates's preference for inane jazz sounds and May Welland's blank vacancy to the architectural inauthenticity of Peter van Degen's mansion and the 'fatiguing' linguistic opportunism of flapper patois. Associated adjectives ('wild', 'unmeaning', 'loose') spring up to characterise America, all suggesting a primary fear of the inexpressive, the ambiguous, the senseless, the opaque; order, deliberation, and pattern comfort her; not unmoved by scenic spectacle, she nevertheless prefers the surprising effects of unique Italian villas and their gardens.

The war and its sequent modernist decade offered her the clearest example of the order–disorder, meaning–unmeaning opposition. Her activities during the conflict were born of a commitment to her host country; she was a pattern of what might be termed the *citoyenne*-expatriate with civic responsibilities, a sense of *patrie*. Wharton defended France with all her might; the effort broke her health, and she was one of the walking wounded by war's end; but she had imposed the order of her own moral responsibility on its cruelty and confusion, an order fittingly symbolised by her efforts to *place* the displaced in something like communities of work and recuperation. The wild expatriate American behaviour she depicts in some of her postwar novels is the obverse of that coin: the Wheaters, the Vanderlyns, and the Lansings endure, inflict, *are*, the social consequences of modern behaviour in the fragmentation and chaos of their familial and social arrangements. Her modernist thematics in *Twilight Sleep* and *Fighting France* are clear and vigorous; but the formal experiments of literary modernism – which Wharton did not practise – seemed to her symptomatic of social evils: modernist narrative and social irresponsibility amount to the same thing; her fictional expatriates clearly embody it.

The motives for late-nineteenth-century American expatriatism were often cultural and economic: Europe was cheap where America was expensive, and it was common especially after the Civil War for Americans to idle away a few years there while collecting handsome rents on vacated properties at home. The Grand Tour and fashion (first and foremost, both of society and of garment), originated in Europe, specifically in France. Such purposes still prompted early-twentieth-century travel to Europe. In addition, Europe continued to offer marriage prospects and aristocratic titles; invisibility; social rehabilitation; and the collection of culture. A notable expatriate strain was that of self-advertisement: Arnold's comment that Americans 'lack the discipline of awe and respect'[34] was even more cogent in the Gilded Age, with the very rich American almost literally throwing money around, the American for whom Europe provided chances to show off. In Wharton's fiction expatriatism is not usually so carefree; it can offer escape, from scandal, restriction, or social marginalisation; her Grand Tourists, however, like Lewis Raycie, are doomed to ignominy and failure; escape condemns Kate Clephane and her acquaintances to a Dantesque fate in the obscure wateringplaces of southern Europe, where the drifting souls of this expatriate limbo gibber and murmur monotonously; the *mal rive* claims Fanny Frisbee for the shadows of the faubourg. Wharton's expatriate narratives, unlike her own history, end mostly unhappily.

This chapter will consider a number of aspects of Whartonian expatriation. About three quarters of her canon was produced substantially or entirely from abroad; most of her fiction takes America or the American expatriate as its subject; that which does not is nonetheless expatriate 'product'. The constant comparison of New World with Old by Wharton and her contemporaries led to the construction of a mythic America, a place of comedy and horror, of chaos, modernism, jazz, a place constantly producing 'specimens' who transport their doubtful national ethos to a quailing old world. This mythic America was one Wharton enjoyed sending up, but at the same time it was one which yielded significant situations and dilemmas, whose worthiness as subjects of fiction she defended in her own practice. This American mythography forced her to meditate upon its difference from her adopted world, to consider the role of the stranger in the aboriginal world. To do this, she contemplates several kinds of expatriate American – the coolly observant outsider, the ignorant, 'vacant' tourist, the buccaneer plunderer, the exile, and the assimilator – each of whom represents a distinct relationship to the Old

World, a relationship comprising various elements of submission, immersion, rejection, and mastery. Some expatriates go native in their adopted country; some retain their national traits; some invent a new identity that is unspecified, transatlantic. The War, hardly mentioned in her post-war fiction outside the two war novels, became the unacknowledged test of the expatriate. For Wharton – the Chevalier of the Legion d'Honneur whose favourite poet was Whitman – loyalty to an idea, a complex idea of tradition, belonging, patriotism, which for convenience we may call 'France' (as she has Campton say in *A Son at the Front*, 'if France went, western civilisation went with it' (*SF* 366)[35]) becomes the index within which she develops registers of delicacy in the relation between visitor and native, insider and outcast, sympathiser and plunderer. The war, more than anything else that France offered, admitted Wharton to a citizenship which it was impossible ever to renounce.

Home thoughts from abroad: America and Americanity

'"What do you know of New York?"
"Only what I have read in Dante."'
(Edgar Saltus)[36]

'I must avoid the subject of America,' Wharton declared in 1904 in an especially truculent mood.[37] Her permanent move to France was still several years off; she had not yet completed a full-length work on an 'American' subject. But the injunction to herself was to prove ironic: the next year she published *The House of Mirth*, and the rest of her literary career would be largely taken up with works about America or Americans, and with an Americanity mediated through her sense of its foreignness.

Locke likened the vast spaces of the almost unpeopled North American continent to the infantile mind.[38] Wharton believes in Whitman's diagnosis of the 'unconsciousness' of its scenery, and extends it to the 'unaware', unstocked minds of her compatriots in the midst of dense European vistas.[39] However, such constructions of America and Americans as blank have always been notoriously unstable: American romantics such as Thoreau, Whitman, Melville, Wallace Stevens, and A.R. Ammons have found in this blankness an enfranchising license to be original and unimpeded by received Old World culture; they also invoke it as a symbol of terror and despair.[40] James and (sometimes) Wharton found it at best mildly comical, at worst horrifying. In James's *The Europeans*, the 'clear-coloured' underfurnished rooms of the Wentworth house are assaulted by Eugenia's prodigal disposition of scarves, shawls, and curtains in Acton's house, almost as if James had been able to read *The Decoration of Houses* in 1878. In Wharton's *The Reef* (1912) the 'blank insensibility' to France of Miss Painter, who refuses to remove her slipcovers after 30 years' residence, is conveyed in her protective instinct toward upholstery against the depredations of 'those people' (corrupt foreigners); it is a gesture denoting the provisional habitation typical of a certain kind of American. Slipcovers insulate furniture from the environment much as the nationality of the novel's *dramatis personae* guarantees minimal exposure to the French. 'After living ... in an atmosphere perpetually tremulous with echoes and implications, it was restful and fortifying merely to walk into the big blank area of Miss Painter's mind.' (*R*212). Wharton's equivocation of comic insensibility and tragic or disturbing vacancy imbues many of her characters with dangerous power. Miss Painter's fortifying blankness is only barely distinguished from the terrifying void exhibited by May Welland, Undine Spragg, Lilla Gates, and Lita Wyant, the 'American nightmare'-women[41] Wharton would later imagine as tenuous and vacuous; the niceness of nice girls in *The Age of Innocence* is transmuted disturbingly into Lilla Gates's large white unintelligibility. If Miss Painter's offended slipcovers constitute a mild *outre-mer* joke, hygienic America (where the 'demicrobed' life has been architecturally imposed even in the rounded, dust-resisting moldings of Pauline Manford's super-efficient household) doesn't see the humour.

Ellen Olenska, an Old World partisan, thinks that American life is very 'public' (*AI*132); this is simply a generous way of intimating that Americans, seeming to lack inner life, have little to hide. The vacancy and unintelligibility of certain American characters in Wharton's post-war fiction is the triumph of surface over innerness, a condition of personality or society which might also serve to define the assault of modernist literary interests on nineteenth-century conventions of naturalism and point of view. American human relations, consequently, are not as complex as European ones.[42] Her Americans are inclined to speak in 'unmodulated candour' (*MT*44); their dinners are a wilderness of elaborate dishes; their homes over-illuminated. Notions of domestic privacy and reserve, of restraint of all kinds, stand for all those things the 'new America' is not. 'What a country!' she intones repeatedly in her correspondence.[43] Over many years of foreign residence she metonymises odd, half-humorous scraps of experience and anecdotes gleaned from newspapers, correspondence, and gossip, as 'America': in her most rancorous vein she has her Americans eating bananas and cream for breakfast in *The Custom of the Country* (she had observed this seemingly blameless practice with horror in a Massachusetts hotel[44]); she disparages

Cole Porter, skyscrapers, jazz slang, 'cubist sweaters', the American home as presented by Hollywood, and Horton's Vanilla Brick.[45] The place is 'a bad dream' to her as early as 1904; over the next three decades it perceptibly deforms itself in her letters and her fiction. America is 'lemming-land', 'skyscraperville', 'a sea of misery', 'perfectly-dentisted, empty-souled',[46] and worst of all, 'morally unready' for war when it came.[47]

This America, it emerges, is neither the 'tissue of capital jokes'[48] imagined by James, nor the crass horror of the worst summer hotel she can conceive of. Instead, her stories show America and Europe miscuing each other when natives of each continent try to decipher one another's untranslatable gabble. Her Americans, ambiguously presented, are indeterminately admirable and unsubtle: individual, unfiltered, angular, straight, 'regular' (*MR*91), childlike, they speak bad French but do so with the charm of 'a native dish, for which the palate yearns' (*CSS*591); they look more or less all the same (*MR*90); they use superlatives with happy indiscrimination;[49] their military discipline is much admired in war-time France. Europeans are equally but differently ambiguous: they are corporate, corrupt, mellow, sinuous, subtle, soft-spoken, alive to nuance and to social *faux-pas*, morally aware, adult, graceful. Small wonder, then, that Kate Clephane, John Durham, and Undine Spragg all find their foreign counterparts difficult to read. 'Was he as remote and unintelligible to her as she was to him?' Durham wonders during an encounter with Madame de Treymes (*MT*61). Undine is like an alien species to her French husband. For the Europeanised American Kate Clephane people 'were always on the point of being merged into a collective American face' (*MR*65).

Madame de Treymes (1907), at the beginning of Wharton's French residence, is perhaps her plainest examination of this incommunication. The mixture of malice and sympathy in the eponymous Frenchwoman is opaque, hard to analyse or to judge even in the outcome. Madame de Treymes cryptically announces that 'it is in the contemplation of your happiness that I have found my reward' (*MT*119); she later translates this for Durham out of her 'old language': 'It meant that I knew there was horrible misery in store for you, and that I was waiting to feast my eyes on it . . . ' (*MT*131). With Americans entertaining 'charming quaint ideas' about Europe, where they disport themselves innocently as in a playground, and Durham identified as 'an American so picturesquely embodying the type familiar to French fiction' (*MT*56), it is appropriate that the central character, the *quondam* Miss Fanny Frisbee of New York City, becomes in her European incarnation the Marquise de Malrive, a shift from the absurdest sort of American alliteration to the troubling French onomastic meaning 'evil shore'. Fanny de Malrive has been captured and trapped, Persephone-like, in a fatal, almost Stygian, place – either the Left Bank, or France, or something more abstractly non-American – a nether shore from which she can never return.[50] Wharton is as troubled by the native cunning of the French family operating with implacable resolve in favour of its corporate good as she is by any American failing. In what Madame de Treymes delineates to Durham as the fine disinterestedness of the French – 'you consider the individual – we think only of the family' (*MT*135) – the story discovers tragedy and sacrifice.

'America can't be quite so summarily dismissed as our great Henry thinks', Wharton wrote in 1911; 'but at the present stage of its strange unfolding it isn't exactly a propitious "ambiance" for the arts...'[51]. Those unpropitious Americans, translated to Europe, present her with interesting fictional *données*. She is far less interested in Americans like herself – assimilated and appreciative of the Old World *because* it is not America – as fictional subjects than in the exciting energy of the more unsophisticated American character, whose Yankee chemistry of naïveté and swagger pitched against European urbanity and disdain is volatile. Booth Tarkington's Lawrence Ogle, the refined middle-class observer figure in *The Plutocrat*, snootily characterises the vulgar, rich Babbitt-style American tourist as a member of another race ('we are never conscious of them unless we travel and then we are but too unhappily made aware of their existence'[52]). But Mme Momoro, the mesmerising French *grande dame*, scathingly corrects him: 'As an American *you* are absurd.... What do we respect *any* of you for except your money?'[53] Wharton, like Mme Momoro, gets her best stories from gorgeous, naive American barbarians; her Europeanised or Europe-gazing American men – Darrow, Durham, Ralph Marvell, Nick Lansing, Newland Archer – are virtually all failures or ineffectual non-entities. Like James, who always prefers this American innocence (in Daisy Miller, in Bessie Alden of *An International Episode*, in Isabel Archer, in Roderick Hudson) to the detachment and sophistication of Europeanised Americans, Wharton finds more matter in an Undine than in a Ralph Marvell.

She prefers innocence and vulgarity in her American characters because the European 'insider' is not easily assailable in fiction. In her non-fiction, her travel- and war-writing, and in her French etiquette guide, however, her own insiderliness is to the fore, and here she is her own protagonist. In *Italian Backgrounds* she deliberately heads against the tourist flow, seeking out places unvisited by the crowds. Writing about Milan she never once mentions the Duomo. Evelyn Waugh would have recognised Edith Wharton as the classic travel-snob, the one who thinks that the tourist is the other fellow. She was careful to dissociate herself from the general run of Americans in Europe by a number of strategems. Shirley Foster has identified in nineteenth- and early-twentieth-century travel-writing two typical responses to foreign experience, which she designates 'feminine' and 'masculine'.[54] Although the gendering of these responses is probably supererrogatory, the essential dichotomy is a clear one: Foster's 'feminine' is a kind of total immersion, a surrender to the power of otherness; the 'masculine', by contrast, seeks to master that foreignness (intellectually and technologically) by forcing it into clarity, by making it yield up its secrets. With her motor-cars, her fluency in various languages, and her élite social contacts, Wharton commanded her European experience, and mastership is her usual fictional mode. In the art-historical *tour de force* of 'What the Hermit Saw' in *Italian Backgrounds* (1905) we see her in it most clearly. Her emotional immersion in the war effort, and the writing that immersion produced, is evoked in the more 'feminine' essays which make up *Fighting France* (1915), as well as the tone and poetry of *Summer* (1917). Each style provides her with a distinct opportunity to take superior possession of Europe, to 'inhale and appropriate' it (as James said), to 'plunder' it in a fashion which excludes the large majority of tourists and their 'vast, comprehensive, and yet deeply self-satisfied unawareness.'[55]

Italian Backgrounds broadcasts the riches of her European experience with a princely largesse which establishes her as a highly unusual tourist, scholarly and initiated. In a Tuscan shrine she authoritatively notices and reassigns to Della Robbia the terracotta figures at San Vivaldo (something of a *coup*); she shows herself seeing into Italian art, a vision which – at least at San Vivaldo – surpasses that of acknowledged experts. She introduces Tirano in the Valtelline, 'one of those unhistoried and unconsidered Italian towns which hold in reserve for the observant eye a treasure of quiet impressions' (*IB*25). When she launches into hermits and wild men in Renaissance painting we are prepared to see her out-Berenson Berenson, and this she does with great precision, demonstrating her superior observation in a discussion of peripheral figures in painted Renaissance landscapes. In the opening chapter she fleetingly compares the rushing three-day tourists to the damned in medieval representations of hell, herself to one of the angels gazing down on them (*IB*5); the distinction becomes clearer as she goes deeper into Italy, the connoisseur's Italy: the world is divided into the observant and the unaware. Near the end of the book, after the astonishing pyrotechnics of her learning and her richly descriptive pictorial style, she remarks with exquisite sarcasm: 'The current notion of the picturesque is a purely Germanic one, connoting Gothic steeples, pepper-pot turrets, and the muddled steepness of the northern burgh...Italy offers little...to satisfy these requirements' (*IB*157). This sardonic gesture, coupled as it is with her apparently invincible expertise, is typically masculine in Foster's sense. The vast authority, long study, and wide experience, her concentration on sights not mentioned or lingered on by the guide-books, separates her intellectually, spiritually, and economically from the tourist with Baedecker or Murray and only a few days to give to Italy. She has the leisure, the inclination, and the opportunity to *know* Italy as they never can; *Italian Backgrounds* graciously condescends to the uninitiated reader.

Fighting France – a later work, one written *de profundis*, urgently, with emotional design – is much more 'feminine': nearly every scene features some version of the miasmic chaos of war, a confusion of sensory impressions much more like the 'immersed' condition of the 'feminine' mode. She converts the maelstrom of Armageddon sensations available to male writers who actually fought, and commonly represented by them in modernist linguistic description,[56] into strange confusions of expectation and logic. Arrived for vespers at a church in the war-zone, she finds herself instead in a hospital; Parisian faces are transformed into ancient bronze medals and young soldiers into Pheidian sculpture; the Seine reflects the unwonted dapple of moonlight during the black-out; soldiers are unexpectedly seated where once old women sat in the doorways of now-abandoned villages; a hospital in Verdun springs up in an hour when 4000 wounded arrive in a single day. *Fighting France* is crammed with such prestidigitation, shape-changing, and mystical transformation. By 1915 the doomed souls of the short-stay trippers in *Italian Backgrounds* have been converted into victims of the Dark Angel of Devastation with the keys to the Bottomless Pit in *Fighting France* (*FF*147).

Wharton was proud of being one of the few civilians to be allowed into the war-zone, to be shown the trenches, an actual battle, to gaze through the look-out of a surveillance post on the front, to be given secret passwords, to pass among the wounded in the front-line hospitals. Her mission there was ostensibly to distribute precious supplies assembled by her war charities to the medics; but she was also gathering impressions of war for her money- and consciousness-raising articles in the American press, articles which eventually were gathered together as *Fighting France*. She obviously enjoyed having access to a France no casual tourist would ever see, and was especially indignant that bad behaviour by some titled ladies who visited before her in a less serious frame of mind had nearly prevented her receiving her own passport to the front;[57] she scorned the remarks of a woman whose summation of such a trip taken just after the war was disappointment in the quality of hotel accommodation in the Devastated Regions.[58] If '"doing" hospitals like museums'[59] became, in war-time, the grotesque counterpart to the three-day tourist in Italy who is in Europe because he *can* be rather than because he must, Wharton again aligned herself, as she does in *Italian Backgrounds*, with the real traveller who abides in foreignness. The Devastated Regions and the front were not to be found in any guide-book; for her they are as remarkable as the misattributed statues at San Vivaldo.

The impressionism of *Fighting France* is purposeful: partly it conveys her 'dumbfounded'-ness, the overwhelming experience of the war (*FF*64): the great conflict is not a sight to be mastered and understood like an obscure hill-shrine. Yet her war-travels, like those of her leisure in Morocco, the near east, Greece, Spain, England, France and Italy, give her a clear superiority of experience. In 1922 she was reading the memoirs of Mrs Charles Amory, an American on a wedding-trip in Europe in the early 1830s, and laughing at her complete ignorance of her surroundings. 'When we think of what was stirring and boiling and flashing and flowing in London and Paris at that time, the stolid complacency of the average rich American traveller of her day makes me feel – well, the rare quality of the few who *were* aware!'[60] Her own response to the war, to be discussed at greater length later in this chapter, was in part that of the sophisticated traveller, the collector of rare experience; it was socially and politically figured for her in the dichotomy of native and visitor, patriot and pleasure-seeker, French and American, aware and unaware.

In Europe Wharton travelled east and south as far as Egypt. Other places, such as the America beyond New England and the mid-Atlantic seaboard, however, were places for rich men to go fishing and for ailing husbands to be sent on therapeutic tours; Oriental travellers in her fiction tend to be escaping or escapist young men (Newland Archer wants to run away to Japan; Nick Lansing has visited India with bores, and is preparing to write a thin little book on eastern art). She herself had unfulfilled ambitions to journey up the Nile and to see India; but when Walter Berry took passage to India she approved the taking of sea air for his health while saying nothing at all of his destination.[61] Western Europe was her chosen territory, and she once accounted for this exclusive fascination with Europe and the Old World surrounding the Mediterranean.

There is a part of the world that seems made for loafing and basking, and a vague sort of superficial desultory contact with places that are all width and no depth; the Stevenson-Conrad-coral-island wilderness. And then there is the other little cupful of blue water, with almost all that has proved worthwhile in history and art and religion almost on its shores – and life is so short that I can't conceive hesitating between the two![62]

With that verb 'loaf', so essentially American, Whitmanian, she implicitly writes off the foregrounded 'blankness' of non-European places. Perhaps the complexities, linguistic and cultural, of mastering non-western art and literature deterred her from exploring the east; Europeanisation gave her her own 'force of negation' which eliminated everything beyond her own range of perception. Those parts of the planet outside the western, Graeco-Roman tradition are like her idea of 'the west' in America, or like Switzerland – all width and no depth, a kind of unmanaged and meaningless wilderness.

Plunder: buccaneers go to Europe when they die

> '"They say . . . that when good Americans die they go to Paris.'
> "Indeed? And when bad Americans die, where do they go to?"
> "Oh, they go to America."'[63]

In 1842 Dickens noted the 'restless and locomotive' quality of Americans in their own country.[64] Post-Civil War wealth coupled with new travel technology (faster ocean-liners, extended railway systems, the automobile, and the invention of the American luxury hotel) transported that restlessness to Europe; and the traditional, leisurely Grand Tour became an event which, with enough money, could be undertaken many times, at relatively short notice, and for relatively brief periods. Wharton herself spent six years of her childhood wandering around the fashionable European capital cities and watering places with her parents, and she returned for a further 16 months in her late teenage years when her father's health failed. As Frances Hodgson Burnett points out in *The Shuttle* (1907), in the early days of recreational ocean-crossings and long-distance travel, 'a man did not lightly run over to London, or Paris, or Berlin, he gravely went to "Europe".'[65]

Wharton's Undine Spragg dashes to and fro across the Atlantic at the turn of the century; Lily Bart can take up a sudden invitation to cruise in the Mediterranean; everyone in *The Glimpses of the Moon* rattles around from Scotland to Biarritz and Sicily. The American buccaneer, in particular, found in extensive travel the natural complement to the establishment of great wealth and social prestige in New York: the European excursion is a form of Veblen's 'honorific waste' [66] which converts economic capital into cultural capital; [67] it is also, in Victor Turner's phrase, a 'cultural performance' [68] in which social prestige is accrued. Making a splash in Europe – all over Europe – is sequent to a splash in Wall Street, as reasonable (merely more evolved) as the initial compulsion to build and entertain extravagantly in Fifth Avenue. Wharton's buccaneer characters exercise their powers of conquest by laying out for Venetian palazzi left mostly empty, for huge steam-yachts and motor-fleets kept waiting at their beck and call; their sumptuous dinners in fashionable restaurants across the continent given to impecunious aristocrats allow one set of opportunists to entertain another.

The extreme form of buccaneer social outlay and cultural performance is practised in *The Glimpses of the Moon*, where the dizzy Violet Melrose dimly conceives of cultural patronage as a fashionable activity. A minor couple called the Fulmers are 'claimed' by Mrs Melrose and her rival, Mrs Gillow: they dispute ownership of the husband, a painter, each regarding him as her own pet genius. Mrs Melrose seems to have won out: 'Yes – I *did* discover him', she shrieks;

> I *did*. . . . You mustn't believe a word that Ursula Gillow tells you about having pounced on his 'Spring Snow Storm' in a dark corner of the American Artists' exhibition. . . . When, in reality, any one who saw me at the exhibition on varnishing day . . . as if one could remember the people about one, when suddenly one comes upon a great work of art, as St Paul did – didn't he? – and the scales fell from his eyes. Well . . . that's exactly what happened to me that day. . . . (*GM* 146–7)

Expatriate 'connoisseur' sensibility is summed up in this speech: Mrs Melrose 'pounces' on art and artists as she might on a chinchilla cloak; her aesthetic discrimination consists only in being the first to have discovered the artist (and even this primacy is invented); neither the art nor its maker, but the sense of her own acuteness and the contention with Mrs Gillow, excites her; such an expatriate contest could as easily be (and, indeed, *is*, in *The Children*) about fashionable dressmakers. Mrs Melrose's wildly off-beam Biblical allusion violently wrenches a signal myth of spiritual transformation into the service of her paltry little rivalry with Mrs Gillow, a disengaging cultural appropriation as characteristic of her class as Mr Raycie's Old Masters shopping list in *False Dawn*. Poe remarked that the Republic seems to produce individuals 'of large purse and little soul'. [69] Wharton's expatriate novels of the twenties are essentially about that contention between soul and purse, highlighted and exemplified by displacement of republican products to Europe.

The war is never mentioned in *The Glimpses of the Moon* (1922), and the book (advertised in its time as 'a novel of society today'[70]) exists in a moral and historical vacuum, in a Europe of expatriates on whose thoughts and conversation the war appears to have made no perceptible impact. Like other forgetful Americans (Undine Spragg, Kate Clephane), they seem to have forgotten (or never noticed) that it happened. Among these vacant, vagrant characters, Susy and Nick Lansing appear to be the very type of the American abroad. They are a pair of impecunious young socialites accustomed to living off their rich friends, friends who value them because she is pretty and conversable, he intelligent and 'literary'. Quite against their habitual pragmatism, they fall in love, and reckon to support their rich international style by accepting only cheques for wedding presents, and getting their friends to lend them houses for as long as possible. They agree, in a hard-headed business arrangement, to break up if either of them gets a better offer of marriage from someone very rich. This initial premiss has almost the comedic artifice of *Volpone* or a Restoration play or *Cosi Fan Tutte*; and Nick and Susy's experiment is likewise acidulated: it is Wharton's experiment with American conditions of matrimony in a European setting, with matrimony standing for modern (read 'American') morals in general, where Purse is victor over Soul; the Lansings's unexpected and debatable triumph over mere self-advancement has a kind of sexual pragmatism rather than any larger virtue attached to it.

Though parasites, the Lansings are only partly typical of the Whartonian international set; Nick has some intellectual pretensions, even if he is unable to translate them into anything worth reading; Susy has an agreeably sensible head on her shoulders, and acknowledges the compromises both of them have made about:

> people with a balance . . . the people one always had to put one's self out for . . . she knew nearly all that there was to know . . . and judged them with the contemptuous lucidity of nearly twenty years dependence. (*GM*5)

We have seen this type before – the individual taken up and used for decorative, conversational, sexual, or missive value – in Lily Bart, that consummate hanger-on and work of art. Although Lily will perform little crucial services for her rich friends – writing their letters, making seating arrangements, distracting suspicious husbands – she is unable to lower herself to certain kinds of behaviour, and suffers the consequent refusal of her friends to go on supporting her. Although Nick is a male version of Lily in this respect, Susy has fewer scruples. In *The Glimpses of the Moon* Wharton had been urged by Appleton's to write another *House of Mirth*; and the novel betrays itself as a cruder copy of the early master-piece: the 'deal' Lily refuses (money for favours) is the economic founda-tion of the Lansing marriage. At the dinner party where Susy first meets Nick she says robustly, 'I'd rather have a husband like that than a steam-yacht!' (*GM*6), and although the glossy sentimentality of glimpsed moon-light which Wharton keeps invoking from first to last page seems to obscure this hard-nosed business sense in Susy, the moon is actually a sick joke *about* sentimentality: for Susy, pretty, available, and well-connected, it *is* a choice between an agreeable but badly-off husband, and an unpleasant rich one with a steam-yacht and all the other luxur-ies she can imagine. Susy knows 'just what [things] are worth, and for what reasons'; to her credit, she chooses Nick over the steam-yacht, des-pite the tendency of her rich friends to regard the marriage as a kind of joke. In addition, the sickness of the joke is centred around Nick, the one through whose eyes the evocation of moon and June is glimpsed, who rapturously contemplates the luxuriance of Susy's eyelashes while she is thinking 'cheques... nothing but cheques' (*GM*22); he is the partner who abandons his mate for a cruise in a steam-yacht.

Nick, unlike Susy, doesn't have any idea 'what things are worth': he can evaluate neither his luxuries nor his necessities, especially not his wife. Their marriage legitimates the ethos of rich or rising Americans, the ethos of getting things out of people. For the impecunious, such getting will not bear much scrutiny. Although he is aware that in their mode of existence 'there were certain links in the chain... certain arrangements and contrivances that still needed further elucidation [which] he was lazily resolved to clear... up with her some day' (*GM*23), he thinks it 'rather fine to be able to give himself so intensely to the fullness of each moment instead of hurrying past it...' (*GM*243) while his wife is busy totting up 'the necessities that enslaved her... so much... for her dresses, so much for her cigarettes, so much for bridge and cabs and tips' (*GM*271). Nick is content to drift along, to be shielded from the realities of their life together ('he had taken care not to ask'), to play at author (a ridiculous project called *The Pageant of Alexander* in which a half-baked art-historical theory will be cast as a novel to disguise the thinness of the material) while Susy manages the money, the servants, attends to various hosts' neglected children, and fends off importunate friends so that her husband can write.

The Lansings exploit their rich friends and are exploited by them, an internal cannibalistic economy which turns the voracity of the buccaneer on itself, making the expatriate social economy a closed system. This enclosure is significant. In several of Wharton's expatriate novels we find American characters resolutely resisting contact with the native population, sometimes on the principle that Europeans are too corrupt, but more usually because the local American expatriate cell provides its own amusements.[71] Assimilation is rarely the point of the exercise: Americans abroad want to impress *each other*, not the French or the English; theirs is 'a little world sparsely peopled by compatriots in the same attitude of chronic opposition toward a society chronically unaware of them' (*MT* 44). Although Undine Spragg briefly samples French aristocratic life, she soon chucks it in to remarry her first American husband, a circular move which emphasises that enclosure; in the last scene of *The Custom of the Country* (in Paris) she awaits dinner guests who are nearly all American. When buccaneers finally settle in or briefly colonise Europe, most of them have either rid themselves of, or never had, any desire to Europeanise; as the marriages and remarriages of the 1920s novels show us, they always pair up with other Americans. Mrs Melrose is championing an American artist she discovered in America, against the rival claims of other Americans. There is virtually no sense in *The Glimpses of the Moon* or the subsequent novels of interaction between Americans and anything or one genuinely European.

In *The Custom of the Country* the relentless buccaneer mode of Undine Spragg and Elmer Moffatt becomes with repetition its own justification, and the complaints and qualms of potential adversaries like Ralph and Raymond are overpowered by the narrative's pattern of demand and satisfaction. But in *The Glimpses of the Moon* Wharton chooses to complicate matters by introducing a moral voice (Nick's) which seems powerful within the story in inverse proportion to its essential weakness outside of it. The story revolves around the discovery by Nick that Susy is helping a rich American friend who has lent them a Venetian palazzo to deceive her millionaire husband while she dallies with an even richer lover. Nick, who throughout the story takes the moral high ground, accuses Susy of selling out; Susy correctly reminds him that her 'managing', as they call the performing of services, is how she has always got along and is the basis of their joint existence. Nick runs off in a passion of priggish disapproval, and they spend the second half of the novel being courted by interested third parties – Nick by a large and rich heiress from that same Apex, the hometown of Undine Spragg; Susy by an English friend who unexpectedly inherits an earldom.

Except for Strefford, the English earl, every other important character in the story is a wandering, immensely rich, American. They inhabit identical, indistinguishable Nouveau Luxe hotels, spend their time in expensive pleasure-seeking, shopping for jewels, being fitted for clothes, and entering into intrigues with one another's spouses. They have what Wharton calls 'hard little appetites' and are constantly on the move, either to join the newest and most exciting crowd, to fetch a new set of clothes, to make new arrangements with a lover. Wharton had certainly met people like this, and her anatomy of the life-cycle of the nomadic rich, if exaggerated, is roughly accurate. Unloosed from whatever natural surroundings they have ever had (and, probable *nouveaux riches*, they are by definition *without* native habitat), these people can only be defined in terms of what they can buy and where they can go. This is certainly not Old New York; nor is it the slicker, mesolithic *milieu* of *The House of Mirth*, where even 'the most irresponsible pretty woman . . . had her inherited obligations, her conventional benevolences, her share in the working of the great civic machine . . .' (*HM*445). These are tycoons put out to pasture; there is no visible sign of business being transacted; the rich men of *Glimpses* are Moffatts and Rosedales no longer on the make. Their eyes no longer fastened on the market, they are engrossed in the teleology of restaurants and the Rue de la Paix. Unlike Undine and Fanny Frisbee, their predecessors, they have never had any interest in invading or experiencing the ancient aristocracies, which for them hardly exist. Expatriatism in this form is the attenuated afterlife of the buccaneer.

The world of *Glimpses* is one in which smiling ladies are assumed to be rejoicing in recent divorces, where a rich child charmingly prefers jewellery to books, where Venice seems to consist of Florian's, the Lido, and dinners in expensive hotels; it is the Playground Europe of F. Scott Fitzgerald, who wrote the titles for the 1923 silent film of this novel. Although the book's design has the adamantine, glacial quality of an exquisite jewel or of the 'hard little appetite' for such gauds displayed even by the youngest children in it, it is here that Wharton first displays her interest in the unmoored workings of mere appetite and pleasure. Undine Spragg, after all, had her way to make, and her story, terrifying as it is, nonetheless comprehends a logic of ascent which is completely probable and predictable within the terms of the novel. But the rich of *The Glimpses of the Moon* are already vastly endowed, socially beyond need; there is no rationale provided for them, and there can be none: 'rich aimless people' move around and behave as they do because nothing better presents itself. In a crucial scene Susy rises above her conditioning to reprove this self-justifying behaviour in her palazzo-owning friend Ellie Vanderlyn, the one who intends to divorce her exceedingly rich husband in order to marry her even richer lover: '"I think you're abominable", she exclaimed . . . "with . . . all the money you can possibly want. . . . Abominable!" ". . . I hardly know how to answer you", [Ellie] stammered. "But you simply don't know what you're talking about. *As if anybody ever had all the money they wanted!*"' (*GM* 215). Wharton's italics give the phrase the lapidary quality of a motto.

There are two sorts of buccaneers here, though. When Nick becomes 'perpendicular' (*GM* 113) about Susy's 'management' of their domestic life, he runs away to hitch a ride with the Mortimer Hickses, roving midwesterners with a steam yacht and a naive enthusiasm for Culture. They represent another, rarer kind of rich American, who prefers to devour Old World culture rather than Old World commodities; the Hickses pay Nick in exposure to sights rather than in pearl tie-pins. They are the only characters to take the trouble to examine the Tiepolos in Venice, the only millionaires in the novel determined that their millions will buy them this more ineffable experiential plunder. These innocents are rather admirable in their expenditure, which, if it does include the inevitable steam-yacht, also includes tutors and excursions to places worth seeing. Their rectitude is all the more emphatic in contrast with Nick, who, although he has been bored by them on other occasions, is not above accepting their lavish hospitality when nothing better offers, and does not scruple to encourage Coral Hicks's intention to buy him in marriage. Coral, unlike Susy, won't have to choose between Nick and a steam-yacht, since she can afford the price of both.

Against the peripheral, amoral 'money' characters, we are given only this pompous, self-righteous cad, an opportunist and a hypocrite who affects ethical propriety without ever putting himself to the test, making Susy bear all the blame for the 'compromised' existence he has been content, heretofore, to lead. Susy has what Nick thinks of as a 'masculine' regard for her word: she doesn't break promises, she pays her social debts even at great cost to herself. Susy reacts with characteristic logic: she treats such contrivances as business arrangements, and asks 'Did you ever in your life get anything for nothing?' (*GM* 108). When Nick abandons her, she squares her shoulders and takes a position as (essentially) a servant, the honest, contractual version of what she has always been. Nick, by contrast, instead of finishing his book, runs to Coral, another 'masculine' woman – massive, solemn, imposing, even faintly mustached – and carries on battening on the rich as he has always done, allowing Coral to think of him as a practising archaeologist as he has encouraged Susy to think of him as a serious writer. Wharton does not admire Nick's red-and-white virtue, which merely aligns him with the senseless rich rather than with the Hickses. Although not a strict materialist (he doesn't require a yacht of his own as long as there is someone to let him come aboard theirs) Nick offers Susy no 'republic of the spirit' – even that weak construction of Selden's is beyond his ken.

The novel's interesting contention between principles and wealth is one more narrowly posed in *The House of Mirth* as a woman's problem. Susy's strict self-auditing of 'mays and mustn'ts' makes her an interesting buccaneer – perhaps the only one of this stripe in all Wharton save for Carry Fisher in *The House of Mirth* – an honest parasite who contemplates and longs for 'the blessed moral freedom that wealth conferred' (*GM*177), moral freedom which would enable her to reject compromises, a sybarite who – uniquely – never forgets her experience or her obligations. But that freedom is, ironically, also the freedom of Ellie Vanderlyn to divorce and marry even more richly. Lily Bart knows that 'the only way not to think about money is to have a great deal of it' (*HM*110); Susy's decision to work as a nurserymaid for a troop of children is the more promising equivalent of Lily Bart's last acts – writing out the cheques to pay her final debts and futilely hallucinating herself nurturing new life.

Significantly, both *Glimpses* and *The House of Mirth* resolve themselves in children, real and imagined. The title of *The Children*, another expatriate novel of the twenties, refers both to the young and to their childlike parents. At the centre of the story is a collection of full-, step-, and half-siblings related to each other through their parents' incessant remarriages; the complications of these relationships are only tenuously established. Headed by fifteen-year-old Judith Wheater, the group includes the twins Terry and Blanca, whose American parents are also Judith's; her half-sister Zinnie, the daughter of their father and an ex-wife (a movie star); Bun and Beechy, two Italian step-siblings to the other children, offspring of the ex-husband of Judith's mother and *his* ex-wife, a circus acrobat; and the baby Chipstone, the child of Judith's newly *remarried* parents. Because they are neglected by the parents, who disport themselves all over fashionable Europe, divorcing and remarrying with bewildering abandon, the children's loyalty is to each other, and they resist being reclaimed by various sets of parents, pitting the relatively unimportant genetic claims of the adults against the moral authority of the protective, invented familial unit which the children have made for themselves.

Their pathetic solidarity momentarily combats the unstable, nomadic world in which they have been raised. These children are in some ways practically wild: even the eldest can hardly spell, and like puppies they clamour for treats from any grown-up who notices them, making little distinction between parents and other adults. Their manners are rough; the littlest girls are allowed to conduct precocious and inappropriate flirtations, and even the fifteen-year-old Judith speaks caressingly to older men in the manner of her mother's friends, drinks cocktails, steals money from her father, and is open to the romantic speculations of a man several times her age. But as Boyne notes, these children are no more primitive than their parents. Acquainted, like all Whartonian expatriates, with luxe hotels and ocean liners but not with school-rooms or family dwellings, these children are the peculiar product of rootlessness; flux prompts them to form a little nation or tribe of their own, whose loyalties and laws outweigh any other traditional duty or feeling, whose very language is part French, part Italian, part English, part infantile idiolect.

The children's genetic relation to each other is as complicated as anything in *The Age of Innocence*, and like that novel, the tribal onomastics are slightly fantastic; it takes Boyne some time to master the names and the relationships. Bun and Beechy are juvenile corruptions of Astorre and Beatrice Buondelmonte; Zinnie is named after her mother, Zinnia Lacrosse; how the twins Terry and Blanca come to have such ethnically distinct names is never explained; 'Chipstone' seems to represent the dynastic enthusiasm with which Mr and Mrs Wheater recommence married life and produce a sturdy second son; as the atavistic Wheater, Chip is idolised and adored by the other children for his serenity and stolidity. When these careless parents suddenly decide to divorce a second time and start to divide the spoils of the marriage, the children enlist the help of the fascinated Boyne and run away to the Tyrol to escape the inevitable diaspora. While the parents are squabbling at the Lido or racing at Cowes, the children are strapped for money, and are reduced to borrowing the governess's life savings to make ends meet. It is not that the parents are ungenerous; they are simply distracted; their quarrels produce the same evanescent chaos as the battle among the children over the upsetting of a goldfish bowl. Most of the novel is taken up with the children's contrivances to elude the parents; yet when all is said and done the disposition of the children is completely random: by the end of the story they are dispersed, dead, or grown up. Ordinary human undertaking is completely compromised and derailed by the erratic excitability of the parents.

Though not naturally parental, Cliffe and Joyce Wheater are obsessed with Baby Chip because he is the 'spare heir' in case the sickly Terry dies young; they seem almost indifferent to, or forgetful of, the six other children surrounding Chip. When they embark on divorce proceedings, Chipstone becomes the token child over whom the parents bicker for custody, the totem of the children's tribe who cannot be yielded up. Boyne's analysis of their behaviour reverts to the characteristic Whartonian anthropological concepts:

> before each other they shouted and struck attitudes ... like savages. But the chief point was that nobody could stay angry – not however much they tried. It was too much trouble, and might involve too many inconveniences, interfere with too many social arrangements. When all was said and done, all they asked was not to be bothered. ... (*C*175)

They are as forgetful as savages (*C*174), and forgetfulness is the reigning character-trait in *The Children*: parents seem to forget about their children, couples suddenly forget their enthusiasm for marriage. Joyce Wheater, having made three improbable unions already (two of them to the cartoon-animal Cliffe Wheater), capriciously takes up the solemn lawyer Mr Dobree and the sacrament of bridge. At first unexpectedly slim and youthful to Boyne (who remembers a much larger woman), she is last seen plump again and middle-aged, the third of her known incarnations (fat–thin–fat). Mrs Wheater, who changes body-shape as quickly as she changes husbands, seems not to remember the flirtation she had with Boyne in her youth – at least, she seems not to remember it *as* flirtation. Boyne *does* remember, so that his surrogate parenthood to her children and step-children is enhanced by the sense that he might indeed have been their father; this distant recollection disables and discomfits him in his attachment to Judith, with its hint of emotional incest.

Although Boyne is one of the few Wharton characters to earn his living, and to earn it practically and usefully as an engineer (others are Guy Thwarte, Ethan Frome, and the narrator of *Ethan Frome*, and even the heroine of 'The Valley of Childish Things'), still he spends a great deal of time doing it away from his homeland and as an excuse to *be* away. The actual job of building bridges and railways and mines is only slightly alluded to by either Boyne or Wharton, so that this world of work exists only in the merest margins of the story's imaginative space; nevertheless, it is interesting that whenever Wharton wants to denote a kind of reliable and honourable solidity, she makes the man an engineer rather than a lawyer or some other 'genteel' profession. Wharton is enough of a modernist to feel the imaginative pull of the great constructions of the early-twentieth century, and to give them a kind of oblique moral pitch. In Boyne the designation of engineer is especially poignant: he is the only character in the novel who remembers that the world exists and needs attending to.

Once caught up in the vitality and cynicism of the children, Boyne becomes unfit either for the glittering and insubstantial world of their parents, or for the future he has planned with the attenuated Mrs Sellars, a woman whose considered responses are measured and mediated, precisely the antithesis of the chaotic Wheaters. The novel fluctuates between Mrs Sellars' almost sepulchral domestic stillness in the middle of the Alpine grandeur, the senseless whirl of the parents' lives, and the messy but authentic and rationalised society of the children. Complicit with the children, Boyne is momentarily stranded in the last of these; but he cannot remain there, and can abide in neither of the other two, so he flees to South America, to the Ibsenesque consolation of 'the glorious soul-releasing world of girders and abutments, of working stresses, curvatures and grades' (*C*240). Boyne cannot belong anywhere; he can only console himself with work. Boyne is finally a man without an emotional country of his own.

The horror of moneyed expatriatism is not what it can *get* for its possessors, but what is *relieves* them of, namely, any sort of social responsibility, or social memory. Expatriates live in undifferentiated and anodyne luxury hotels because housekeeping would limit movement and strain their practical ingenuity (apparently they do not keep houses in America, either: the children are literally homeless); and the indistinguishable hotels spare them the effort of remembering the difference between one place and another. Expatriate children are socialised by their proximity to other placeless 'international' children like the drug-addicted suicide, Doll Westway, and young lift-boys and bellhops.

The hotel-culture of *The Children* is symptomatic of that remote relationship of buccaneer expatriates to the host country. Hermetically enclosed in their Americanness, it would never occur to them to test life far from Palace hotels or colossal steam-yachts. Such rootless expatriates are more horrifying than Undine Spragg: they are, if possible, *more* transient, more restless, than she. Undine is a social destroyer, but she works from the inside. The 1920s expatriates don't care about the social codes so eagerly studied by Undine Spragg because they belong to a wholly new and even more deracinated order, one which brings no special plans to Europe, and breaks foreign bounds not because it doesn't understand them, but merely because it hasn't noticed them. Undine is the product of the Belle Epoque and the Edwardian afternoon, and her history of destructive impulse is only meaningful set against carefully maintained order; but what Wharton described as 'the mountains of wreckage now dividing two geological ages' (*FG1*) stands between Undine's world and the tumult of the Jazz Age: her post-war characters are not so much destroyers of an existing order as symptomatic of the prevailing disorder which has succeeded it. Post-war existence is in Wharton's view rudderless and without principle; by setting the spare neoclassical elegance of her prose style and controlling design against the moral and behavioural chaos of a fallen world, she reproduces the contention between order and disorder. Where money is excuse enough for anything, where persons and households zoom around the continent in search of fashion and pleasure, where flimsy and empty marriages can be dissolved in the blink of an eye, the delicate Jamesian perceptions of Mrs Sellars are merely tedious and mannered, and all the effort of a practical man like Boyne is ultimately without effect or meaning. *The Children* falls into fragments in the final chapter, with the diaspora of the siblings and Boyne's flight out of the story.

   The Glimpses of the Moon and *The Children* were enormous commercial successes, but critics were less pleased by them. Together with much of Wharton's 1920s output (*Twilight Sleep* and *The Mother's Recompense*) they continue to elicit a certain amount of disdain from readers. *The Age of Innocence* and the 'Old New York' tetralogy are brilliant retrograde responses to the chaos of war. But Appleton's hope for another *House of Mirth* was clearly confounded by the six years Wharton needed to produce *The Glimpses of the Moon*, a mark of her exile from her earlier subjects. She noted in 1918 that 'these four years have so much changed the whole aspect of life that it is not easy to say now what one's literary tendencies will be when the war is over.'[72] Although her literary tendencies were as altered as the landscape of the front by the war, readers and publishers alike have always resented the shift away from *The House of Mirth*; that she had passed through divorce, geographical transplantation, middle age, and world war could not, seemingly, excuse her from the demand for more of 1905 or of the 1870s. That the world had suffered cataclysm is thought sufficient to explain the new twentieth-century modes of other writers, but Wharton's address to the same post-war world is written off as a decline from greatness.[73]

In her final work, Wharton attempted the portrayal of an attractive expatriate American, although she had to retreat to the post-war period of the 1870s to do so, a retreat generally approved by Lewis and other disparagers of her contemporary subjects. The American Annabel St George is the passionate opposite of the vapid, nomadic expatriate, and her involvement with Guy Thwarte shows a slightly less black-and-white contrast between rich Americans and cultured Europeans. The money behind Annabel permits her, against the European grain, to escape her marriage and elope with Thwarte; on the other hand, the great noble families of Tintagel and Brightlingsea are small-minded and mean-spirited, less concerned with heritage than with deference and money, so that the violation has Wharton's approval. Annabel, too, has been 'brought up in hotels and watering holes all over America', but nevertheless (and somewhat improbably) has an intuitive appreciation of old houses, landscapes, and the Fleshly School of poetry which is quite alien to her identically-reared sister and friends. Capable of appreciating paintings, gardens, and architecture, she is relegated in Wharton's notes for the unfinished ending to the outer darkness of South America in consequence of her crimes against matrimony.

Even if the late-nineteenth-century setting aligns the novel with *The Age of Innocence* and the Old New York novellas, *The Buccaneers* is more like a melodramatic rural fable in the style of Frances Hodgson Burnett's *The Shuttle* (1907).[74] Wharton's England is rosy and well-stocked with susceptible young Dukes and dashing 'detrimentals', derangingly pretty and rich young American girls, and trout-like duchesses under the impression that indians haunt the New York suburbs teaching archery to young ladies. The details are cartoon-like and corny: the name of Guy Thwarte's beautiful house Honourslove appears to be some sort of pun on a line of Lovelace's; Italian reunification gets mixed up in it in the person of Annabel's heroic governess. But in spite of its faults the novel deals in the same themes as its predecessors: the system of exchange (in this case of fortune for title) thrives; Consuelo Vanderbilt, the unhappy Duchess of Marlborough, is a clear model for Annabel St George.[75] The exchange of capital for honour is ultimately fatal: the American wives of English noblemen either destroy their husbands' heritage or find that no amount of money can salvage it; or they are themselves injured by the friction of contact. The subject is potentially important and serious; but where it might have climbed out of its nursery-pudding charm and into something more bracing, it remains unfinished. Nostalgia, as Millicent Bell reminds us, is 'not an adequate standpoint for someone as intelligent and realistic as Edith Wharton',[76] and *The Buccaneers* is too nostalgic to achieve the detachment of *The Age of Innocence* or *Twilight Sleep*, too sentimental and romantic to stand up as satire, its improbabilities merely silly and amusing. The affair between Nan St George and Guy Thwarte, however, is far from amusing, and is bound to create damage. The damage is to the traditions of England, and to the very future they both so cherish: Honourslove is lost to them as Guy is disinherited; Nan's ingenious and loyal governess sacrifices her own future in order to aid her eloping former pupil. The clash between the old world and the expatriate is only superficially funny; the real consequences are tragic and irremediable.[77] Wharton's final fictional enterprise follows the career of a sympathetic American in Europe, her only such protagonist since *Madame de Treymes*; but the book itself, like Nan's attempt to achieve the best of England and Englishness, is ultimately a failure.

'Did you ever see anything so French?': assimilators

> 'It is always well for a stranger in an old society to err a little on the side of what you call its prejudices but I should rather describe as its traditions.' (*R*95)

Chapter 3 examined Wharton's uncanny likeness to Undine Spragg and the buccaneer figure. The James circle's comic rendition of Wharton as the angel of devastation, the *faisan d'or*, provided them with a vocabulary for what Gilbert and Gubar have analysed as her obsessive desire for 'emotional and intellectual emancipation' from the institutionalised diminution of women's accomplishment and ambition.[78] James's complicated relationship with Wharton had among its elements jealousy of her great commercial success and the condescension of master to acolyte; the caricature of Wharton as a kind of sentient female hurricane is both affectionate and usefully limiting for James as well as for other members of the group.[79] But, as they recognised in their mystical terminology, Wharton was *not* an American buccaneer in the mould of Isabella Stewart Gardiner, whom James described as 'the American, the nightmare ... looming up – dim, vast, portentous.'[80] Percy Lubbock, ever alive to Wharton's social and intellectual powers, repeatedly admires her almost supernatural curiosity and self-transforming ability. After her death, Lubbock marvelled at 'the yawning hiatus between Pussy Jones at her first party and the "faisan d'or" of her early Quacre days',[81] as if she had at some moment before he knew her metamorphosed from debutante and matron of Old New York into glittering legend. In 1925, Wharton having embarked on one of her typically comprehensive and detailed excursions to northern Spain, he reports: 'Here comes an airy card from E.W., with a picture of Coruña – the very end of Europe – the continent gives out, so she can go no further, but she would if she could – she beats against the confines of the world.'[82]

As 'Mrs Jack', with Berenson's assistance, pounced on Renaissance masterpieces, Wharton's possession of Europe consisted of a less predatory diet of sightseeing and experience. Instead of pouncing, she and Gaillard Lapsley would 'gloat' over their voyeuristic spoliation of art treasures.[83] To be sure, she was an avid acquirer of Old World goods in the form of crates of *marmi* [marbles] arriving at the Mount from Italy;[84] she had searched long and hard but without success for an eighteenth-century glass ceiling for her house in Newport;[85] and her friends recalled her manner of hard bargaining with *antiquaires* when she had her eye on some especially covetable piece of furniture.[86] But she was more covetous of foreign experience than of foreign wares. 'It's all really so glorious and amazing and deep and dense and cuts such long vistas in so many different directions, that I've been stretched to bursting with it all', she intoned in 1903.[87] In others 'the absence of vibrations' gave her 'a feeling of suffocation': she was appalled by 'stupid Italians' who are insensible to the treasures surrounding them; 'I begin to think it is better to be an American, and bring to it all a mind and eye unblunted by custom'; equally, she said, 'I look with amazement at the Americans and English who come [to Rome] for a few weeks, and give all their time and strength to forcing their way into a society not particularly anxious to receive them.'[88]

Although in Paris Edith Wharton immediately settled in the Rue de Varenne, an austere street of imposing *hôtels particuliers*, including the Hôtel Matignon, and although she was in many ways well-connected to faubourg and French intellectual society through people like Paul Bourget, she did not, from this base, infiltrate that closely-knit society in the manner of some of her characters, and it is not clear that she ever wished to do so. Her circle of friends was a celebrated one, to be sure, but she initiated no *salon*, participated only sparingly in the existing ones, never contemplated marriage with any French aristocrat.[89] Her likeness to expatriate buccaneers of fiction and reality is mostly coincidental: unlike them, she was in France to *work*, and she spoke of literature there as her 'business';[90] she was impatient with the wasted energy and money expatriate Americans spent on mad rushing around. But she herself was addicted to 'motor-flights', forever crossing and recrossing the Atlantic, guilty as a young married woman of having spent an entire year's income on an Aegean cruise. She did not, for example, let news of the Sarajevo assassinations in the summer of 1914 interrupt her travel plans: she experienced 'a momentary shiver', but since Archduke Ferdinand was only a name, and since she had extensive excursions in the offing, she was more taken up with anticipation of places she had always wanted to see than with the prospect of war (*BG*336–7). Still, this is not Wheater or Vanderlyn or Spragg behaviour: her greed is for the cultural and social heritage of Europe rather than for its parties; she never fails to condemn the unconscionable frivolity of expatriate gadflies.

It is not every American in Wharton's fiction who traverses and plunders the Old World with such rapacious vigour as the buccaneer expatriates, or with such supernatural energy as Wharton herself. Her most interesting characters (Olenska, Fanny de Malrive, Sophy Viner) are all transatlantic. The novella *Madame de Treymes* (1907) and *The Reef* (1912) feature American protagonists and supporting characters of quite different tendencies. The former Fanny Frisbee is not an ugly American: her 'long European discipline', derived from her unfortunate French marriage to a *marquis*, has refined her 'random fluency' (*MT*6) and modelled and finished her 'fresh uncomplicated personalit[y]' (*MT*35). 'I never saw anything so French!' exclaims one of her American visitors (*MT*35); but Madame de Malrive (as she has become) is a hybrid, neither French nor American: 'There were, with minor modifications, many other Fanny Frisbees; whereas never before . . . had there been a Fanny de Malrive' (*MT*34). Her modulation and 'delicacy' is uncommon in the expatriate American and is surprising to the French, and yet her real Europeanising is moral, not physical: despite her unhappy experience, she means to raise her boy as a Frenchman among his own people. But after 15 years' absence from the States and torment by her French husband, she is ready to 'be with dear, good, sweet, simple, real Americans again', to be in 'clear American air where there are no obscurities, no mysteries' (*MT*23), a desire which is to be thwarted by the existence of her French son. Her pro-Americanism has the same naivete as Ellen Olenska's.

Fanny de Malrive's French *nuance* is coupled with American moral simplicity; her very names suggest the contrast between American innocence and French policy: 'Fanny Frisbee' has an almost preposterous New World quality in it; but next to the sinister 'Malrive' it has an appealing freshness. By contrast, the stolid Mrs Elmer Boykin (whose name is no more absurd than Fanny Frisbee's, and evokes the perpetual childishness Wharton perceived in the American character) is unmistakably American even after a quarter century's residence in Paris; her drawing room still has 'the hard bright atmosphere of her native skies' (*MT*44), her gaze is direct and her voice unmodulated, and she remains 'true to national ideals in electric lighting and plumbing' (*MT*44). Fanny has assimilated; Mrs Boykin is still a visitor. Unlike Mrs Boykin – insulated in her suspicion of the French – Fanny is at risk; assimilation lays traps for the unwary American. Since Fanny is no Undine, and neither can nor wishes to buy out her boy's French relations, the consequence of her divorce is a Hobson's choice between her child and her lover. The sombre-tinted faubourg snares Fanny and Durham with its cunning; but the dark opposition between New and Old World which Wharton seems to set up is not simple. Americans like Mrs Boykin are not 'dear, good and sweet'; and Madame de Treymes, the scheming faubourg insider, proves at the eleventh hour to be honourable and sympathetic to Fanny's predicament, even though she is also helpless to solve it.

Another assimilator is Anna Leath in *The Reef*. Her late husband, an American watercolourist settled in rural France, is a caricature of the Jamesian precisian, whose collection of social instances is structured like his collection of snuff-boxes. Fraser Leath (dead before the novel begins) had understood French manners, facts, and punctilious observances as if from a guide-book or a *catalogue raisonné*; but these, like the snuff-boxes, had little intrinsic relation to the totality of French life or his own. His outlook had been what Wharton had recognised in *Italian Backgrounds* as 'foreground' (*IB*177). Givré, Fraser Leath's beautiful chateau, has no hereditary connexion with him; it was the property of his French step-father, and came to him as his mother's heir. Even the shabbiness of certain rooms is a contrived, 'sought-for' effect engineered by Leath, ultimately unconvincing and immediately detected by an American visitor.

Fraser Leath is not alone: all the speaking parts in *The Reef* belong to Americans, acclimated Americans without countries of their own. Fraser Leath's mother, the American Mme de Chantelle, and her American son, are thoughtless social mimics; Anna Leath is a kind of quenched American spirit with a deep attachment to her French life; her stepson Owen Leath is raised in France but educated at Harvard, and given to identifiably American outbursts; George Darrow, a successful American diplomat in London and soon to become Anna's second husband, is about to take his next posting in South America; Sophy Viner is a floating young American woman adrift on the tide of opportunity, 'with the loose native quality strained through a closer woof of [European] manners...' (*R*12); a version of Mrs Boykin, Miss Adelaide Painter is a spinster from South Braintree, Mass., who has not been in America in 30 years, yet is 'protestingly and provisionally camped [in France] in a state of contemptuous protestation' (*R*157). '[She] might have left South Braintree yesterday', says Anna, 'if she hadn't, rather, brought it over with her in her trunk' (*R*157). Expatriate Americans, in other words, are capable of taking on extreme protective colouration to blend with their adopted nation, as Madame de Chantelle and her son – perhaps absurdly – do; of retaining an agreeable American freshness which is not offensive or unsympathetic to the host culture, as do Anna Leath, Sophy Viner, and Fanny Malrive; or of maintaining a comic and adamant foreignness which defies it, as in the case of Miss Painter or the Boykins. All these registers of expatriatism, however, imply a dialectical relation with the Old World: the quality of American behaviour overseas depends on the decision to embrace, reject, or honour at a distance the behaviour of the natives. Thus, Fanny Frisbee de Malrive is a perfect amalgam, an expatriate whose equipoise between the two cultures is both exact and wonderful, and ultimately self-damaging. She, and Sophy Viner after her, commute 'the showiest national attributes', 'the loose native quality', into something slightly enigmatic, hybridised by European influence, 'a closer woof of manners' (*R*12), 'finish, modelling' (*MT*35), restraint. Europe in some sense defaces and deforms these Americans, a transformation whose meaning is ambiguous: compared to other Americans in the novel, Fanny de Malrive is a miracle of grace and deportment; and Sophy Viner competes, as fresh-faced and blameless rival to Anna Leath, for our approval and sympathy. But both are crabbed and injured by their Europeanisation: 'feudal' French law leaves Fanny stranded by the cruel choice between her own freedom and possession of her child. Sophy, innocence and experience mixed, heroically exiles herself from hoped-for felicity – a very 'angular', but somewhat mysterious American decision – in renouncing both Owen Leath and George Darrow.[91] A true transient, she is last heard of in India in tow to a rich American woman, powerless, stateless. Wharton's Sophys, Fannys, Kates, and Ellens, all upright and admirable Americans, are alchemically altered by cultural immersion, and are finally women without countries of their own, internal exiles in their adopted worlds, forever unfitted for American residence. Americans who merely dally with Europe but are themselves impervious and impermeable – Undine, May, and the various socialites of *The Glimpses of the Moon* and *The Children* – are the moral equivalent of three-day tourists who do not catch the tremulous echoes disturbing the rich atmosphere of the Old World. Americans like Fanny and Ellen have descended into some underworld which will never relinquish them.

The greatest challenge of Wharton's French life was the development of *patrie*. She could not, it seems, write about French or European subjects; she retained distinctive American traits and never attempted to become French in the manner of Fanny de Malrive or of certain American *salon* hostesses; she never even relinquished American citizenship. It was the war, the huge crisis in the middle of her French years, which defined her relation to France.

Children of Flanders: how the war made Europe a real place

> '...writers have to have two countries, the one where they belong and the one in which they live really. The second one is romantic, it is separate from themselves, it is not real but it is really there'.[92]

In *The Metropolis*, Upton Sinclair's muckracking novel of 1908, we are shown a palatial country house in Long Island. Above gilded stucco garlands and Queen Anne gables rises an octagonal Norman tower; nearby is the dome of a Turkish mosque with a dove-cote on top, a Methodist steeple on the dove-cote, and a statue of Diana on the tip of the steeple. 'Has there ever been any *insanity* in the family?' a visitor asks.[93]

The madness of Gilded Age architecture, especially in the private residences of its New York millionaires, consisted of giddy agglomerations not very much less ridiculous than Sinclair's description. This accumulation, both of exterior and interior effects, seemed to Wharton and her contemporaries to reflect not only the remote relation of American money to European styles and epochs, but also the voracity of those who paid for it. Dreiser, Fitzgerald, Sinclair, and Tarkington (to name only a few) mimic the sheer appetite of buccaneer tycoons in catalogues and congeries of almost Whitmanian freedom and size. These commingled miscellanies seem to suggest the promiscuous and unreflecting taste of such men; Wharton herself succumbs to this particular form of analogical enactment when she loads *The Custom of the Country* with the plenitude of things which Undine notices and wants, and when she indulges in renditions of the vulgar interiors of Mrs Pulsifer in *Hudson River Bracketted* and Pauline Manford in *Twilight Sleep*. After all, the men who could compare railroads to Rembrandts and collect them with equal fury, whose cultural *reclame* consisted of the nostrum 'Buy May wheat. It'll beat art hollow'[94] were unlikely to obey any canon of architectural and decorative proprieties approved by Mrs Wharton.

Architectural order, presented in the serenity of consistent style, in the preservation of structural lines and features, and especially in the organic relation between use and decoration, between architecture and ornament, could never have interested buccaneer tastes whose principal ingredient was the speed at which taste had to be formed and the pace at which it had to be displayed, and whose requirement was that houses should shout at their viewers. In earlier novels – *The House of Mirth* and *The Custom of the Country* – but especially in the fiction of the twenties, Wharton pitches the aesthetic of architectural or domestic consistency against a threatening, competing aesthetic of accumulation. This encounter is a powerful index of crudity in her fiction; but it is nowhere more starkly invoked than in her war writing.

She identifies that competition in *The Custom of the Country*, suggesting in the language of architecture an index of moral character:

> What [was] called society was really just like the houses it lived in, a muddle of misapplied ornament over a thin steel shell of utility . . . the union between them was as monstrous and factitious, as unlike the gradual homogeneous growth which flowers into what other countries know as society, as that between the Blois gargoyles on Peter van Degen's roof and the skeleton walls supporting them. (*CC*44)

Peter van Degen is himself a gargoyle, 'sauroid', predatory and untrustworthy; if the van Degen house is guilty of being inauthentically built, it is only because the Blois allusions are not integral to van Degen or to twentieth-century America; his physical likeness to his architectural embellishments is anything but factitious. The Greiner house in *The House of Mirth* can claim no such unity: a complete farrago, it is unashamedly inauthentic, 'a complete architectural meal; if he had omitted a style his friends might have thought the money had given out' (*HM*257). This remark reflects a common sense that aesthetic chaos had arisen out of cultural chaos, the chaos Paul Bourget noticed in the amusingly indiscriminate use of adjectives in the lexicon of the American society girl.[95] Edgar Allan Poe in 1840 had assessed glitter, glare, glass, and gas as unmodulated, unnuanced, exhausting, 'huge and unmeaning', like the New York mansion of Senator Clark of Montana, whose sole virtue was that it could 'holler the loudest'.[96] It is an *unmeant* collection of detail, unmoored from tradition or social development, adrift of utility. [Plate 7b]

In what Wharton called 'Thermopylae[s] of bad taste',[97] such as the new Vanderbilt house in Newport and Senator William Clark's palace in Fifth Avenue, architectural and decorative badness is a condition she figures as semantic confusion, visual clutter, social disarray, even national catastrophe, symbolised in the battle in which the Spartans were trounced; and they were, conveniently, a kind of Greek whose name has become a byword for restraint. For Wharton, who likened her craft to masonry (*WF*117) – whose similitude of language and the built environment is obvious in *The Decoration of Houses*, where she declares that the elements of decoration must rhyme, and sort their features metrically – the destruction of *linguistic* order is akin to the assault of garish, functionless architecture on the eye: 'In America', she says, 'we preserve a few humble old buildings and try to copy them, but we trample on and destroy every hour of the day that magnificent house not built with hands, that temple of our race, the English tongue. The French [by contrast] respect both their houses and their speech.'[98] In *A Backward Glance* this link between language and architecture is made again: she gives equal attention to her early linguistic training and her domestic experience: the brownstone houses have their own decorative, idiomatic absurdities, to be sure, and certainly possess for her at times an unexampled monotony; yet, like an orderly lexical community, they are in some sense *meant*: they arise in their shape, colour, and grammar of ornament out of some tradition, out of 'gradual homogeneous growth' which is both legible and socially coherent, even if ultimately insignificant. As such, brownstones represent the Spartans of New York domestic architecture, the last failing stand against the epic Xerxes and his Persians in the persons of the Vanderbilts, the Belmonts, and the Bradley-Martins. Consequently, suffocation, muteness, and unmeant phatic utterance in the form of habitual exclamation are constant features of Wharton's fiction, the symptoms of unsettling or downright damaging sensibilities, usually those most likely to build monstrous houses.

But the depredations attending on the construction of the early-twentieth-century prodigy house nevertheless fill her with horror because they ruin longstanding architectural landscapes; on the New York scene the spoils of conquest, usually displayed indiscriminately, represent an incoherence which is akin to linguistic disruption and disablement. In *The Decoration of Houses* her opening theme is the disparagement of heterogenous and superficial ornament, of incongruous effects which only sever what should be the natural connexion between the interior and the exterior of a house. Again, the linguistic metaphor is implicitly invoked: decorative superfluity is the architectural equivalent of the sign unmoored from meaning, of a linguistic collapse in which the conventions of use are discarded in favour of a kind of surreal anarchy of expression. Her distrust of fashionable decoration is *always* couched in such linguistic terms: rooms and houses should *mean* what they are, rooms should have named and established uses. Libraries should not be garbled as drawing rooms and hallways; things which are called 'Marie Antoinette' or 'petite Trianon' should have more connexion with those styles than the gilt chairs which seem to suggest 'Frenchness' to the vulgar; she deplores the coy colour-onomastics of the modern 'artistic' decorator ('jonquil-yellow', 'shell-pink', 'ashes-of-roses' (*DH*32)); doorways should not be cluttered with *portières* which obscure the lines of the room; 'upholsterer' is a dirty word. Rooms should be honest: they should announce their structures, and structure should announce use. Wharton fears and detests occlusion, pretence, confusion, veiled effects, in architecture and in language, an attitude she disparages in her fiction, when absurd Old New York gangs up linguistically on things it doesn't like by hiding them in euphemism, or by refusing to name them at all.

If moral and social chaos are figured by Wharton in architectural senselessness, the Great War provided her with exact images of that unmeaning disarray. In an article in the New York *Sun* in the spring of 1915, based on her visits to the Devastated Regions of northeastern France, she describes the shattered landscapes and the wilful destruction of the retreating German army, who are cast in her general sense of the war's *dramatis personae* as the Persians, the destroyers of Frenchness.[99] If there are people in this landscape, they are not noticed: instead, the houses are the protagonists, slaughtered, mutilated architectural corpses lying splintered, fragmented, disembowelled.

> One searches in vain for any trace of furniture or domestic utensils. There is not a fragment of a chair or a bed, not a torn scrap of blanket or sheet or clothing. . . . Near each murdered house are ruined farming utensils, choked up wells and orchards with prostrate fruit trees. Trees there was no time to cut down have had the bark stripped off or a deep ring hacked into the trunks.[100]

In *Fighting France* she imagines the little church in Heiltz-le-Maurupt as 'so stripped and wounded and dishonoured that it lies there by the roadside like a human victim' (*FF*82); the streets are full, again, of 'murdered houses' (*FF*93). She was attempting, she said of *A Son at the Front*, 'a study of the world at the rear during a long war' (*BG*368). The 'rearview' is accomplished not in that novel, however, but in *Fighting France*.

She gets that view as she motors through resting columns of soldiers shining their boots and drinking tea by the roadside, and other glimpses not of the war itself, but of its social consequences. She is dumbfounded by a 'visible episode of the great subterranean struggle' (near Clermont-in-Argonne) (*FF*64), but the silence of Ypres ('we had seen no emptiness like this' (*FF*152)), the perfect order of an abandoned lace-making class in a convent, the pathetic war-memorial tended by a surviving priest in a razed village, these evidences of 'the motionless horror'[101] and the inexpressible 'sadness of all things'[102] practically defeat her powers of description. In the town of Cassel – not destroyed, but existing in a state of suspended animation within sight of Ypres and Dixmude – she finds 'a place so intensely itself that all analogies dropped out of mind' (*FF*145).

The image that haunts her especially is the vulnerability of the blown-up houses to voyeurism: everywhere she goes she can see inside them; their interiors are exposed to any passer-by. [Plate 8] It is a vulnerability especially horrifying to her: in *The Decoration of Houses* she insists that the door of a sitting room should never be on an axis with the desk or the hearth, the places where one might sit; rooms should spare their inhabitants the scrutiny of those passing the doorway. In *French Ways and their Meaning* she says:

> The world since 1914 has been like a house on fire. All the lodgers are on the stairs, in dishabille. Their doors are swinging wide, and one gets glimpses of their furniture, revelations of their habits, and whiffs of their cooking, that a lifetime of ordinary intercourse would not offer (*FW*v).[103]

In *Fighting France* she pities 'the poor little household gods [who] shiver and blink like owls ...' (*FF*153). The faces of buildings and towns have been shattered by the bombs (Ypres is 'a town without a profile' (*FF*151)), the sliced-off walls which reveal the separate storeys of the houses remind her of a stage-set (for farce), a set decorated with shreds of wallpaper, framed photographs and diplomas, icons, sofas, 'the poor frail web of things that had made up the lives of a vanished city-full' (*FF*154). Anthropologically, she expects to discover the key to these various expressions of social organisation (French ways, after all, *have* 'meaning'), but the houses seem to say to her 'use unknown'. The horror of war denies such order; Pont-a-Mousson, she reflects, 'is not at home to visitors' (*FF*111), a terrible inversion of the creaking Old New York locution: euphemism, like analogy, has perished along with populations, and householders are *literally* not there to receive guests. For Wharton, the overturning of domestic, agrarian order in acts of wanton destruction elicits her most powerful war-writing; there is nothing remotely like this intensity in *The Marne* or *A Son at the Front*.[104] To most the Great War turned the world upside down; to Wharton it must have seemed inside out. Inside-outness is only another form of unmeaning: the jumbled spoils of the buccaneer interior and its untethered exterior allusions are replicated in the spoliation, the publicised, gazed-upon domesticity of ordinary houses. The war – 'the greatest thing that life is likely to show'[105] – prompted her to epic and biblical language: it presaged the last trump, it was a dark angel of devastation and a Great Shadow, a process of cosmic ripening and rotting. Its victims became strangers in a strange land, and the conflict itself bore a Medusa-face. But the metamorphic images, the inside-outness of the domestic landscape in the Devastated Regions are far more powerful: grand allusions do far less work than her more homely sense of domestic disruption. From the woman whom a misplaced flower in an arrangement could distress, such disruption evokes her most remarkable analogies.

To organise her sense of the war and its meaning into something concrete, expressible, and personal, Wharton turned not to war novels – those would come later, and would not capture the same sense of spellbound horror – but to 'rear-view' activity which might offer coherence in the midst of disarray. She need not have visited the war-zone to see war: not even Big Bertha's shells, one of which fell on a nearby house in the Rue de Varenne, could move her as did the sight of the unemployed, the homeless, and later on, the sick and wounded in the streets of Paris. Her *ouvroirs* for Parisian seamstresses, her hostels for refugees, her orphanages for the Children of Flanders, and her tubercular hospitals all shared the principle of reconstituting home and community for those whose understanding of the world had always 'been measured by the shadow of their village steeple' (*FF*34). It is not within the scope of this discussion to dwell on Wharton's war charities in detail, themselves an epic undertaking.[106] It is, however, interesting to note that that charitable reconstitution for Wharton takes the form of domestic reconstruction, as if the tide of disruption, chaos, and discontinuity might be stemmed by shelter, work, lessons, suits of clothes, hot meals, and a restored sense of purpose. *Home*lessness, the personal analogy of statelessness, is for her the most terrible consequence of war. Re-homing the *sans foyers* was an obvious practical contribution to the war-effort, and has obvious symbolic resonance for this peerless home-maker on two continents who was herself in a sense homeless. But domestic restoration, the imposition of simple order and coherence onto the thousands of disrupted lives she assisted, was also a strike against the perceived German voracity, the military buccaneers. They destroyed landscapes, particularly civic and domestic ones, and left in their place an indiscriminate disorder of ruined buildings and ways of life, much as the buccaneer palace-builders had deformed Manhattan with their excesses, and the buccaneer expatriates had devoured or ridden roughshod over the old societies of Europe. In *Fighting France* Wharton records stumbling upon a monument on a hilltop near the Front commemorating the repulse of the Teutonic hordes by Jovinus in 362 (*FF*108), its modern symbolism too obvious to require explication, Wharton herself too overwhelmed by the conflict to bother with the obvious. Her silence on the subject of Jovinus is the silence of dead towns.

She supported her charitable enterprises by selling fiction and extracting large amounts of money from her friends in Europe and America. She converted much of this activity, moreover, into a kind of guidebook to war-riven France for a yet-univolved America: Mrs Wharton's War Charities had huge propaganda value, with facts and figures about the refugees, photographs of their lace-making *ouvroirs*, anecdotes about individuals,[107] even classic tourist 'work-displays' for influential persons, all produced to coax money and commitment from her fellow citizens. Wharton, in other words, was responsible to her adopted land, and paid back what she gained from it in a coin minted in her observation of French ways,[108] her experience of travel and tourism, her delight in and talent for perfecting the domestic machine. 'The fluffy fuzzy people'[109] of pre-war international Paris were driven away by the war, she noted, 'dead flies shaken down out of a summer hotel window curtain! We shall never lodge in *that* summer hotel again'.[110] In this wistful domestic metaphor, she distinguishes herself from the plundering, irresponsible, thrill-seeking expatriate American of her fiction, who regards the Old World as a playground, and, to her disgust, abandoned it to its fate when the war made pleasure inconvenient.

Wharton's war fiction has been excoriated and defended. At least one critic has proposed *A Son at the Front* (1923) as Wharton's modernist experiment;[111] another has suggested that her social satire could not function any longer in a world now too chaotic to admit classical satiric agency,[112] that she moved to 'tremolo'[113] productions during and after the war to engage sympathy for its victims. These are honourable but in some ways unnecessary explanations: nothing can excuse *The Marne* (1915), a dreadful little production, indefensible in literary terms – thin in style, careless of composition,[114] simplistically jingoistic, toe-curlingly sentimental and melodramatic, whose perpetual rendition of the pounding of soldierly hearts, the dashing away of patriotic tears, and the Blimpish-ness of American charity-workers is an insult to her readers and a blot on the rest of her writing. *A Son at the Front* is better: not a very good novel, though an interesting one, it attempts the 'rear-view' – the view of expatriate Americans in Paris – of the battles of the home front, battles as essential and as important as those of the Marne so audible in the city.

The war, it seemed to her, had burnt away all pettiness from the French character (*FF*15, 41); likewise it burnt away the softer Wharton, so that satire, whose viability Sinclair Lewis and Anita Loos among others had been gloriously demonstrating, was the mode Wharton returned to triumphantly in *The Children* and *Twilight Sleep*. Somehow, she could not translate the war itself into art; her failure in the two war-novels is eloquent testimony to war's effect on her: although *Summer*, one of her masterpieces, was written at the height of her involvement in war-relief, the catastrophic conflict effectively silenced her ability to make stories directly about it. An adequate fictional engagement with what the war had *meant* – to her and to civilisation – was not to appear until 1927, in *Twilight Sleep*.

In a letter of 1923 to Gaillard Lapsley, Wharton sent an article from the *Manchester Guardian* on the presentation of American domesticity in films. Among the anecdotes (for instance, that 'flowers are continually arriving in long boxes') she underlined: 'A good fifth of the American people . . . dwell constantly in . . . hotel lobbies.'[115] Films were reprodu-cing the intolerable publicity of war and wealth by expressing, in places of congress like hotel lobbies, the private experience of domestic life. In the vulgar glare and display of Fifth Avenue mansions, the pathetic exposure of bombed-out houses, 'the elliptical and metaphorical are going to be . . . as much of a "dead language" as English is rapidly becoming'.[116] The nuances of privacy and domesticity, their oblique social messages, are as doomed as those of language and of architecture and decoration. *Twilight Sleep* is the novel which replicates this sense of modern, war-induced gibberish and converts it into an equivalent mod-ernist image of social and domestic confusion.

This novel is her most extended engagement with modernist themes and styles. It generates a full-blown myth of America as Wharton con-ceived it by 1927 (by which point she had spent a total of three and a half weeks in America since 1911),[117] a daemonology of America manufactured from reading, anecdote, and newspaper articles, bizarre and essentially a caricature. It comprehended, says Percy Lubbock, 'the horrid details of the invasion of her own world – her droll and dear world that was perishing...under the trampling of strange new legions'.[118] This version of America Wharton *knew* to be outrageous; her satirical purpose adopts it as a sounding-board for her grievances against the modern world in general, and, moreover, as a replication of the confusion of war as she had experienced it. If *The Children*, written a decade after the end of the war, uses the fractured family as metaphor of that disruption, a secret anatomy of the varieties of penance which the war exacted from its victims, the America of *Twilight Sleep*, a year earlier, is less modulated; it is a fantasy whose implicit standard is embattled by the very narrative effect of the novel, which is deliberately unsettled, atomised, self-contradictory. Aldous Huxley congratulated Wharton on having, in *Twilight Sleep*, beaten him to the subject and atmosphere of *Brave New World* (1932), a compliment which pleased her enormously; Huxley recognised in this rendition of America a novel akin to the grim futuristic fantasies of the modernist writers and painters.

If any aspect of literary modernism dismayed Wharton, it was in the upsetting of narratorial point of view. The 'formless rush of sensation' of *Mrs Dalloway* is, she complains, inexplicably broached by the thoughts of a couple sitting on a park bench;[119] in *The Mother's Recompense* she practised an opposite craft, rigorously excluding the background on Lilla Gates which she had contemplated in a sketch for the novel, realising that Kate must *not* understand her niece, for the sake of psychological consistency.[120] But *Twilight Sleep* challenges narratorial control by choosing to linger on individuals who are essentially chaotic and not subject to conventions of narratorial omniscience.

In *A Son at the Front* the artist John Campton gazes at the view of wartime Paris through his studio window and thinks of a line from *Faust*: '"Take care! You've broken my beautiful world! There'll be splinters ..."' (*SF* 190). For Wharton, although she mourned 'the beautiful visible world (of man's making)',[121] the splinters were made of experience itself. *Twilight Sleep* is set in an incipient unreality: the title, a reference to a modish anaesthetic regime in childbirth, is a metaphor of the avoidance of reality practised by all the characters, a practice through which mothers are 'aimlessly kind and fathomlessly pure' (*TS* 5), in which 'bewildered and disenchanted' post-war youth finds the universal panacea in the latest dance-step, in which newborn babies are as efficiently produced and regulated as Ford motor-cars, where elaborate dinner-parties are expected to produce 'the flash of revelation for which the whole creation groaned' (*TS*323). Twilight sleep in childbirth is the induced, institutionalised form of forgetting which characterises all her post-war novels with contemporary settings. Dale M. Bauer has shown how current debates about the New Woman and eugenics inform *Twilight Sleep*, and she argues that the chaotic and anaesthetic features of the life depicted in it are Wharton's response to 'the contradictory nature of [the] choices offered to women'.[122] The reality is surely even simpler: *Twilight Sleep* is Wharton's rebuke to the nation that won the cruellest of wars without suffering. Forgetfulness is the only option for a triumphal America and her citizens who prefer not to remember what that war exacted from the rest of the world. This America – a clubwoman's New York rather than Old New York – is about to be bought out by Hollywood and its gauzy fantasies, a buy-out much less antagonistic to its essential spirit than the principal characters can admit.

One kind of avoidance is Pauline Manford's. She shields herself from reality with an impenetrable wall of engagements, plans, and projects geared to the perfection of existence. Manic forethought replaces spontaneity, emotional engagement, or the addressing of facts; money and words buy off or deny the existence of suffering. By contrast, other characters – Lita Wyant and Arthur Wyant – have no idea what time it is, and drift in alcohol and drug-induced suspension. Arthur belongs to the conquered aboriginal race of palaeo-New York, and his chivalrous solution to his daughter-in-law's infidelity is the duel; he talks incessantly but never takes action; he is written off as ineffectual against the twentieth century in which he is merely relict.[123] Lita, at the opposite extreme, is modernist, nihilist, an ethereal flapper who sleeps in the day and lives at night, who never knows what time it is because she can't imagine anything worth taking time *for*.

The novel trails a confused cloud of un-thought-out ideologies. Pauline's various regimes (eurhythmics, eastern mysticism, inspirational guidance, birth control, anti-wrinkle radium treatment), Lita's bizarre household of absurd minimalist decoration and 'jazz' tastes, Mrs Standish's cult of Nordic genius, are brilliant send-ups of topical American events and fads as Wharton perceived them from across the ocean, a *Babbitt*-esque portrait of the socially improving activities of the American New Woman. This welter of fads, cults, self-improvement treatments, and quasi-social programmes has a preposterous and ultimately exhausting quality not unlike Undine Spragg's world of *things*. A motor-manufacturing heiress, Pauline's life, apparently disciplined and organised as if on Taylorist or Fordist principles, is in fact inchoate: birth control and unfettered reproduction are somehow consonant in her mind (indeed, interchangeable, it transpires); a Swami, a Rabbi, a Cardinal, and a Bishop all together at one of her dinner parties are thought potentially capable of yielding a beautiful ecumenical *rapprochement*; her elaborate burglar alarm catches out Dexter, the master of the house, but is carefully disabled by a conspiracy of servants who do not 'see' the actual intruder. The profusion of detail which makes the tone of the novel so memorable is not matched in the Wharton canon except by *The Custom of the Country*. In the earlier novel, Undine's appetite, the successive rhythm of desire-fulfillment-dissatisfaction, is an analogy of its thematic rhythm: Undine's inclination is ever upward, or more-ward, and this must be fleshed out in depictions of *more*. *Twilight Sleep* offers a similar analogical relation between theme and texture, only this time there is nothing like 'rhythm' to sustain the plot. Instead, meaning and individual purpose are engulfed in the morass of available convictions and behaviours, and ceaseless activity becomes an essential distraction from cold reality. Pauline's rigorous exclusion of anything unpleasant from her thoughts includes personal betrayals by family members; the novel itself excludes the war by failing to admit it even in allusion.

Pauline's 'list', introduced in the novel's first page, is the objective correlative of this wilderness. She is 'martyrized' by her punishing schedule – a word which, along with 'regularize', 'Taylorize', 'slenderize', and 'Fletcherize' stands in the Whartonian lexis as the linguistic trace of crimes against reasonable comportment.[124] The comedy of the list's contiguous but unrelated appointments (Pauline's hair-waver and her psychoanalyst have equal purchase in it) becomes more suspect when, first, Pauline's daughter finds its rigid forward-planning unyielding even to filial need, and second, when we are told that a corresponding 'night-list' exists, a special framed tablet containing the next day's schedule on Pauline's bedside table for those uncomfortable nocturnal moments when she is alone with her thoughts. The list has its own life, and Pauline follows its Taylorized schedule because it is there to be followed; one of the entries on the list must surely be 'make new list', the rationale of the *mise en abyme*. And the list spawns its own culture: Pauline's first husband Arthur, a weekly item in it, is always referred to in it as 'A.', from which Pauline's children develop the nickname 'Exhibit A', reduced for most of the novel to 'Exhibit'; this semblance of affectionate family onomastics has its origin in Pauline's maniacal determination to do the right thing by her ex-husband, combined with her need to reduce the uncomfortable fact of her failed first marriage to a single-letter abbreviation. Arthur is *indeed* a specimen of Old New York, a survival, like the coelacanth, of almost unimaginable antiquity.

To more typical Wharton types (for Arthur Wyant is a Newland Archer double, Pauline Manford a female version of Elmer Moffatt) she adds a character from Beckett in the person of Lita, a creature with no known history who lives in a state of apparently permanent amnesia; and another from Greek tragedy in the shape of Pauline's nineteen-year-old daughter Nona. Caught in this web of vicious comedy, Nona is drifting, pessimistic, confused, unable to command the attention of her parents, in love with a married man, aware of the deteriorating marriage of her half-brother and Lita; she is conscientious and affectionate toward 'Exhibit A' and the family crises of servants; she dutifully keeps up with Lita in moving around aimlessly from Cubist Cabaret to private minstrel-show, always 'going somewhere else in order to do exactly the same thing' (*MR*102); she is given to grand gestures of self-denial. But, as with Martin Boyne in *The Children*, none of these actions has any consequence. A casualty of the fragmentation of modernist existence, Nona, the very person who is morally 'awake' and unforgetful in the novel, makes *Twilight Sleep* a satire with darker consequences than either *Glimpses* or *The Children*: the escalating pace and purposelessness of fashionable modern life culminates in attempted murder and in her accidental maiming while trying to forestall the incident. Nona is literally damaged by her mother's resolutely heedless world.

By the end of the novel it is not clear that Pauline accepts that her husband Dexter has been having an affair with Lita, that Arthur Wyant, Lita's father-in-law, has tried to end it by shooting Dexter but has wounded Nona instead, and that everyone, including the servants, collude in pretending to each other and to the police that the crime was committed by a burglar who escapes capture. Instead, she rushes off with her husband on a long international tour as soon as possible. In spite of Pauline's dauntless, aggressive optimism,

> somebody in every family had to remember now and then that such things as wickedness, suffering and death had not yet been banished from the earth; and with all those bright-complexioned white-haired mothers mailed in massage and optimism...perhaps their children had to serve as vicarious sacrifices. There were hours when Nona Manford, bewildered little Iphigenia, uneasily argued in this way.... (*TS*48)

This, as Wharton privately noted, is 'an Aeschylean tragedy without Aeschylean sanctions',[125] and Nona's final response to the disorganised, ecclectic world of enthusiasms which has generated near-tragedy is to wish for a world 'where nobody believes in anything' (*TS*373).

Critical consensus since the 1920s has more or less agreed that Wharton's finest works are elegiac: among her post-war fiction, *The Age of Innocence* and the Old New York novellas have – perhaps justly – elicited more admiration than works located in the American or expatriate-American present day. Such judgements have limited our perception of the very powerful experience of foreignness which is the subject of her other fiction, foreignness mediated through the estranging experience of Europe, of America itself, and – most profoundly – of the world war. In pre- and intra-war works like *The Custom of the Country*, *Ethan Frome*, and *Summer*, she attempts to perform acts of imaginative relocation (in the hard reality of rural New England or in the psyche of a female American buccaneer). Neither attempt is entirely authentic, brilliant as these works are. It was only after the engulfing and exacting experience of war in Europe that she could take, in *Fighting France*, *The Glimpses of the Moon*, *The Mother's Recompense*, *Twilight Sleep*, and *The Children*, the measure of her own modern age, her compatriots as they really were, and her two homelands (native and adopted). Only through the war's refracting and distorting lens could she produce a diagnosis of modernity which is harder, fiercer, sadder, and more open-ended than either her rural fables or her Old New York retrospectives. In the war and after, Edith Wharton joined the twentieth century.

Notes

Preface and Acknowledgements

1. Donnée Book (c. 1900), 39 (Yale).
2. E.W. to Robert Grant (25.vii.1900) (Yale).
3. E.W. to Sally Norton (24.ii.1902) (Yale).

Chapter 1 Tribes

1. Reminiscence of Edith Wharton (unpublished MS) (Yale), 2.
2. I have borrowed these expressions from Sylvia Adamson, 'The What of Language?' in *The State of the Language* ed. Christopher Ricks (London: Faber and Faber, 1990), 503–14.
3. For some useful reflections on this phenomenon, see Kenneth Burke's essay 'The Negative as a Marvel of Language' in *Language as Symbolic Action: Essays on Life, Literature and Method* (Berkeley: University of California Press, 1966), 419–25. See also Adamson, 509–10.
4. E.W. to A.H. Thorndike (18.xii.17) (Yale).
5. The widowed Mrs John Smith would only eventually style herself 'Mrs Mary Smith' after a suitable period of linguistic 'mourning', the alteration recognising her status of married singleness; a divorcée would immediately become 'Mrs Mary Smith'. The protean capability offered to someone like Mrs Ralph Marvell, who looks 'so unmarried' to French eyes, is encoded in her divorced title, 'Mrs Undine Marvell', a name she retains in widowhood. See Nancy Bentley's discussion of the American divorcée in *The Ethnography of Manners: Hawthorne, James, Wharton* (Cambridge: Cambridge University Press, 1995), 185–9. Wharton's own retention of 'Mrs Wharton' through marriage, divorce, and widowhood is an interesting parallel with Undine. Mrs Wharton would be horrified by 'Wharton', the mode to which I am reluctantly compelled by modern academic fashion.
6. E.W. to Edward Sheldon (6.v.24) (Yale).
7. Lloyd Morris, *Incredible New York: High Life and Low Life of the Last Hundred Years* (New York: Random House, 1951), 153–4. For a fascinating *précis* of American card-leaving protocol, see Kenneth L. Ames, *Death in the Dining Room and Other Tales of Victorian Culture* (Philadelphia: Temple University Press, 1992), 35–43.
8. Leonore Davidoff, *The Best Circles: Society Etiquette and the Season* (London: Croom Helm, 1973), 42–3.
9. The Mingott–Welland-Dallas/Beaufort family tree might be rendered as follows:

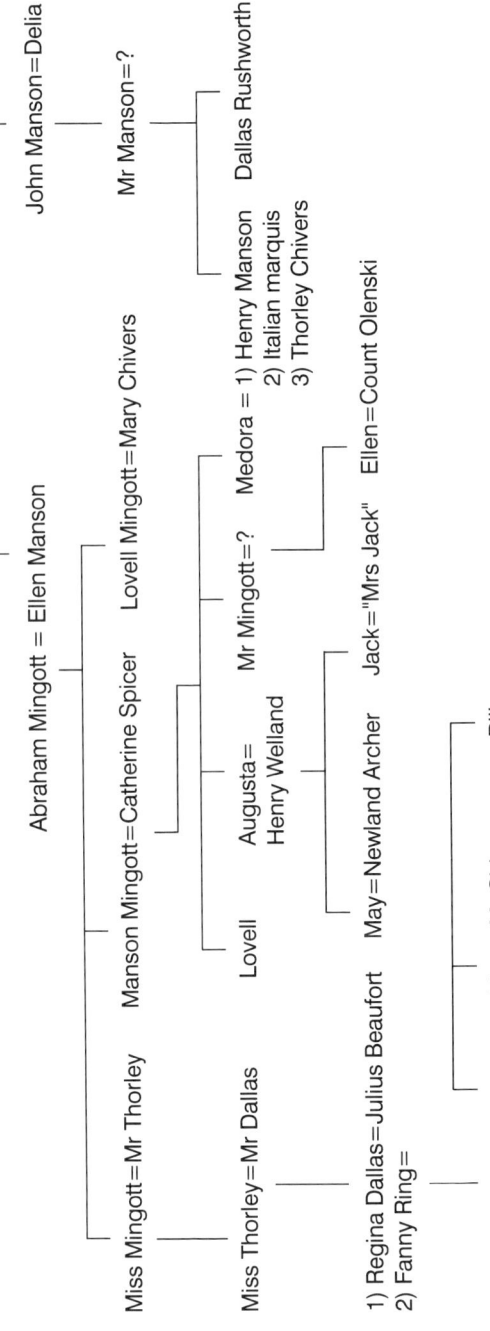

*See various remarks in The Age of Innocence, and 'Notes & Subjects I' (Yale) for Wharton's own attempts at this genealogy. The relationship of Medora Manson is not entirely clear. She is either a daughter of Mrs Manson Mingott, and therefore the aunt of May and Ellen; or she is Mrs Manson Mingott's first cousin by marriage, the widow of Manson Mingott's uncle John Manson's son. I have preferred the former solution because it explains Ellen's habit of calling Medora 'Aunt'.

10. The *Ladies' Home Journal* rejected *The Old Maid* as too 'vigorous' for their readership (Benstock, 363). The *Woman's Home Companion* worried that the elopement in *The Buccaneers* would be 'difficult' for their conservative readers (Benstock, 442); *Summer* aroused 'puritanical' recoil in parts of the American literary press (Lewis, 398).

11. The old Academy of Music, with 18 boxes, was superseded by the new Metropolitan Opera House, with 118. The Met was built with the backing of Mrs W.K. Vanderbilt and other new-rich social titans. Within two years of its opening in 1883, its competition closed the Academy (see Morris, 191).

12. Dio Lewis, *Our Girls* (New York: Harper and Brothers, Publishers, 1871), 211.

13. Although I disagree with his conclusion, James W. Gargano interestingly reads Newland's search for freedom as 'a Faustian impulse to ignore the humane values that underlie responsible social intercourse' ('Tableaux of Renunciation: Wharton's Use of *The Shaugraun* in *The Age of Innocence*' *Studies in American Fiction* 15 (Spring, 1987), 2). Commitment to May, I suggest in Chapter 3, is rather a validation of irresponsible – unhealthful – fetishising of female innocence.

14. Stages and theatrical situations are a favourite Whartonian trope: they occur with special significance in *The House of Mirth*, *The Reef*, *The Custom of the Country*, *Summer*, *The Marne* and *The Age of Innocence*.

15. Catharine H. Waterman, *Flora's Lexicon: an Interpretation of the Language of Sentiment* (Boston: Crosby, Nichols, Lee & Co., 1861), 125.

16. S.C. Edgarton, *The Flower Vase; containing the Language of Flowers and their Poetic Sentiments* (Lowell, Mass.: Merrill and Heywood, 1847), 91. Wharton may only require a white flower for May at this point, but she is too astute a recollector of her native culture not to remember the popularity of flower-languages. The violets which May carries at other times represent, variously, 'faithfulness' and 'modesty'; the violet is a flower which 'retains the bashful timidity of the nymph' (Waterman, 216). Yellow roses, Newland's gift to Olenska, represent infidelity in love and friendship. 'This scentless flower, which profits neither by attention nor liberty, seems only to prosper when under restraint.' (Waterman, 179). On the semantics of phyllanthography, see Jack Goody, *The Culture of Flowers* (Cambridge, Cambridge University Press, 1993).

17. Cynthia Griffin Wolff, however, reads this as May's (and therefore Old New York's) deep and generous intuition (*A Feast of Words: The Triumph of Edith Wharton* (second, revised, edition) (Reading, Mass.: Addison-Wesley Publishing Company, 1995), 313–17.

18. 'Visibility in Fiction' (1929) in *Edith Wharton: The Uncollected Critical Writings* (Princeton: Princeton University Press, 1996), 164–5.

19. 'A totem', Freud says, quoting Frazer, 'is a class of material objects which a savage regards with superstitious respect, believing that there exists between him and every member of the class an intimate and altogether special relation.' (*Totem and Taboo* in *The Complete Psychological Works of Sigmund Freud* vol. 13 (London: Hogarth Press, 1955), 103) I use this word somewhat generously: Freud specifies totems as animals or objects rather than persons, but the bloodless, almost mummified quality of the van der Luydens seems to place them within this domain; in every other particular (the awed respect of the Archers, the endogamous connexion between the van der

Luydens and the Archers and presumably with most other members of the tribe) they satisfy the conditions of totemhood.

20. Bernard Berenson was troubled by Wharton's onomastics in *The Custom of the Country*, which he considered extreme; but she was able to cite 'two "actualities"' who occur to me instantly': Lurline Spreckels and Florida Yurlee. 'As for similar instances, the 'Herald' register will give you a dozen any morning'. (Lewis, 349). Wharton's notebooks contain many lists of names, some gathered, some invented. 'Blondelle Malone' caught her eye in the 1910–14 period; in 1918–23, names for a 'Boston novel' have generic predictability, as do those in a list for *The Age of Innocence*; and 'Themistocles Apotheosis' and 'Carmelita Ring' are proposed for a story called 'The Cadums' Governess'.

21. This anecdote is described but unattributed by Lewis, 12.

22. Mrs William Astor eventually prevailed (Morris, 155).

23. E.W. to Eunice Maynard (3.iii.09) (Yale).

24. Gargano points out that no such stage direction exists in the text of the play (Gargano, 10); however, the production at Wallack's Wharton remembered is commemorated in a photograph of the episode (see Plate 2).

25. Henry James, *The Europeans* ed. Tony Tanner (Harmondsworth: Penguin Books, 1985), 79.

26. To appreciate Wharton's structural mastery in this opera scene, with its restrained and delicate implications, it should be compared to the opening *Faust* scene in Frank Norris's *The Pit* (1902). Norris uses the melodrama of 'grand opera' to open up Laura Dearborn's responsive character; but it could be any theatrical event, any public occasion. There is no integration of situation, repertoire, and point of view, and the narratorial control of the scene is merely procedural; the cool detachment of Wharton as a controlling lens is nowhere to be found.

27. This was also Mrs Astor's practice on the third Monday of every January, before her ball (Morris, 146). Thorstein Veblen would classify such behaviour as the '*performance* of leisure'.

28. Alexis de Tocqueville, *Democracy in America* (1835,1840), 2 vols, trans. Henry Reeve, intro. Daniel C. Gilman (New York: Century Co., 1898), II, 264.

29. Mrs Trollope's unequivocal design is to discourage 'the wild scheme of placing all the power of the State in the hands of the populace'. ('Preface to the First Edition', *Domestic Manners of the Americans* (1832) ed. Richard Mullen (Oxford: Oxford University Press, 1984), xxxiii.

30. The tradition appears as early as Crèvecœur, whose *Letters of an American Farmer* (1782) investigates such problems as 'what is America like?' and 'what is an American?'

31. See also Julian Street (an American) in *Abroad at Home* (1915), for additional observational essays.

32. See Gertrude Himmelfarb, *Darwin and the Darwinian Revolution* (New York: W.W. Norton & Co., Inc, 1959), 412. An extended discussion Wharton's use of Darwinian theory appears in Chapter 2.

33. Sandra H. Gilbert and Susan Gubar think she must have done ('Angel of Devastation: Edith Wharton on the Arts of the Enslaved' in *No Man's Land: The Place of the Woman Writer in the Twentieth Century*, II (New Haven: Yale University Press, 1984), 130). 'Sociologists without a drop of American blood in them', Wharton writes, 'have been the first to recognise what the traditions

of three centuries have contributed to the moral wealth of our country' (*BG*5).

34. Thorstein Veblen, *The Theory of the Leisure Class* (1899) intro. J.K. Galbraith (Boston: Houghton Mifflin Co., 1973), 48.

35. 'Remedial Exchanges' in *Relations in Public: Microstudies of the Public Order* (London: Allen Lane, 1971), 38.

36. See Wolff on oppression and inarticulacy, 25–6. The muteness of animals seems to have had a special horror for Wharton (see my discussion in Chapter 2).

37. See Nancy Bentley, '"Hunting for the Real": Wharton and the Science of Manners' in *The Cambridge Companion to Edith Wharton*, ed. Millicent Bell (Cambridge: Cambridge University Press, 1995), 55–7.

38. Wolff, 323–5.

39. Lewis, 8; Veblen, 51.

40. Lewis, 13.

41. de Tocqueville, II, 264.

42. Lewis H. Lapham, *Money and Class in America: notes and observations on our civil religion* (New York: Weidenfeld and Nicholson, 1988), 4; Paul Fussell, *Class: Style and Status in the USA* (London: Arrow Books, Ltd., 1984), 15; see also Richard P. Coleman and Lee Rainwater, *Social Standing in America: New Dimensions of Class* (New York: Basic Books, 1978), 18–19.

43. McAllister may be a model for Sillerton Jackson (Morris, 144). Wharton is essentially kindly to this elderly male snob whose chief qualification is having been made much of at the Tuilleries in the 1840s.

44. de Tocqueville, 213–14.

45. Wharton must have been thinking of her young collaborator on *The Decoration of Houses*, Ogden Codman, and of her niece Beatrix Jones Farrand, the well-known landscape architect.

46. Newland reflects: 'He had done little in public life, and would always be by nature a contemplative and a dilettante; but he had had high things to contemplate, great things to delight in; and one great man's friendship to be his strength and pride'(*AI*346). The sudden access of Teddy Roosevelt in the novel is too fulsome to be comfortable. Wharton knew Roosevelt well, but the recollected scene of the former governor of New York and future President of the United States banging his fist on the table as he tries to persuade Newland Archer to enter public life is strained: Newland has never shown the least inclination for any such connexion beyond the obligatory charitable behaviour and committee-work, any more than Wharton herself had for complex political assessments. This final note in *The Age of Innocence* is one of her few errors of fictional judgement.

47. James, *The Europeans*, 193.

48. The governess was Anna Bahlmann; the friend, Emelyn Washburn, the daughter of the Jones's rector.

49. Martha Louise Rayne, *What Can a Woman Do?* (Petersburgh, NY: Eagle Publishing Co., 1893), 34.

50. Rayne, 462.

51. Alcott's Jo and Christy marry late; and Christy is quickly widowed. Jo writes for her living (although only after she abandons her hearty adventure-romances for the sentimental 'In the Garret', a poem presumably in theme

a lot like *Little Women*); Christy finally becomes a labour activist on behalf of women workers, using her oratorical skills to galvanise her audiences.

52. David B. Lynn, *Daughters and Parents, Past, Present and Future* (Monterey, California: Brooks/Cole Publishing Co., 1979), 54.
53. Deborah Gorham, *The Victorian Girl and the Feminine Ideal* (London: Croom Helm, 1982), 103.
54. Exceptions to this rule in the Wharton canon are Grace Fulmer and Anne Clephane of *The Glimpses of the Moon* and *The Mother's Recompense*. Grace is a violinist, but excused by the fact of her bohemian marriage to an artist. Anne Clephane has used her wealth and her opportunities to study painting; but she is also notably unlike the typical young woman of her set in most other ways. Both novels, being set in the 1920s, acknowledge the change in women's roles, post-war and post-franchise.
55. Lady Grenville, *The Gentlewoman in Society* (London: Henry and Co., 1892), 28.
56. Mrs John King van Rensselaer, *Newport, Our Social Capital* (Philadelphia: Lippincott, 1905).
57. F. Scott Fitzgerald, *The Great Gatsby* (1926) ed. Tony Tanner (Harmondsworth: Penguin Books, 1990), 22.
58. Louis Auchincloss, *Pioneers and Caretakers: A Study of Nine American Women* (Minneapolis: University of Minnesota Press, 1961), 3.
59. Mrs John King van Rensselaer, *The Social Ladder* (New York: Henry Holt & Co., 1924), 16–17.
60. Veblen, 359.
61. Robert Frost 'Desert Places' (*The Collected Poetry of Robert Frost* (London: Jonathan Cape, 1977), 296).
62. Herman Melville, *Moby-Dick, or the Whale* ed. Charles Feidelson, Jr. (Indianapolis: Bobbs-Merrill, 1964), 254–5. See also Stevens's 'white of an aging afternoon' in 'The Auroras of Autumn' (*The Collected Poems of Wallace Stevens* (New York: Alfred A. Knopf, 1981), 411–21.
63. Paul Bourget, *Outre-Mer: Impressions of America* (London, T. Fisher Unwin, 1895), 92.
64. Wolff, 315, observes that Diana is the deity of childbirth and fertility; but although Diana's virginity is being invoked by the often deluded Newland, he is surely (for once) apt: May and the other white-clad archers at Beaufort's competition allude to the divine huntress and virgin, not to reproduction; this is in direct contrast to the disturbingly frank sexuality of Olenska, who wears a low-cut dress without the modesty of a tucker, and displays troubling expanses of bare arm. It is May who circumlocutes in the scene in which her pregnancy is revealed, whereas Olenska asks Newland 'Shall I – once only come to you; and then go home?'(*AI*312), which makes the blood rush to his head.
65. Bourget, 69.
66. See Bentley, *Ethnography* (169–71) on wax-works, and my discussion in Chapter Two of Enid Drover in *The Mother's Recompense*.
67. Bourget, 87.
68. Gilbert and Gubar, 147.
69. It is important to note that Wharton and James were Whitman's devoted admirers. Wharton borrowed the title of her autobiography from his

'a backward glance o'er travell'd roads', and read him eagerly all her life in the original, in translation, and as the subject of biography; he appeared early in a list of her favourite books (Lewis, 86). Henry James declaimed poems from *Leaves of Grass* on the terrace of the Mount one autumn evening, out of which came the mutual discovery that he and Wharton held Whitman supreme among American poets (*BG*185–6). Kenneth Clark says that Wharton too loved to read Whitman aloud at I Tatti, and that she claimed to have been taught to do it by James (Kenneth Clark, *Another Part of the Woods: A Self-Portrait* (New York: Harper and Row, 1974), 204).

70. Lilla Gates in *The Mother's Recompense* is a related 'blank' character.
71. In Martin Scorsese's 1993 film of the novel, Olenska's strangeness is neatly encapsulated in a visual gag in which Archer studies a painting on the wall of her drawing room. The camera pans for several breathless seconds across what turns out to be an immensely long post-impressionist canvas. In *A Further Glance* Wharton describes the effect of her own decorating schemes on more traditional sensibilities: 'I remember that one of the many things I did which shocked & pained my mother-in-law not the least was the elimination in our house in the country of all the lace and dotted muslin draperies which should have intervened between ourselves & the robins on the lawn.' (*FG*9–11). Edith Wharton's first literary endeavour was an influential little book called *The Decoration of Houses*, which espoused a style utterly distinct from the fussy, overdraped taste of her mother and of Old New York. Her taste was not Olenska's, by any means, but it was similarly daring.
72. Olenska proposes to divorce Olenski. Divorce made a woman, whether its instigator or not, a social pariah until the 1870s, and socially suspect until the outbreak of the war (van Rensselaer, *Social Ladder*, 49).
73. The effort of trying herself to become this vacant being may have induced some kind of collapse in Wharton. Something happened to her in 1898; whether it was a physical or a mental breakdown is much debated. The nature of Wharton's psychological and physiological ailments is hard to pin down. What Lewis categorically states to have been a psychological crisis requiring the stringent Weir Mitchell treatment (Lewis, 82–4) is contradicted by Shari Benstock, who finds only evidence of persistent bouts of bronchial and sinus infection (Benstock, 93–7). There is little point in quibbling, however, since, whether she officially recognised a nervous complaint with an authentic rest-cure, it seems certain from Benstock's exhaustive documentation of her various recurrent maladies that many were psychosomatic, brought on by stress. Earlier in her life, that stress was probably emotional; later it seems more likely to have been the consequence of overwork and exhaustion.
74. During and after the war, of course, her charities and her domestic arrangements (including the pensioning of elderly servants) necessitated a large and steady income.
75. van Rensselaer, *Social Ladder*, 128.
76. The author of 'The Culprit-Fay' is Joseph Drake, whose poem is a narrative fantasy of the mid-century about fairies.
77. Morris, 151.
78. Pauline is like Jay Gatsby, whose authentic library of real books is at odds with his general inauthenticity. His books, like hers, are unread (the pages

are uncut). (*The Great Gatsby*, 47). By the mid-twenties the realness of libraries is not taken for granted either by Fitzgerald or Wharton.

79. On the intrusion into the Trenor library, see Judith Fryer, *Felicitous Space: the
Imaginative Structures of Edith Wharton and Willa Cather* (Chapel Hill: University of North Carolina Press, 1986), 84.

80. See Fryer 120–1, for a discussion of Eastlake's principle of simplicity as moral
superiority in art and design.

81. Candace Waid says both these works were Wharton's own (*Edith Wharton's
Letters from the Underworld: Fictions of Women and Writing* (Chapel Hill: University of North Carolina Press, 1991), 130). Wharton did leave notes for an
essay on Whitman as rhythmist and sound-artist (Yale). The languishing
long poem is the sort of thing Wharton herself might have attempted and
abandoned. She wrote dramatic monologues by characters from the *Oresteia*
(Yale), and published a blank-verse poem on the Renaissance anatomist
Vesalius in 1902 ('which has made me want to hide under the furniture ever
since I've seen it in print.' (Lewis, 113)).

82. This is probably a reference to J.P. Morgan's library annexe in a forbidding
building on Madison Avenue.

83. The tale is based on the experience of James Jackson Jarves, who bought
Italian Primitives before the Civil War, only to find them unwanted and
ignored in New York. This collection eventually went to Yale (Morris, 161).

84. George Templeton Strong, 'Diary' in *The Hone and Strong Diaries of Old Manhattan* ed. Louis Auchincloss (New York: Abbeville Press, 1989), 158. Lewis
Jones was one of Wharton's forebears of her grandfather's generation.

85. Elizabeth Fries Ellet, *The Court Circles of the Republic or the Beauties and Celebrities of the Nation* (Hartford: Hartford Publishing Company, 1869), 585.

86. James to E.W. (17.viii.1902) (Yale).

87. Burton Rascoe, 'An Entomologist of Society' [review of *The Glimpses of the
Moon*] New York *Tribune*, 23 July 1922, reprinted in *Edith Wharton: the Con-
temporary Reviews* eds James W. Tuttleton, Kristin O. Lauer, and Margaret P.
Murray (Cambridge: Cambridge University Press, 1992), 310–12.

88. Her fictions *not* set within this world are not tribal. She cannot, or does not
attempt to, delineate the sort of sociological categories and behaviours of Starkfield and North Dormer because she has only imagined them from the outside
(probably during motor-trips around Lenox). The Spragg family and the recol-
lections of Moffatt's exploits in Apex are exaggerated for satirical effect.

Chapter 2   Outcasts

1. Edith Wharton, introduction to *The House of Mirth* (Oxford, 1935) (in galley
proofs, Yale).

2. Walter Berry to E.W. (28.xi.1900) (Yale), of T.H. Huxley.

3. The Trenors belong to an old Dutch family, but the only evidence of this
is the library of their Hudson River 'manor-house', Bellomont, which is the
only remaining part of the original house. Although it contains family portraits
and family books, the present Trenors have made 'no perceptible additions'
to these, and the library is relegated to the status of secluded meeting-place
for guests. There is little sense of continuity between Trenors past and present.

4. Gillian Beer, *Darwin's Plots: Evolutionary Narrative in Darwin, George Eliot and Nineteenth-Century Fiction* (London and Boston: Ark Paperbacks, 1985) (1st edn 1983), 14.

5. Veblen, 45.

6. Rosedale is seen playing with Carry Fisher's child, a behaviour which surprises Lily as uncharacteristic of his type.

7. Wharton, introduction to *The House of Mirth* (Yale).

8. Janet Flanner, 'New York Letter', *New Yorker* 2 March, 1929 (Yale).

9. Donald Pizer observes that Nettie seems like a refugee from some other novel, a realist one ('The Naturalism of Edith Wharton's *The House of Mirth*' (*Twentieth Century Literature* 41 (1995), 243).

10. The novel ends with a meditation on the *mycteroperca bonaci*, a fish with 'an almost unbelievable power of simulation . . . power to deceive'. Like the unscrupulous predator in the animal kingdom, or its counterpart in the social arena of New York, the financier is 'concerned only to see what was of vast advantage to him' (*The Financier* (1912) (New York: New American Library, 1967), 78).

11. Wharton was fairly sceptical of the ability of most critics. 'American and English reviewers of fiction are so disinclined to recognize that novels may be written from a dozen different standpoints, and that the "heart-interest" need not always predominate'. (E.W. to Sally Norton (24.ii.02) (Yale).) It is surprising how late in the century critics were still taking Wharton to task for being hard and 'unfeminine'. *Ethan Frome* is marred, thought the *Saturday Review*, by 'the mere craving for . . . exaggerated terror'; *The Bookman* called it, and her, 'relentless' and 'remorseless'; she was deemed 'subhuman' in *Summer* by *The New Republic*. 'She watches the movements of the insects and records them minutely, accurately and dispassionately, with a sort of scientific interest'. (Tuttleton *et al.*, 311.)

12. If this was an accusation levelled against Wharton by her critics (see previous note), Gerty Farish silently convicts Lily Bart of experimenting with people's lives, of being unconnected to the specimens under her gaze (*HM* 262).

13. R. Harré, 'The Evolutionary Analogy in Social Explanation', in *The Philosophy of Evolution*, eds U.J. Jensen and R. Harré (New York: St. Martin's Press, 1981), 164.

14. Sally Norton, reminiscence of Edith Wharton (unpublished MS, Yale).

15. Of Huxley's many works it is difficult to guess which she might have read, but obvious ones would have been *The Advancement of Science in the Last Half-Century* (1887); *American Addresses* (1877) (three lectures on evolution); and *Darwiniana* (1893). She knew Wallace's *Darwin and Darwinism* (1889). Spencer's blend of biology, sociology, ethics, and psychology are clear influences on much of her writing; the *Works* was published in 1897. Romanes was an evolutionist and zoologist (*Darwin and After Darwin* (1892–5); *Mental Evolution in Animals* (1883); *Mental Evolution in Man* (1888)). Von Haeckel's popular work *The Evolution of Man* (1896) was her source for ideas about amphioxus.

16. Walter Berry to E.W. (23.v.1900) (Yale), and Walter Berry to E.W. (22.xi.1900) (Yale).

17. Augustin St Hilaire (1769–1853) was a botanist and explorer of the South American interior. Baron Georges Cuvier (1769–1832) was an animal taxon-

omist and comparative anatomist whose great work was *The Animal King-dom* (1827–32). H.G. Wells wrote many popular books on science (Wharton was later to meet Wells).

18. Edvard Westermarck's *A History of Human Marriage* (1889) may also have interested her. The physical anthropologist Paul Topinard's most important book was *Anthropology* (1876).

19. Walter Berry to E.W. in Lenox (24.x.1900) (Yale). The poem was not, apparently, written. Egerton Winthrop sent her (rather patronising) instructions about reading such work ('Darwinism, etc. Suggestions') which include the following: 'Learn a few definitions, like that of evolution for instance "by heart", – while your hair is being done!' (quoted in Price, *The End of the Age of Innocence: Edith Wharton and the First World War* (London: Robert Hale, 1996), 90).

20. He was, she said, writing a book called *The Origin of Life*, but the book was published as *The Physical Conditions of Life* (1908).

21. It was this book that made Teddy ask '"Does that sort of thing really amuse you?"', at which point 'I heard the key turn in my prison-lock'. (Quoted in Benstock, 186).

22. E.W. to Daisy Chanler (25.iii.32) (Yale). Her reading is reported in *A Backward Glance*, 94; and discussed in Lewis's biography, 56–7. See also James W. Tuttleton, 'Edith Wharton: The Archeological Motive', *Yale Review* 61 (1971–2), 562–74. It is likely that she read Malinowski in the 1920s, well before Huxley introduced her to him.

23. She had been reading Haeckel's chapter, 'The Structure of the Body of the Amphioxus and of the Ascidian' in *The Evolution of Man* (1896).

24. Haeckel, 462.

25. In the 'Quaderno dello Studente' [notebook] (begun 1924) (Yale), no page-number or date.

26. *Life and I* (undated, probably 1920s), 22 (Yale).

27. E.W. to Walter Berry (24.x.1900) (Yale).

28. On the subject of social debt, see Wai-Chee Dimock, 'Debasing Exchange: Edith Wharton's *The House of Mirth*', *PMLA* 100 (October, 1985), 783–92.

29. This relationship with early-twentieth century money-novels is discussed more fully in Chapter 3.

30. Dreiser, *The Financier*, 8.

31. Undine possesses this capability in its most fully developed form.

32. De Tocqueville notes that American women never acknowledge the polite attentions of men; they expect them to be rendered. (Cited by Christopher Mulvey, *Transatlantic Manners: Social Patterns in Nineteenth-century Anglo-American Travel Literature* (Cambridge: Cambridge University Press, 1990), 71).

33. Waid, especially Chapter 1, 'Women and Letters', 15–49.

34. It has a fanlight, pilasters, wooden mantels with 'neat classic ornaments', and plaster mouldings on the ceilings (S183).

35. E.W. to Daisy Chanler (27.xi.1930) (Yale).

36. E.W. to Minnie Jones (5.iii.1925) (Yale). In the event she chose 'his ancestral estate in Kansas' ('Velvet Earpads' (*CSS*, II, 481)).

37. See the discussion of western place-names in Chapter 3.

38. The modern Grand Central terminal was being planned as Wharton was writing *The House of Mirth*. The old Grand Central Station, on the same site,

was nevertheless a huge structure, with platforms 530 feet long and a glass roof 60 feet high.

39. In the moments after the Bry *tableau* Lily greets her admirers as they flock from the ballroom into an empty drawing-room, again stemming the flow of 'lesser' mortals. When Selden joins her, the two of them walk 'against the tide' of guests toward the conservatory; 'the faces about her flowed like the streaming images of sleep' (*HM* 220–1). Not to bend with the tide, but to impede it, or even to go against it, is here an image (perhaps the only one of the novel) of Lily's momentary power; it alludes, however, to the drifting and broken reed she will shortly become.

40. This bow-window bronze was one of Wharton's 'données' for the novel from about 1900 ('Donnée Book' (Yale), 125).

41. From notes for 'A Moment's Ornament', *Donnée Book*, 79 (Yale). Compare this to final version (*HM* 516).

42. Gaston Bachelard, *The Poetics of Space* (1958) trans. Maria Jolas, intro. John R. Stilgoe (reprinted Boston: Beacon Press 1994), 86.

43. That it is Selden, the amphioxus of the novel, who points this out to Lily is mildly ironic.

44. Erving Goffman, *Stigma: Notes on the Management of Spoiled Identity* (New York: Simon and Schuster, Inc., 1963), 1.

45. Wolff contends that the narrator's story of Ethan Frome is in fact a fantasy and unreliable (Wolff, 172–4).

46. Wolff, 168–70.

47. Robert Frost, *Complete Poems* (New York: Henry Holt & Co., 1949), 173.

48. In *Eumenides*, of course, Clytemnestra is condemned for the murder of Agamemnon; Orestes is acquitted for killing Clytemnestra.

49. Henry James, *The Europeans*, 193.

50. E.W. to Minnie Jones (25.i.19) (Yale).

51. E.W. to Gaillard Lapsley (4.ii.28) (Yale).

52. 'Autre Temps', 258.

53. E.W. to Daisy Chanler (27.vi.29) (Yale).

54. The snobbish Mr Raycie in *False Dawn* is described as a well-kept agricultural estate (*FD* 11).

55. Goffman, *Stigma*, 3.

56. Goffman, *Stigma*, 28.

57. Frazer, *The Golden Bough* ed. Theodor H. Gastor (New York: New American Library, 1959), 615.

58. The phrase 'the house of mirth' was current in 1905 as the press's buzz-word describing the Equitable Life Assurance Scandal of that year, a scandal that threatened the stability of the American financial system (see Wayne Westbrook, *Wall Street in the American Novel* (New York: New York University Press, 1980, 137–8)).

59. Clark, 203.

Chapter 3   Buccaneers

1. Veblen, 29.

2. '"What's in a name?" Sometimes nothing; sometimes a whole biography.' Henry Fuller, author of another money-novel, *The Cliff-Dwellers* (1893), gives

the onomastic biography which parallels the curious career of Miss Ann Wilde: she moves through Annie (at fourteen), Annette, Anne, Anna, and finally Ann (at an unmarried thirty-five), each name portending her self-image of the moment (Henry Fuller, *The Cliff-Dwellers* (New York: Harper and Brothers, Publishers, 1893), 15–16).

3. To the learned it may recall a Shakespearean adjective meaning 'clever', or an eighteenth century word for 'lively young man' (*SOED*: sprag (a.); sprag, sb. 1.). This meaning is as unlikely to have occurred to Wharton as Montaigne's *ondoyante* to Mr and Mrs Spragg.

4. See Thomas L. McHaney, 'Fouqué's *Undine* and Edith Wharton's *The Custom of the Country*', *Revue de Littérature Comparée* 45 (1971), 180–6. In the folktale, the undine is markedly unlike her foster parents, a detail Wharton may have had in mind in depicting Mr and Mrs Spragg.

5. *Certes c'est un sujet extraordinairement vain, divers et ondoyant, que l'homme'* is from Montaigne's essay '*Par divers moyons on arrive á pareille fin*', on the theme of unpredictable and erratic behaviour. Walter Berry had urged Wharton in these terms much earlier, in 1899: 'You have reached a point where you can be "ondoyante et diverse"' (Walter Berry to E.W. (27.xii.1899) (Yale)). The likeness between Undine and her maker is hinted at even here.

6. For the accounts of the historical financiers, see Matthew Josephson's somewhat polemical but hugely readable classic *The Robber Barons: The Great American Capitalists, 1861–1901*, second edition (New York: Harcourt, Brace and World, Inc., 1962) (1st edn, 1934). Charles Francis Adams and Henry Adams' *Chapters of Erie* (1886) and Thomas William Lawson's *Frenzied Finance: The Crime of Amalgamated* (1906) offer first-hand accounts of derring-do and criminal behaviour among the post-Civil War financiers.

7. Mark Schorer finds this beautifully apt dedication mysterious, and wonders whether it signifies 'the recognition of a real indebtedness'. (*Sinclair Lewis: An American Life* (London: Heinemann, 1961), 347.) The indebtedness seems obvious in the light of *The Custom of the Country*.

8. Upton Sinclair, *The Metropolis* (London: T.W. Laurie Ltd., 1908), 173.

9. The economic novel is still, of course, being written, although it is now firmly in the province of popular fiction, much of it by and about women. To the works of Judith Krantz and Barbara Taylor Bradford and Michael Ridpath's *Free to Trade* (1995), Jeffrey Archer's, *Not a Penny More, Not a Penny Less* (1976), Paul Erdman's *The Crash of '79* (1976), might be added more serious efforts like Tom Wolfe's *The Bonfire of the Vanities* (1987), William Gaddis's *JR* (1975), Caryl Churchill's *Serious Money* (1987), Tony Marchant's *Speculators* (1988), and the films *Trading Places*, *Rollover*, and *Wall Street*.

10. Wharton greatly admired *Unleavened Bread*; a letter to Grant survives which praises it as one of the best American novels in years (Grant and his wife were visitors to The Mount, and he became a valued, though not an intimate, member of the literary circle which gathered there). 'Selma . . . [is] as good in her way as Gwendolen Grancourt.' (E.W. to Robert Grant, 25.vii.1900 (*Letters*, 40–1)). Selma White has Undine's implacable self-interest and monolithic character, but in her it is disguised by an unreflective patriotic smugness; also, Selma, although she has certain social ambitions, is puritanical enough to despise the super-rich with whom Undine consorts, and

wishes rather to make them recognise her as being *above* their sphere. Like Undine, Selma is much-married (by the end of the novel she is Selma White Babcock Littleton Lyons; she settles for Lyons, a national politician, because his cant matches hers). Selma's egotism is distinct from Undine's, however. She is unwaveringly confident of her brilliance and aptitude for virtually any sphere of human activity, and is infuriated when she is not instantly recognised and feted as a journalist, nurse, socialite, politician's wife. She scorns those who with patience and long effort achieve expertise and excellence: 'Her idea of doing things was to do them quickly and brilliantly, arriving at conclusions, as became an American, with prompt energy and despatch.' (*Unleavened Bread* (New York: Charles Scribner's Sons, 1900), 177). Selma is monstrous and essentially implausible where Undine is extraordinary but entirely probable as a character.

11. Stephen Orgel, in his recent introduction to *The Custom of the Country*, remarks that 'the new American world of capitalist enterprise is . . . nearly . . . opaque to Wharton. *The Custom of the Country*, ed. Stephen Orgel (Oxford: OUP, 1995), x.

12. 'Donnée Book' (Notebook 1910–14, Yale), 9.

13. Begun in 1907, the novel was produced intermittently until 1913, when it was serialised in *Scribner's Magazine*.

14. E.W. to Dr Morgan Dix (5.xii.05) (*Letters*, 99).

15. In her notes accompanying the manuscript of *The Custom of the Country* Wharton makes a chronology of the novels' events (Yale):

> 'The story takes place between 1899 and 1906–7.
> February 1900: Undine marries Ralph
> January 1901: Paul born
> July 1903: Undine goes off with van Degen
> September 1903: Undine goes to Dakota
> January 1905: Undine meets de Chelles
> July 1905: Ralph dies
> January 1906: Undine marries de Chelles'

We can infer from this note and the evidence of the story that Undine first married Moffatt in 1896, and remarries him in 1907, the year in which the novel was begun.

16. Edgar Allan Poe, 'The Philosophy of Furniture' (1842) (Harmondsworth: Penguin Books, 1973), 414.

17. See Roderick Nash, *Wilderness and the American Mind*, third edition (New Haven: Yale University Press, 1982), 1–83.

18. Ray Ginger, *The Age of Excess: the United States from 1877–1914* (New York: Macmillan, 1965), 93.

19. Ellet, 585ff.

20. Sinclair, 252–3.

21. Sinclair, 192.

22. Sinclair, 269.

23. Louis Auchincloss, *The Vanderbilt Era: Profiles of a Gilded Age* (New York: Charles Scribner's Sons, 1989), 3.

24. van Rensselaer, *Social Ladder*, 108.

25. Mrs van Rensselaer was a cousin of Wharton's closest friend, Walter van Rensselaer Berry, a member of the old Dutch élite. Wharton's editor at Appleton notified her in Paris in 1923 of the publication of this book, and it appears that she read it (Jewett to E.W., (16.ii.23) (Yale)).
26. van Rensselaer, *Social Ladder*, 58.
27. Strong, 'Diary', 262.
28. *Men and Mysteries of Wall Street* (Boston: Fields, Osgood & Co., 1870), 156.
29. The originator of this cod-anthropological manner is of course Thorstein Veblen.
30. Sinclair, 192.
31. Booth Tarkington, *The Plutocrat* (Garden City, New York: Doubleday, Page & Co., 1927), 342.
32. Tarkington, 112.
33. F. Scott Fitzgerald, *The Great Gatsby* (1926) (Harmondsworth: Penguin Books, 1990), 10.
34. *The Financier*, 448.
35. Frank Norris, *The Pit* (New York: Doubleday, Page & Co., 1903), 302.
36. Cynthia Griffin Wolff seems to introduce the subject of the money-novel in relation to *The Custom of the Country*, but almost immediately dismisses it with the following remark: 'Horatio Alger's myth in all its manifestations was for men, not for women.' Wolff, 221. It is part of the purpose of my argument to show otherwise.
37. Henry James to E.W. (8.ii.05.) (Yale).
38. Henry James, *The American Scene* (New York: Harper & Bros., 1907), 158. The grandeur of Wharton's own magnificent house in Lenox, Mass., The Mount (inspired by Belton House in Lincolnshire), is suspiciously close to James's description.
39. Medbery, 1–2.
40. Veblen, 25.
41. Veblen, 26–8.
42. Veblen, 273.
43. Financial sleight-of-hand could have had, at the same time, an almost comic aspect. Daniel Drew is said to have perfected the 'handkerchief trick': at a meeting with other traders, he would draw out his handkerchief to wipe his brow, and in doing so a bit of paper would flutter to the floor. One of the other traders would furtively put his foot over it so that Drew would leave without noticing that he had dropped it. Written on it would be some tip which would invariably be followed by the traders, allowing Drew to start sudden and unexpected runs in the market (Josephson, 19). Medbery describes a trick on the trading floor: an employee equipped with a signet ring containing a squirt of perfume would pass behind an enemy trader; the perfume would be squirted, and the enemy would automatically begin to raise his hat as if to a lady, thereby inadvertently placing a bid (Medbery, 144–5).
44. Sinclair, 214.
45. This metaphor had been used by Dreiser in *The Financier* in the early and over-portentous duel between a lobster and a squid.
46. On the Van Swerigens, see John R. Stilgoe, *Borderlands: Origins of the American Suburb, 1820–1939* (New Haven: Yale University Press, 1988), 240–51;

on Miller and Mulholland, see Mike Davis, *City of Quartz: Excavating the Future in Los Angeles* (London: Verso Press, 1990), 23, 379–82.

47. Josephson, 137.
48. Sinclair Lewis, *Babbitt* (New York: Grosset & Dunlap, 1922), 2.
49. Anita Loos, *Gentlemen Prefer Blondes* (1925) (London: Folio Society, 1985), 58. Wharton met and highly approved of Loos in Paris (for Wharton's remark, see *Letters*, 491n).
50. Loos, 57.
51. It would be unjust to Morgan, however, to ignore his strongly held ideas of honour and of communal service in business by lumping him indiscriminately with the men Teddy Roosevelt described as 'malefactors of wealth'. Moffatt is like Morgan only in the volume of his art collecting.
52. Wharton's free indirect narration consistently allies her with Moffatt in her art descriptions, but never with Undine.
53. Josephson, 343.
54. Undine, as we know, has no extended family, her siblings having died in the typhoid outbreak in Apex which prompted her father's Pure Water Move. The undine of legend, a difficult sprite adopted by a pair of old cottagers, replaces a drowned child and dominates her elders with her imperious ways. Nothing in Undine Spragg's genetic or folkloric background equips her to understand 'heritage'.
55. For a discussion of Undine's self-commodification within the framework of early-twentieth century American consumerism and divorce practice, see Debra Ann MacComb, "New Wives for Old: Divorce and the Leisure-Class Marriage Market in Edith Wharton's *The Custom of the Country*", *American Literature* 68:4 (Dec.1996), 777–83.
56. Stephen Orgel notes that fashionable intellectual opinion of the day would have concurred in disparaging Bernhardt, and suggests that Undine's assessment is not at all contemptible (Orgel, xi). This may well be a glimpse of Wharton's own highly developed aesthetic snobbery, but it is still too generous to Undine, who, if she rejects Bernhardt coincidentally with the *savants*, does so for reasons of supreme indifference to plays, literature, and dramatic style.
57. Robert Grant to E.W. (18.xi.1913) (Yale).
58. Orgel, xi.
59. Veblen, 232. See also Veblen, 'The Barbarian Status of Women', *American Journal of Sociology* 4 (1899), 503–14 (reprinted in *Sex and Equality* (New York: Arno Press, 1974)).
60. Loos, 78.
61. Trollope, 309.
62. Apex City is not specified as being in a particular state, although Stephen Orgel and others have suggested that it is in Indiana or Kansas or Illinois, or even Arizona. The much later *The Glimpses of the Moon* (1921) again alludes to Apex, the native city of Mr and Mrs Mortimer Hicks and their daughter Coral. From this novel, we know that Apex is a prairie state; and from *The Custom of the Country* it is certain that it is east of Opake, Nebraska, since Moffatt and Undine head into the sunset toward their illicit marriage there. Wharton's western geography must never be taken literally, of course; but the prairies technically extend from western Illinois to the Rockies; only

from Iowa, northernmost Missouri, or the southern Illinois banks of the Mississippi could one head due west from prairies to any part of Nebraska. Its exact location hardly matters, since for Wharton, 'the West and the Northwest and the new Northwest and the Far West and all the other Wests yet to be invented' (Fuller, 16) are more or less undifferentiated, a blur of the unknown continent (in her mother's terms, 'not-New York'). Like some of her favourite novelists (Balzac, Thackeray, Trollope, Conrad), Wharton was fond of reusing names and places in her novels.

63. There is no such place as 'Dakota'; this is the term used by those too ignorant or lazy to recognise North Dakota and South Dakota, which had become states in 1889, 15 years or so before the moment of the story and two decades before Wharton wrote it. The use of 'Dakota' is of a piece both with Undine's vagueness and incuriosity about other people and places, and with Wharton's own snobbery about 'the West', a distant place somewhere on the other side of the Hudson.

64. See MacComb, 772–7, on the divorce states.

65. 'Tiring of Moffatt, who turns to little Paul Marvell for solace. Undine sick of Paris, & yearning to go to London, where James J. Rolliver has just been made an ambassador – that what she always needed was "a man with a career".' (Notes for *The Custom of the Country*) (Yale).

66. MacComb, 786–7.

67. See note 65. The likelihood of Undine's flight from Moffatt is latent, however, in the entire book, not just in the fugitive ending.

68. Mulvey discusses the reduced sensibility of the average nineteenth-century American tourist, and the potential vulnerability to cultural overload and breakdown in the highly receptive ones such as Emerson, James, Eliot (Mulvey, 4).

69. Hotels seem to provide Americans with a sense of continuity: as the success of chains like Holiday Inn, Howard Johnson, and Best Western testifies, the more alike the hotels of different cities are, the less dislocating the experience of travel to new places, the better they are appreciated and patronised. F. Cholmondeley Frink's poem about the homelike effect of hotels in *Babbitt* sums up the emotion: 'When I get that lonely spell, I simply seek the best hotel, no matter in what town I be – St Paul, Toledo, or K.C., in Washington, Schenectady, in Louisville or Albany. And at that inn it hits my dome that I again am right at home' (*Babbitt*,185).

70. Quoted by Eleanor Dwight, *Edith Wharton, An Extraordinary Life* (New York: Abrams, 1994), 46.

71. Bourget, 53.

72. Georg Simmel, *The Philosophy of Money* (Berlin, 1907); second edition edited and translated by David Frisby and Tom Bottomore (London, 1990), 244.

73. Bourget, 55.

74. Cornelius Vanderbilt's famous *mot* ('What do I care for the law? Haint I got the power?') can stand beside Lily's 'Beyond!', an injunction which might have been Undine's, had she time for such things as mottoes (Undine's motto, insofar as she has one, is 'Go steady, Undine!' (CC17)).

75. Veblen, *Works*, 359.

76. Sinclair, 250. See Veblen, 'Barbarian Status', 507.

77. *The Financier*, Dreiser, 225–6.

78. For accounts of Moses, see Robert Caro, *The Power Broker: Robert Moses and the Fall of New York* (New York: Knopf, 1974); and especially Marshall Berman, *All That Is Solid Melts Into Air: The Experience of Modernity* (New York: Simon and Schuster, 1982), 290–312.
79. Two Women, Victoria Woodhull and Tennessee Claflin, duped Commodore Vanderbilt by persuading him that their stock-market advice was derived from the spirit-world. With his help they set up a brokerage firm in 1870, and published *Woodhull and Claflin's Weekly* (which supported Woodhull for President in 1872). These two sisters had previously enjoyed a successful career in the midwest selling fake cures and working other scams (Morris, 129–31). Except to such tricksters, finance was not a career option for women in this period.
80. In *The House of Mirth*, Lily – still clinging to her fatal principles – refuses to be painted by society portraitist Paul Morpeth. 'I don't care to accept a painting from Morpeth', she says coldly (*HM*405), and no discussion ensues, as if one's presence in a portrait immediately places one within the cash nexus. Undine has no such qualms.
81. Auchincloss, *The Vanderbilt Era*, 126.
82. Fitzgerald, 50.
83. Fitzgerald, 95.
84. Infantile sexuality is, likewise, reflexive and unformed; and indeed, Undine, we know, does not like being touched. She is in a sense sexually undeveloped.
85. Mrs Bradley-Martin, whose fabulous and scandalously extravagant fancy-dress ball of 1897 symbolised for many the vulgarity of the new wealth, was said also to have worn Mary Antoinette's ruby necklace, as well as diamond clusters made for Louis XIV (van Rensselaer, *Social Ladder*, 209).
86. Percy Lubbock, *A Portrait of Edith Wharton* (New York: D. Appleton-Century Company, Inc., 1947), 11.
87. Henry James to Howard Sturgis (9.ix.12) (*The Letters of Henry James* ed. Leon Edel, 4 vols (Cambridge, Mass.: Belknap Press of Harvard University Press, 1974–84), IV, 622).
88. Quoted in Millicent Bell *Edith Wharton and Henry James: The Story of their Friendship* (New York: George Braziller, 1965), 177.
89. Henry James to Howard Sturgis (20.vii.12) (Edel, 620).
90. James to Gaillard Lapsley (4.v.1909) (quoted by Lewis, 247).
91. James to Howard Sturgis (20.vii.1912) (in Edel, *Letters* IV, 620–1).
92. Lewis, 262.
93. Henry James to Howard Sturgis, November, 1908 (Edel, *Letters* IV, 239).
94. Her friend Charles Eliot Norton, the distinguished Harvard professor, affected a studied rusticity in Ashfield, near Lenox, without any of these conveniences; a fact of which she complained in her letters when communication was slow.
95. Dwight, 141.
96. See Wharton to Eunice Maynard (24.v.06) (Yale). James also imagines her 'recoiling', 'rebounding', 'charged with booty', 'gyrating', 'plundering and pillaging', producing 'a great side-wind', like some amazing machine (H.J. to E.W. (6.ix.13) (Yale)).
97. From a letter from James to Mrs Humphrey Ward (date not given), quoted in Bell, 185.
98. Lubbock, 67–8.

99. E.W. to Bernard Berenson (29.vi.12) (*Letters*, 272–3).
100. *A Motor-Flight Through France* (1908) (DeKalb, Ill.: Northern Illinois University Press, 1991), 1.
101. A similar incident occurred near Lenox, when, again, a local army had to pull the Wharton motor car out of a muddy ditch (E.W. to Sally Norton 7.viii.06 (*Letters*, 105)).
102. Between 1893 and 1903 she owned her New York house(s) (882–884 Park Avenue), Land's End at Newport, and latterly the Mount in Lenox; from 1903 to 1910 she had Park Avenue, the Mount, and rented one of two flats in Paris; in the period 1918 to 1921 she lived in Paris while renovating Pavilion Colombe in St Brice, north of the city, and St Clair le Chateau in Hyères on the Riviera. At all times except during the war years, when she owned no property and rented 53 rue de Varenne, Wharton always had two functioning households.
103. James to Howard Sturgis (no date given) (Lewis, 262).
104. *The Reef* (1911), her first novel to be published by Appleton, commanded an advance of $15,000, compared with $5000 offered by Scribner's.
105. Quoted in Lubbock, 68.
106. She was so successful in 1924 that she had to ask her editor at Appleton to send her no more cheques for the time being because she feared the tax bill (Lewis, 459).
107. E.W. to William Crary Brownell (25.iv.99) (*Letters*, 37–8).
108. E.W. to William Crary Brownell (14.ii.02) (*Letters*, 57–8).
109. This surprising attitude appears as early as the 1920s. Vernon Parrington says 'if she had lived less easily, if she had been forced to skimp and save and plan, she would have been a greater and a richer artist'. (quoted by Millicent Bell, ed., introduction to *Cambridge Companion to Edith Wharton* (Cambridge: Cambridge University Press, 1996), 7). See also, for example, Robert M. Lovett, *Edith Wharton* (New York: Robert M. McBride, 1925). Alfred Kazin and others have written Wharton off as the helpless captive of her own inherited gentility; they prefer, on this basis, the rugged social realism of Dreiser and Sinclair (by which they mean they prefer fiction about the masses rather than fiction about the élite). One feels these critics to be very much of their moment, in the grip of the intensely fashionable (but not necessarily enduring) muscularity of the grim and the earthy, on political rather than aesthetic grounds. (See Alfred Kazin, 'Two Educations: Edith Wharton and Theodore Dreiser' in *On Native Grounds: An Interpretation of American Prose Literature* (New York: Harcourt, Brace & World, Inc., 1942); and Vernon Parrington *Main Currents in American Thought* (New York, 1954). This archaic reasoning has also been more recently put forward by Michéle Roberts (*The Independent*, 23 October, 1994 review of Benstock).
110. Benstock, 60–1.
111. E.W. to Bernard Berenson (16.v.11) (*Letters*, 239–40).
112. 'It takes care of itself, all *to* admiration, and one has to the highest and happiest point the sense of a full-orbed muchness to come – the large mass of the orb hanging and looming there, with all the right dimness, in the light actually forecast.' (Henry James to E.W. (3.ii.13) (Yale)).
113. Henry James to E.W. (11.vi.13); and (2.v.13) (Yale). 'She' was also Wharton's and James's nickname for her car; but whether 'she' in this letter refers to

Undine or a machine, the likeness of the two to each other, and of either to Edith Wharton, is still pointed.

114. Henry James to E.W. (16.i.14) (Yale).
115. Edmund Wilson, 'Justice to Edith Wharton' in *Edith Wharton: A Collection of Critical Essays*, ed. Irving Howe (Englewood Cliffs: Prentice-Hall, Inc., 1962), 22.
116. Clark, 204.
117. *The Financier*, 182.
118. Lewis, 378.

Chapter 4   Expatriates

1. 'New York Letter' in *The New Yorker*, 2 March, 1929 (Yale).
2. Mary Cadwalader Jones, *European Travel for Women: Notes and Suggestions* (New York: Macmillan, 1900), 1.
3. Cited by James Buzard, *The Beaten Track: European Tourism, Literature, and the Ways to Culture* (Oxford: Clarendon Press, 1993), 230.
4. Henry James to Charles Eliot Norton (1872) (quoted in R.W.B. Lewis, *The Jameses. A Family Narrative* (New York: Farrar, Straus & Giroux, 1991), 223.
5. Henry James to Hamlin Garland (quoted in Millicent Bell, *Henry James and Edith Wharton* . . . , 75); Henry James to E.W. (4.xii.1912) (Yale).
6. I use this term rather than 'antimodern' to avoid confusion with what T.L. Jackson Lears identifies as the modernist attempt to reauthenticate experience *via* a primitivism of production, behaviour, and belief which would stem the tide of industrialised sterility and 'overcivilization'. (*No Place of Grace: Antimodernism and the Transformation of American Culture, 1880–1920* (New York: Pantheon Books, 1981).
7. *Life and I*, 19–20.
8. Millicent Bell, 'Edith Wharton in France' in Joslin and Price, 63.
9. Percy Lubbock to Gaillard Lapsley (2.xi.1909) (Yale).
10. See Roger Asselineau, 'Edith Wharton – She Thought in French and Wrote in English' in Joslin and Price, 355–63.
11. This Racinianism 'helps to account a little for something *qui me chiffoné* throughout; which is why the whole thing, unrelated and unreferred . . . to its milieu and background . . . takes place *comme cela*, and in a specified, localised way, in France – these non-French people "electing", as it were, to have their story out there. . . . But the point was, as I see it, that you couldn't really give us the sense of a Boston Eriphyle or Boston Givré, and that the exquisite instinct, "back of" your Racinian inspiration . . . absolutely prescribed a vague and elegant French colonnade or gallery . . . as the harmonious *fond* you required . . . ' (Henry James to E.W. (4.xii.1912) (Yale)).
12. Auchincloss, *Pioneers*, 4.
13. Shari Benstock points out that Wharton's conception of the faubourg was an anachronism in the post-war period (Benstock, 'Landscapes of Desire: Edith Wharton and Europe' in Joslin and Price, 23), and Millicent Bell makes a similar point about Wharton's admiration for French tradition as expounded in *French Ways and their Meaning*: the France she conceived was 'somewhat illusive' because it had never really existed in that form (Bell, 'Edith Wharton in France' in Joslin and Price, 70).

14. Benstock, 280.
15. It would be useful to know how much, and which, Freud Wharton had read, just as it would be useful to know that she had read Veblen. There is only indirect evidence of her acquaintance with either, but it is almost inconceivable that she did not investigate them. She refers casually to the libido in a letter (E.W. to Gaillard Lapsley (9.viii.1936) (Yale)) (*See* Bauer, *Edith Wharton's Brave New Politics* (Madison: University of Wisconsin Press, 1994), 97).
16. E.W. to Minnie Jones (2.xi.1934) (Yale).
17. E.W. to Sally Norton (18.ix.1912) (Yale).
18. 'Mr Ed Wilson Jr. speaks words that are as balm to me, for it has dawned on him that perhaps satire *is* my weapon!' (E.W. to Gaillard Lapsley (5.vii.1921) (Yale)). Wilson's adulatory assessment of Wharton is found in 'Some Things I Consider Underrated: Three Little Essays in Constructive Criticism' in *Vanity Fair* 16:1 (March, 1921) (reprinted in *From the Uncollected Edmund Wilson* eds Janet Groth and David Castronovo (Athens, Ohio: Ohio University Press, 1995), 141–3).
19. E.W. to Daisy Chanler (1.x.1923) (Yale).
20. '"Clever but depressing" – c'est vraiment le ça de la dire, so joyless, graceless, hopeless, futureless, is the horrible U.S. she pictures.' E.W. to Minnie Jones (13.viii.1918) (Yale).
21. E.W. to Minnie Jones (15.i.1923) (Yale).
22. This book was helping her with *The Buccaneers* (E.W. to Minnie Jones (2.ii.1934) (Yale)).
23. *American Magazine*, 1920 (Pocket Diary, 1920 (Yale)).
24. 'The best summing-up of New America that I have yet seen'. (E.W. to Daisy Chanler (19.viii.1928) (Yale).)
25. E.W. to Sally Norton (5.vi.1903) (Yale).
26. E.W. to Sally Norton (5.vi.1903) (Yale).
27. E.W. to Sally Norton (18.ix.1912) (Yale).
28. E.W. to Sally Norton (14.vi.1906) (Yale).
29. E.W. to Sally Norton (5.vi.1903) (Yale).
30. Millicent Bell makes this point in 'Edith Wharton in France', in Joslin and Price, 67.
31. 'Aggressive salubrity and repose' are her strange oxymorons for this landscape.
32. 'Notes and Subjects II' (1924–8), 73 (Yale).
33. E.W. to Sally Norton (19.vii.1906) (Yale).
34. Matthew Arnold, (quoted in Mulvey 32).
35. 'Some one asked [a cousin of Wharton's] if the Anglo-French bonds . . . were "a good investment"; and he answered' "If they are not going to be a good investment life is not going to be worth living."' E.W. to Robert Grant (10.x.1916) (Yale).
36. Edgar Saltus, 'The Most Extraordinary Panorama in the World', quoted in Grace Mayer, *Once Upon a City* (New York: Macmillan, 1958), 3.
37. E.W. to Sally Norton (19.viii.1904) (Yale).
38. See Peter Conrad, *Imagining America* (New York: Oxford University Press, 1980), 5.
39. E.W. to Daisy Chanler (14.vi.1903[?]) (Yale).

40. See my discussion of female blankness in Chapter I, 34–5. Stevens's 'The Comedian as the Letter C' and other 'Adamic' writing depicts the liberating quality of the blank.

41. This is Henry James's vision: 'The figure of Mrs Jack [Gardner], the American, the nightmare . . . the American looming up – dim, vast, portentous – in their millions – the gathering waves – the barbarians of the Roman Empire.' (Quoted in Earnest, 232).

42. E.W. to Daisy Chanler (17.vii.1926) (Yale).

43. E.W. to Minnie Jones (14.vii.1921) (Yale); E.W. to Minnie Jones (2.xi.1934) (Yale); E.W. to Gaillard Lapsley (9.viii.1936) (Yale).

44. E.W. to Sally Norton (17.vi.1905) (Yale).

45. 'I'm . . . languishing with an envie de possesse for a Horton Vanilla-Brick, and then another. My country 't is of thee . . .' (E.W. to Gaillard Lapsley (7.vii.1923) (Yale)).

46. 'Note and Subjects' (1924–28), 67–8 (Yale).

47. 'The crash has come at a moment that seems to find the other nations *morally* ready. I could include the U.S. – but it sticks in my innards that the great peace-treaty-Hague-convention protagonist shouldn't rise in its millions to protest against the violation of the treaties she has always been clamouring for.' (E.W. to Gaillard Lapsley (23.xii.1914) (Yale)).

48. *The Europeans*, 41.

49. 'The American use of superlatives is so excusable when applied to one's self!' E.W. to Sally Norton (14.iii.1902) (Yale).

50. Candace Waid does not discuss *Madame de Treymes* in her study of Persephone images in Wharton.

51. E.W. to John Hugh Smith (6.viii.1911) (Yale).

52. Tarkington, 125.

53. Tarkington, 434.

54. Shirley Foster, 'Making It Her Own: Edith Wharton's Europe', in Joslin and Price, 130.

55. E.W. to Sally Norton (21.vi.1922) (Yale).

56. David Jones, Ezra Pound and T.S. Eliot, for example, produced verbal analogies of the chaos of war in dense, *scriptible* poems in which linguistic fragmentation mimics sensory and emotional breakdown.

57. Price, 43.

58. E.W. to Gaillard Lapsley (21.v.1920) (Yale).

59. Quoted in Price, 45. Teddy Roosevelt urged American sightseers to stay home rather than 'look at the agony in a spirit of vapid and idle curiosity'.

60. E.W. to Sally Norton (21.v.1922) (Yale).

61. Benstock, 293.

62. E.W. to Daisy Chanler (24.xi.1929) (Yale).

63. Although the remark is usually credited to Oscar Wilde, Oliver Wendell Holmes, in *Autocrat of the Breakfast Table* (1857–8), quotes this *mot* as Thomas Appleton's.

64. Charles Dickens, *American Notes*, quoted in Mulvey, 55.

65. Frances Hodgson Burnett, *The Shuttle* (London: Heinemann, 1907), 2.

66. Veblen, 81.

67. Pierre Bourdieu, *Distinction: a Social Critique of the Judgement of Taste* (1979) trans. Richard Nice (London: Routledge and Kegan Paul, 1986), 303.

68. Victor Turner, quoted in William W. Stowe, *Going Abroad: European Travel in Nineteenth-Century American Culture* (Princeton: Princeton University Press, 1995), 20.

69. Poe, 418.

70. Benstock, 369.

71. See, for example, the Boykins in *Madame de Treymes*; the expatriate community of the French Riviera in *The Mother's Recompense*; and Miss Painter's attitude to the French in *The Reef*.

72. Lewis, 396.

73. For example, Auchincloss, *Edith Wharton: A Woman in Her Time*, 169–75; and Lewis, 444–6. I would allow, however, that *Hudson River Bracketted* and *The Gods Arrive*, of which I have said little, are very weak novels indeed.

74. A number of incidents which befall the pathetic Rosalie Vanderpoel in *The Shuttle* are strikingly like Nan's experience as an unhappy duchess, including an attempt to aid poor villagers, injury during pregnancy, and a termagant dowagered mother-in-law.

75. Other historical examples are Jenny Jerome, one of the fabulous Jerome sisters of New York, the mother of Winston Churchill; and Nancy Shaw of Virginia who married William Waldorf Astor.

76. Millicent Bell, 'Edith Wharton in France' in Joslin and Price, 72.

77. The dreadful adaptation of this novel by the American Public Broadcasting System and the BBC (1995) turned the novel into Mills and Boon, a desecration of Wharton for the American TV audience akin to the desecration of English society by the buccaneers themselves. As Guy Thwarte's father remarks after meeting Nan's parents (a Colonel and Mrs Tracey St George, who hail from 'some unspecified region which Mrs St George called "the Sa-outh"'), 'they cannot grasp the meaning of [aristocratic] institutions or understand the hundreds of minute observances forming the texture of an old society . . .' (*B*155).

78. Gilbert and Gubar, 156.

79. Percy Lubbock could be terrified by her in an early encounter ('she is cleverer and more alive and finer than her books I think . . . Henry turned up . . . several times while she was here, the moth to the candle. . . .') but could dismiss her work privately in the same letter ('she has no business to be writing rotten little melodramatic anecdotes like the one I read in Scribner's yesterday'). The rotten melodrama was 'The Bolted Door'. Percy Lubbock to Gaillard Lapsley (10.iii.1909) (Yale).

80. See note 41.

81. Percy Lubbock to Gaillard Lapsley (22.ii.1938) (Yale).

82. Percy Lubbock to Gaillard Lapsley (19.xi.1925) (Yale).

83. E.W. to Gaillard Lapsley (18.x.1933) (Yale).

84. E.W. to Daisy Chanler (18.vii.1903) (Yale).

85. Benstock, 79.

86. Percy Lubbock quotes such an anecdote from an unidentified source (*Portrait*, 116).

87. E.W. to Daisy Chanler (14.iv.1903) (Yale).

88. E.W. to Daisy Chanler (8.iii.1903) (Yale).
89. Shari Benstock states that Wharton 'longed' to be a *salon* hostess; but there is little documentary evidence for this claim. She was not a regular attender of the most advanced *salons*, and those which she occasionally visited, like Rosa Fitz-James's, were conservative; Wharton was in any case disinclined to discuss her work with other writers, preferring the social benefits of literary celebrity (Benstock, *Women of the Left Bank*, 44; and Martin/Martin-Wagner, 'The Salons of Wharton's Fiction', in Joslin and Price, 105). Millicent Bell also describes her as 'building' a 'growing' *salon* (Bell, 127).
90. E.W. to Minnie Jones (25.i.1919) (Yale).
91. Stephen Orgel asks, sensibly, 'why?' (Introduction, *The Reef* (Oxford University Press, 1998), xix).
92. Gertrude Stein, quoted in Frederick J. Hoffman, *The Twenties: American Writing in the Postwar Decade* (New York: The Free Press, 1949, 43).
93. Sinclair, 92.
94. Norris, *The Pit*, 225.
95. See Chapter 1, note 67.
96. From a satirical poem by Wallace Irwin, quoted in Mayer, 39.
97. E.W. to Ogden Codman (8.v.1895) (cited in Dwight, 52).
98. 'Subjects and Notes' (1918–23, I) (Yale), 1.
99. The Germanic culture of excess would naturally have irritated Wharton, whom Bourget called 'Le Velasquez' in recognition of 'her high restraint' (Charles du Bos, reminiscence of E.W., unpublished MS, Yale). Germans and Germany are a type of Wharton's buccaneers. But Kristin Olsen Lauer points out that this aesthetic-political doctrine of saving France and French culture from innate German depredation was old-fashioned and reactionary by the 1920s ('Can France Survive This Defender? Contemporary American Reaction to Edith Wharton's Expatriation' in Joslin and Price, 88).
100. New York *Sun*, 5 April, 1915 (Yale).
101. E.W. to Minnie Jones (17.xi.1915) (Yale).
102. E.W. to Sally Norton (9.i.1917) (Yale).
103. This image of domestic privacy being made suddenly public through calamity resurfaces as the opening of *New Year's Day*, when a fire breaks out at the Fifth Avenue Hotel, revealing the central, illicit arrangement of the story. Lily Bart's lack of privacy in *The House of Mirth* (discussed in Chapter 2) is a related idea.
104. See Annette Larson Bennett's excellent article on Wharton's war writing ('Edith Wharton at War: Civilized Space in Troubled Times' in *Twentieth Century Literature* 42:3 (1996), 322–43).
105. E.W. to Minnie Jones (17.xi.1915) (Yale).
106. See Price, however, for a full discussion of her war activities.
107. 'As for the individual pathetic stories it is hard for us here, on the edge of this awful tragedy, to understand why people in America do not understand that we are too busy to collect anecdotes ... until the horizon lightens it will be hard to sit down and collect anecdotes.' (E.W. to Minnie Jones (21.xii.1917) (Yale)).
108. A good case in point is her abilty to introduce to France the modern 'fresh-air' treatment of tuberculosis. The Red Cross and the Rockefeller Foundation has difficulty imposing this superior regime on the suspicious French

because they did not understand, as Wharton did, French cultural resistance to certain aspects of modern domestic hygiene. See Price, 117.

109. E.W. to Bernard Berenson (30.xi.1914) (*Letters*, 341).
110. E.W. to Gaillard Lapsley (8.xi.1914) (Yale).
111. Judith L. Sensibar, '"Behind the Lines" in Edith Wharton's *A Son at the Front*: Re-writing a Masculinist Tradition' in Joslin and Price, 245–52.
112. Shari Benstock, 'Landscapes of Desire: Edith Wharton and Europe' in Joslin and Price, 35.
113. E.W. to Elisina and Royall Tyler (19.iv.1916), quoted in Price, 91.
114. Among other stylistic infelicities, she repeats phrases almost exactly, as if in her haste she had forgotten she had already used them.
115. Enclosed in a letter from E.W. to Gaillard Lapsley (14.viii.1923) (Yale).
116. E.W. to Edward Sheldon (6.v.1924) (Yale).
117. After she left the Mount for the last time in the summer of 1911, she went back twice to America: to attend Beatrice Jones's wedding in 1913 (a trip of two weeks); and for eleven days in 1923 to collect her honorary doctorate from Yale.
118. Lubbock, 150.
119. 'Documentation in Fiction' (unpublished MS, Yale).
120. 'What is Lilla Gates's history? Perhaps she has felt more, in her primitive way, than the others.' ('Notes and Subjects II' (1924–28), 51 (Yale)).
121. E.W. to Bernard Berenson (28.vi.18) (Yale).
122. Bauer, 95.
123. Wharton made a telling error in her notes when she referred to Arthur Wyant as Arthur 'van Leyden', a slip which refers back nearly a decade to the soon-to-fail aboriginals of *The Age of Innocence* ('Notes and Subjects II' (1924–28), 68 (Yale)).
124. Judith Wheater shocks Martin Boyne by suggesting that 'an old *liaison*' be 'regularised' by marriage (*C*193); the complacent Henry Prest in *New Year's Day* uses the word to propose marriage to Lizzie Hazeldean (*NYD*290). The Fletcher method of nutrition, popular in the early-twentieth century, required prolonged mastication of food; Wharton reported that Henry James had ruined his health by following the regime for six years (*Letters*, 199–200); Taylorizing was a system of time-and-motion efficiency in industry devised by the American industrialist F.W. Taylor, and Wharton describes Lilla Gates's life, in her notes for *The Mother's Recompense*, as 'smoothness – shock-absorbers – the Taylorized life' ('Notes and Subjects II' (1924–28), 51 (Yale)).
125. 'Notes and Subjects II' (1924–28) (Yale), 68.

Bibliography

Manuscripts

Yale Collection of American Literature, Beinecke Rare Book and Manuscript Library, Yale University (YCAL MSS 42).

The Gaillard Lapsley papers, Wren Library, Trinity College, Cambridge.

Printed sources

Adams, Charles Francis, Jr. and Henry. *Chapters of Erie* (1886). Ithaca: Cornell University Press, 1956.

Adamson, Sylvia. 'The What of Language?' In *The State of the Language*. Ed. Christopher Ricks. London: Faber and Faber, 1990, 503–14.

Alcott, Louisa May. *Little Women* (1868). Harmondsworth: Penguin Books, 1989.

——. *Work* (1873). Harmondsworth: Penguin Books, 1994.

Ames, Kenneth L. *Death in the Dining Room and Other Tales of Victorian Culture.* Philadelphia: Temple University Press, 1992.

Ammons, Elizabeth. *Edith Wharton's Argument With America.* Athens, Georgia: University of Georgia Press, 1980.

Asselineau, Roger. 'Edith Wharton – She Thought in French and Wrote in English.' In Joslin and Price (1993), 355–63.

Auchincloss, Louis. *Pioneers and Caretakers: A Study of Nine American Women.* Minneapolis: University of Minnesota Press, 1961.

——. *Edith Wharton: A Woman in Her Time.* New York: Viking Press, 1971.

——. *The Vanderbilt Era: Profiles of a Gilded Age.* New York: Charles Scribner's Sons, 1989.

Bachelard, Gaston. *The Poetics of Space* (1958). Trans. Maria Jolas. Intro. John R. Stilgoe. Boston: Beacon Press, 1994.

Banner, Lois W. *American Beauty.* New York: Alfred A. Knopf, 1983.

Bauer, Dale M. *Edith Wharton's Brave New Politics.* Madison: University of Wisconsin Press, 1994.

Beer, Gillian. *Darwin's Plots: Evolutionary Narrative in Darwin, George Eliot and Nineteenth-Century Fiction* (1983). London and Boston: Ark Paperbacks, 1985.

Bell, Millicent. *Edith Wharton and Henry James: The Story of their Friendship.* New York: George Braziller, 1965.

——. 'Edith Wharton in France'. In Joslin and Price (1993), 61–73.

——, ed. Introduction to *Cambridge Companion to Edith Wharton.* Cambridge: Cambridge University Press, 1996.

Benert, Annette Larsen. 'Edith Wharton at War: Civilized Space in Troubled Times'. *Twentieth Century Literature*, 42:3 (1996), 322–43.

Benstock, Shari. *Women of the Left Bank: Paris, 1900–1940.* Austin: University of Texas Press, 1986.

——. 'Landscapes of Desire: Edith Wharton and Europe'. In Joslin and Price (1993), 19–42.

——. *No Gifts From Chance: A Biography of Edith Wharton*. New York: Charles Scribner's Sons, 1994.

Bentley, Nancy. *The Ethnography of Manners: Hawthorne, James, Wharton*. Cambridge: Cambridge University Press, 1995.

——. '"Hunting for the Real": Wharton and the Science of Manners'. In *The Cambridge Companion to Edith Wharton*. Ed. Millicent Bell. Cambridge: Cambridge University Press, 1995, 55–7.

Berenson, Bernard. *The Selected Letters of Bernard Berenson*. Ed. A.K. McComb. Boston: Houghton Mifflin Co., 1964.

Berman, Marshall. *All That Is Solid Melts Into Air: The Experience of Modernity*. New York: Simon and Schuster, 1982.

Bourdieu, Pierre. *Distinction: A Social Critique of the Judgement of Taste* (1979). Trans. Richard Nice. London: Routledge and Kegan Paul, 1986.

Bourget, Paul. *Outre-Mer: Impressions of America*. London: T. Fisher Unwin, 1895.

Burke, Kenneth. *Language as Symbolic Action: Essays on Life, Literature and Method*. Berkeley: University of California Press, 1966.

Buitenhuis, Peter. 'Edith Wharton and the First World War'. *American Quarterly*, 18 (1966), 493–505.

Burnett, Frances Hodgson. *The Shuttle*. London: Heinemann,1907.

Buzard, James. *The Beaten Track: European Tourism, Literature, and the Ways to Culture*. Oxford: Clarendon Press, 1993.

Caro, Robert. *The Power Broker: Robert Moses and the Fall of New York*. New York: Knopf, 1974.

Clark, Kenneth. *Another Part of the Woods: A Self-Portrait*. New York: Harper and Row, 1974.

Coleman, Richard P. and Lee Rainwater. *Social Standing in America: New Dimensions of Class*. New York: Basic Books, 1978.

Conrad, Peter. *Imagining America*. New York: Oxford University Press, 1980.

Craig, Theresa. *Edith Wharton: A House Full of Rooms: Architecture, Interiors, and Gardens*. New York: Monacelli Press, 1996.

Crèvecœur, J. Hector St John de. *Letters from an American Farmer*. London, 1782.

Culler, Jonathan. 'Semiotics of Tourism'. *American Journal of Semiotics*, 1 (1981), 127–40.

Cuvier, Georges, *The Animal Kingdom* (1827–32). London: Allen, 1893.

Davidoff, Leonore. *The Best Circles: Society Etiquette and the Season*. London: Croom Helm, 1973.

Davis, Mike. *City of Quartz: Excavating the Future in Los Angeles*. London: Verso Press, 1990.

Dickens, Charles, *American Notes*. London, 1842.

Dimock, Wai-Chee. 'Debasing Exchange: Edith Wharton's *The House of Mirth*'. *PMLA*, 100 (October, 1985), 783–92.

Dreiser, Theodore. *The Financier* (1912). New York: New American Library, 1967.

Dwight, Eleanor. *Edith Wharton, An Extraordinary Life*. New York: Abrams, 1994.

Edgarton, S.C. *The Flower Vase; containing the Language of Flowers and their Poetic Sentiments*. Lowell, Mass.: Merrill and Heywood, 1847.

Ellet, Elizabeth Fries. *The Court Circles of the Republic, or the Beauties and Celebrities of the Nation*. Hartford: Hartford Publishing Company, 1869.

Earnest, Ernest. *The American Eve in Fact and Fiction, 1775–1914*. Urbana: University of Illinois Press, 1974.

Fitzgerald, F. Scott. *The Great Gatsby* (1926). Ed. Tony Tanner. Harmondsworth: Penguin Books, 1990.

Flanner, Janet. 'New York Letter'. *New Yorker*, 2 March, 1929.

——. *Paris Was Yesterday, 1925–1939*. Ed. Irving Drutman. New York: Viking Press, 1972.

Foster, Shirley. 'Making It Her Own: Edith Wharton's Europe'. In Joslin and Price (1993), 129–45.

Frazer, James. *The Golden Bough* (1890). Ed. Theodore Gaster. New York: New American Library, 1959.

Freedman, Jonathan. *Professions of Taste: Henry James, British Aestheticism, and Commodity Culture*. Stanford: Stanford University Press, 1990.

Freud, Sigmund. 'Totem and Taboo'. In *The Complete Psychological Works of Sigmund Freud*, vol. 13. London: Hogarth Press, 1955.

Frost, Robert. *The Collected Poetry of Robert Frost*. London: Jonathan Cape, 1977.

Fryer, Judith. *Felicitous Space: the Imaginative Structures of Edith Wharton and Willa Cather*. Chapel Hill: University of North Carolina Press, 1986.

Fuller, Henry. *The Cliff-Dwellers*. New York: Harper and Brothers, 1893.

Fussell, Paul. *Class: Style and Status in the USA*. London: Arrow Books, Ltd., 1984.

Gargano, James W. 'Tableaux of Renunciation: Wharton's Use of *The Shaugraun* in *The Age of Innocence*'. *Studies in American Fiction*, 15 (Spring, 1987), 1–11.

Gilbert, Sandra H., and Susan Gubar. 'Angel of Devastation: Edith Wharton on the Arts of the Enslaved'. *No Man's Land: The Place of the Woman Writer in the Twentieth Century*, vol. 2. New Haven: Yale University Press, 1984.

Ginger, Ray. *The Age of Excess: the United States from 1877–1914*. New York: Macmillan, 1965.

Goffman, Erving. *Stigma: Notes on the Management of Spoiled Identity*. New York: Simon and Schuster, 1963.

——. 'Remedial Exchanges'. in *Relations in Public: Microstudies of the Public Order*. London: Allen Lane, 1971.

Goody, Jack. *The Culture of Flowers*. Cambridge: Cambridge University Press, 1993.

Gorham, Deborah. *The Victorian Girl and the Feminine Ideal*. London: Croom Helm, 1982.

Grant, Robert. *Unleavened Bread*. New York: Charles Scribner's Sons, 1900.

Grenville, Lady. *The Gentlewoman in Society*. London: Henry and Co., 1892.

Haeckel, Ernst. *The Evolution of Man*, 2 vols. New York: Appleton, 1896.

Harré, R. 'The Evolutionary Analogy in Social Explanation'. In *The Philosophy of Evolution*. Eds U.J. Jensen and R. Harré. New York: St. Martin's Press, 1981.

Hills, Patricia. *Eastman Johnson*. New York: Clarkson N. Potter, Inc. and Whitney Museum of American Art, 1972.

Himmelfarb, Gertrude. *Darwin and the Darwinian Revolution*. New York: W.W. Norton & Co., 1959.

Hoffman, Frederick J. *The Twenties: American Writing in the Postwar Decade*. New York: The Free Press. 1949.

Huxley, T.H. *American Addresses* (New York: D. Appleton, 1877).

——. *The Advancement of Science in the Last Half-Century*. New York: Appleton and Co., 1887.

——. *Darwiniana*. London: Macmillan, 1893.

James, Henry. *The Europeans* (1878). Ed. Tony Tanner. Harmondsworth: Penguin Books, 1985.

——. *The American Scene*. New York: Harper & Bros., 1907.

——. *The Letters of Henry James*. 4 vols. Ed. Leon Edel. Cambridge, Mass.: Belknap Press of Harvard University Press, 1974–84.

Jones, Mary Cadwalader. *European Travel for Women: Notes and Suggestions*. New York: Macmillan, 1900.

Josephson, Matthew. *The Robber Barons: The Great American Capitalists, 1861–1901* (1934). New York: Harcourt, Brace and World, 1962.

Joslin, Katherine, and Alan Price, eds. *Wretched Exotic: Essays on Edith Wharton in Europe*. New York: Peter Lang, 1993.

Kazin, Alfred. 'Two Educations: Edith Wharton and Theodore Dreiser.' In *On Native Grounds: An Interpretation of American Prose Literature*. New York: Harcourt, Brace & World, Inc., 1942.

Lapham, Lewis H. *Money and Class in America: notes and observations on our civil religion*. New York: Weidenfeld and Nicholson, 1988.

Lawson, Thomas William. *Frenzied Finance: The Crime of Amalgamated*. London: William Heinemann, 1906.

Lears, T.L. Jackson. *No Place of Grace: Antimodernism and the Transformation of American Culture, 1880–1920*. New York: Pantheon Books, 1981.

Lewis, Arnold, James Turner and Steven McQuillin. *The Opulent Interiors of the Gilded Age*. New York: Dover Press, 1987.

Lewis, Dio. *Our Girls*. New York: Harper and Brothers, 1871.

Lewis, R.W.B. *Edith Wharton: A Biography*. New York: Harper and Row, 1975.

——. *The Jameses. A Family Narrative*. New York: Farrar, Straus & Giroux, 1991.

Lewis, Sinclair. *Babbitt*. New York: Grosset & Dunlap, 1922.

Loos, Anita. *Gentlemen Prefer Blondes* (1925). London: Folio Society, 1985.

Lovett, Robert M. *Edith Wharton*. New York: Robert M. McBride, 1925.

Lubbock, Percy. *A Portrait of Edith Wharton*. New York: D. Appleton-Century Company, 1947.

Lynn, David B. *Daughters and Parents, Past, Present and Future*. Monterey, California: Brooks/Cole Publishing Co., 1979.

MacCannell, Dean. *The Tourist: A New Theory of the Leisure Class*. New York: Macmillan, 1976.

MacComb, Debra Ann. 'New Wives for Old: Divorce and the Leisure-Class Marriage Market in Edith Wharton's *The Custom of the Country*'. *American Literature*, 68:4 (Dec.1996), 777–83.

McHaney, Thomas L. 'Fouqué's *Undine* and Edith Wharton's *The Custom of the Country*'. *Revue de Littérature Comparée*, 45 (1971), 180–6.

Mariano, Nicky. *Forty Years With Berenson*. London: Hamish Hamilton, 1966.

Martin, Robert A. and Linda Wagner-Martin. 'The Salons of Wharton's Fiction'. In Joslin and Price (1993), 97–110.

Mayer, Grace. *Once Upon a City*. New York: Macmillan, 1958.

Medbery, James. *Men and Mysteries of Wall Street*. Boston: Fields, Osgood & Co., 1870.

Melville, Herman. *Moby-Dick, or the Whale* (1851). Ed. Charles Feidelson, Jr. Indianapolis: Bobbs-Merrill, 1964.

Montez, Lola. *The Arts of Beauty, or, Secrets of a Lady's Toilet*. New York: Dick and Fitzgerald, 1858.

Morris, Lloyd. *Incredible New York: High Life and Low Life of the Last Hundred Years*. New York: Random House, 1951.

Mulvey, Christopher. *Transatlantic Manners: Social Patterns in Nineteenth-century Anglo-American Travel Literature*. Cambridge: Cambridge University Press, 1990.

Nash, Roderick. *Wilderness and the American Mind*, third edition. New Haven: Yale University Press, 1982.

Norris, Frank. *The Pit* (1902). New York: Doubleday, Page & Co., 1903.

Orgel, Stephen, ed. Introduction to Edith Wharton, *The Custom of the Country*. Oxford: Oxford University Press, 1995.

——, ed. Introduction to Edith Wharton, *The Reef*. Oxford University Press, 1998.

Parrington, Vernon. *Main Currents in American Thought*. New York: Harcourt, Brace & World, Inc., 1930, repr. 1958

Pizer, Donald. 'The Naturalism of Edith Wharton's *The House of Mirth*'. *Twentieth Century Literature*, 41 (1995), 241–8.

Poe, Edgar Allen. 'The Philosophy of Furniture' (1842). In *Selected Writings*. Harmondsworth: Penguin Books, 1973, 414–20.

Price, Alan. 'Dreiser's Cowperwood and Wharton's Undine Spragg: A Match Made in Spencer's Heaven'. *Markham Review*, 16 (1987), 37–9.

——. *The End of the Age of Innocence: Edith Wharton and the First World War*. London: Robert Hale, 1996.

Rayne, Martha Louise. *What Can a Woman Do?* Petersburgh, NY: Eagle Publishing Co., 1893.

van Rensselaer, Mrs John King. *Newport, Our Social Capital* (Philadelphia: Lippincott, 1905).

——. *The Social Ladder*. New York: Henry Holt & Co., 1924.

Roberts, Michéle. Review of Shari Benstock, *No Gifts From Chance*. London *Independent*, 23 October, 1994.

Romanes, George. *Mental Evolution in Animals*. London: Kegan, Paul and Trench, 1883.

——. *Mental Evolution in Man*. London: Kegan, Paul and Trench, 1888.

——. *Darwin and After Darwin*. Chicago: Open Court Press, 1892–5.

Ruben, P. 'From Moralization to Class Society or from Class Society to Moralization: Philosophical Comments on Klaus Elder's Hypothesis'. In *The Philosophy of Evolution*. Eds U.J. Jensen and R. Harré. New York: St. Martin's Press, 1981.

Schorer, Mark. *Sinclair Lewis: An American Life*. London: Heinemann, 1961.

Sensibar, Judith L. 'Edith Wharton Reads the Bachelor Type: Her Critique of Modernism's Representative Man'. *American Literature*, 60 (1988), 575–90.

——. '"Behind the Lines" in Edith Wharton's *A Son at the Front*: Re-writing a Masculinist Tradition'. In Joslin and Price (1993), 245–52.

Simmel, Georg. *The Philosophy of Money* (1907). Ed. and trans. David Frisby and Tom Bottomore. London: Routledge, 1990.

Sinclair, Upton. *The Metropolis*. London: T.W. Laurie, Ltd., 1908.

Snyder, Carl. *The Physical Conditions of Life* (1908) (also reprinted *Science Progress* 12 (April, 1909).

Spencer, Herbert. *Works*. New York: Appleton and Co., 1897.

Stern, Robert A.M., Gregory Gilmartin and John Massengale. *New York 1900: Metropolitan Architecture and Urbanism, 1890–1915*. New York: Rizzoli, 1983.

Stein, Susan R., ed. *The Architecture of Richard Morris Hunt.* Chicago, University of Chicago Press, 1986.

Stevens, Wallace. *The Collected Poems of Wallace Stevens.* New York: Alfred A. Knopf, 1981.

Stilgoe, John R. *Borderlands: Origins of the American Suburb, 1820–1939.* New Haven: Yale University Press, 1988.

Stowe, William W. *Going Abroad: European Travel in Nineteenth-Century American Culture.* Princeton: Princeton University Press, 1995.

Street, Julian. *Abroad at Home: American Ramblings, Observations, and Adventures of Julian Street.* New York: Century Co., 1915.

Strong, George Templeton. 'Diary'. In *Diaries of Old Manhattan.* Ed. Louis Auchincloss. New York: Abbeville Press, 1989.

Tarkington, Booth. *The Plutocrat.* Garden City, New York: Doubleday, Page & Co., 1927.

Tauranac, John and Christopher Little. *Elegant New York: The Builders and the Buildings, 1885–1915.* New York; Abbeville Press, 1985.

de Tocqueville, Alexis. *Democracy in America* (1835, 1840), 2 vols. Trans. Henry Reeve. Intro. Daniel C. Gilman. New York: Century Co., 1898.

Topinard, Paul. *Anthropology.* London: Chapman and Hall, 1876.

Trollope, Frances. *Domestic Manners of the Americans* (1832). Ed. Richard Mullen. Oxford: Oxford University Press, 1984.

Tuttleton, James W. 'Edith Wharton: The Archeological Motive'. *Yale Review,* 61 (1971–2), pp. 562–74.

Tuttleton, James W., Kristin O. Lauer and Margaret P. Murray, eds. *Edith Wharton: the Contemporary Reviews.* Cambridge: Cambridge University Press, 1992.

Twain, Mark. *The Gilded Age.* (London: Chatto and Windus, 1892).

Veblen, Thorstein. *The Theory of the Leisure Class* (1899). Intro. J.K. Galbraith. Boston: Houghton Mifflin Co., 1973.

——. 'The Barbarian Status of Women'. *American Journal of Sociology,* 4 (1899), 503–14 (reprinted in *Sex and Equality.* New York: Arno Press, 1974).

Vita-Finzi, Penelope. *Edith Wharton and the Art of Fiction.* London: Pinter Publishers, 1990.

Waid, Candace. *Edith Wharton's Letters from the Underworld: Fictions of Women and Writing.* Chapel Hill: University of North Carolina Press, 1991.

Wallace, A.R. *Darwin and Darwinism* (London: Macmillan, 1889).

Waterman, Catherine H. *Flora's Lexicon: an Interpretation of the Language of Sentiment.* Boston: Crosby, Nichols, Lee & Co., 1861.

Westermarck, Edvard. *A History of Human Marriage.* New York: Macmillan and Co., 1891.

Wharton, Edith and Ogden Codman. *The Decoration of Houses* (1897). New York: W.W. Norton, 1997.

Wharton, Edith. *Italian Backgrounds* (1905). New York: Charles Scribner's Sons, 1905.

——. *The House of Mirth* (1905). New York: Charles Scribner's Sons, 1905.

——. *Madame de Treymes* (1907). New York: Charles Scribner's Sons, 1907.

——. *The Fruit of the Tree* (1907). London: Virago Press, 1984.

——. *A Motor-Flight Through France* (1908). DeKalb, Illinois: Northern Illinois University Press, 1991.

Wharton, Edith. *Ethan Frome* (1911). Oxford: Oxford University Press, 1982.
———. *The Reef* (1912). New York: Appleton and Co., 1912.
———. *The Custom of the Country* (1913). Harmondsworth: Penguin Books, 1987.
———. *Fighting France: from Dunkerque to Belfort* (1915). New York: Charles Scribner's Sons, 1915.
———. *Summer* (1917). Oxford: Oxford University Press, 1982.
———. *The Marne* (1918). New York: Charles Scribner's Sons, 1918.
———. *French Ways and their Meaning* (1919). New York: Appleton and Co., 1919.
———. *The Age of Innocence* (1920). New York: Collier Books, 1992.
———. *The Glimpses of the Moon* (1922). New York: Appleton and Co., 1922.
———. *A Son at the Front* (1923). New York: Charles Scribner's Sons, 1923.
———. *False Dawn* (1924). New York: Appleton and Co., 1924.
———. *The Old Maid* (1924). New York: Appleton and Co., 1924.
———. *The Spark* (1924). New York: Appleton and Co., 1924.
———. *New Year's Day* (1924). New York: Appleton and Co., 1924.
———. *The Mother's Recompense* (1925). New York: Appleton and Co., 1925.
———. *The Writing of Fiction*. New York: Charles Scribner's Sons, 1925.
———. *Twilight Sleep* (1927). New York: Appleton and Co., 1927.
———. *The Children* (1928). London: Virago Press, 1985.
———. *Hudson River Bracketted* (1929). London: Virago Press, 1986.
———. *A Backward Glance* (1934). New York: Appleton-Century, 1934.
———. *The Buccaneers* (1938). London: Everyman, 1993.
———. *The Collected Short Stories of Edith Wharton*. 2 vols. New York: Charles Scribner's Sons, 1968.
———. *Fast and Loose* [1877]. Charlottesville: University of Virginia Press, 1993.
———. *A Further Glance*. Unpublished MS, Beinecke Library, Yale Collection of American Literature.
———. *Life and I*. Unpublished MS, Beinecke Library, Yale Collection of American Literature.
———. *Edith Wharton: The Uncollected Critical Writings*. Ed. Frederick Wegener. Princeton: Princeton University Press, 1996.
———. *The Letters of Edith Wharton*. Eds R.W.B. Lewis and Nancy Lewis. London: Simon and Schuster, 1988.
Wilson, Edmund Jr. 'Some Things I Consider Underrated: Three Little Essays in Constructive Criticism'. *Vanity Fair*, 16:1 (March, 1921) (reprinted in Edmund Wilson, Jr. *From the Uncollected Edmund Wilson*. Eds. Janet Groth and David Castronovo. Athens, Ohio: Ohio University Press, 1995, 141–3.
———. 'Justice to Edith Wharton'. In *Edith Wharton: A Collection of Critical Essays*. Ed. Irving Howe. Englewood Cliffs: Prentice-Hall, Inc., 1962.
Wolff, Cynthia Griffin. 'Lily Bart and the Beautiful Death'. *American Literature*, 46 (1974–5), 16–40.
———. *A Feast of Words: The Triumph of Edith Wharton*. Second, revised, edition. Reading, Mass.: Addison-Wesley Publishing Company, 1995.

Index